POSTCARD HISTORY SERIES

Daytona Beach Florida

A Postcard Tour

POSTCARD HISTORY SERIES

Daytona Beach Florida

A Postcard Tour

Dale Cambre

ARCADIA PUBLISHING

ISBN 978-0-7385-5436-5

Published by Arcadia Publishing
Charleston, South Carolina

Printed in the United States of America

Library of Congress Catalog Card Number: 98-88059

For all general information contact Arcadia Publishing at:
Telephone 843-853-2070
Fax 843-853-0044
E-mail sales@arcadiapublishing.com
For customer service and orders:
Toll-Free 1-888-313-2665

Visit us on the Internet at www.arcadiapublishing.com

Contents

Acknowledgments

Thanks goes to the staff of the Halifax Historical Society for making research material available to me; to Karen Dell of the Volusia County library system for obtaining reference books from institutions outside the system; to postcard dealer Richard Dragoni for access to his inventory; to David Findlay for the loan of cards from his personal collection; to Betty Hall for the use of family photographs; to the Curt Teich Postcards Archives in Wauconda, Illinois for permission to reproduce the Daytona Souvenir Booklet; and to the AAA library for photographs.

I especially appreciate three others who gave me their support: my mentor, who offered advice and correction; Amanda, whose "left brain" skills pulled me through the tedious layout process; and my husband, who encouraged me to have fun with this project.

Introduction

At the height of the Florida land boom, three towns on the Halifax River consolidated to embrace the tourism phenomenon that started shortly after the Civil War.

Florida became a state in 1845, then seceded from the Union in 1861. Reconstruction-era Florida, once again a state, was quickly acknowledged as the country's "new frontier," a land of opportunity for farmers and hunters, invalids and tourists, naturalists and capitalists. In 1870 an entrepreneurial Ohio businessman named Mathias Day purchased 3,200 acres of land on the west bank of the Halifax River and began building the town that came to be known as Daytona.

Day's upstart town was one of the first planned settlements in the Halifax River country. Just across the river from Daytona, two other peninsula villages formed within a few years: Seabreeze, developed by Charles C. and Helen Wilmans Post as the headquarters for their Mental Science Movement, was incorporated in 1901; Daytona Beach formed a municipality in 1905. The three communities—Daytona, Seabreeze, and Daytona Beach—often were referred to collectively as the Triple Cities, yet they maintained separate identities until 1925 when they became one incorporated city named Daytona Beach.

Jacksonville was the gateway to eastern Florida in the late 1800s. One could travel to the port city from New York by ocean steamer, or overland by a network of railroad lines. Going farther south in comparable style was unheard of until the late 1880s. Mathias Day sailed from Jacksonville down the Atlantic Coast in 1870 on a small schooner that entered the Halifax River at Mosquito Inlet (now Ponce Inlet). The only other practical transportation to the coast was a St. Johns River steamboat to Tocoi, then by horse-drawn rail car to St. Augustine. In the 1870s, St. Augustine was the southernmost "resort" destination, mainly due to inadequate transportation and accommodations beyond that point.

Transportation was key to Florida's development. Daytona Beach's growth parallels improvements in transportation to and within the state. Oil magnate Henry Flagler played a pivotal role in bringing tourism and progress to the East Coast when he established his Florida East Coast Railway Company about 1885. He purchased and upgraded a series of independent railroad lines between Jacksonville and Daytona, and built bridges where they were needed.

Not all of Flagler's energy was devoted to railroad construction. He built luxury hotels in St. Augustine and purchased and remodeled an already successful Ormond establishment on the Halifax River north of Daytona. Although Flagler did not work his hotel magic in Daytona, his vision for an "American Riviera" played a major role in the growth of area tourism.

Naturalists were some of the first tourists in Florida. It is reported that John James Audubon spent time at a local plantation while documenting wildlife in the early 1800s. Invalids, primarily those afflicted with lung diseases, came south believing in the curative powers of Florida's climate. Sportsmen found an abundance of wildlife in the forests; fishermen marveled at the size of black bass in Florida's streams. Beach recreation delighted Northern visitors who sought refuge from freezing snow. But it was beach racing that turned public attention to the Ormond and Daytona beaches.

They say every picture tells a story. We can thank early photographers for recording vivid images of both the ordinary and the unusual; for documenting people, places, and scenery that no longer exist; and for capturing random moments in time with such clarity that we can almost imagine what it was like to be there.

One

Destination Daytona
Tourism and Travel

People flocked to Daytona Beach long before the town was associated with spring break. In fact, its busiest time wasn't spring at all. From the mid-1800s, pioneers, naturalists, and entrepreneurs had made their way to Florida's Halifax River region to discover and enjoy its natural resources. Tourism actually began in earnest around the turn of the 20th century, as residents of Northern cities migrated south to escape harsh winters, often staying for months at a time. Word of mouth, photographs, postcards, and promotional brochures put Florida in the limelight as the premier tourist destination of the day. The material in this section offers some insight into the start of it all.

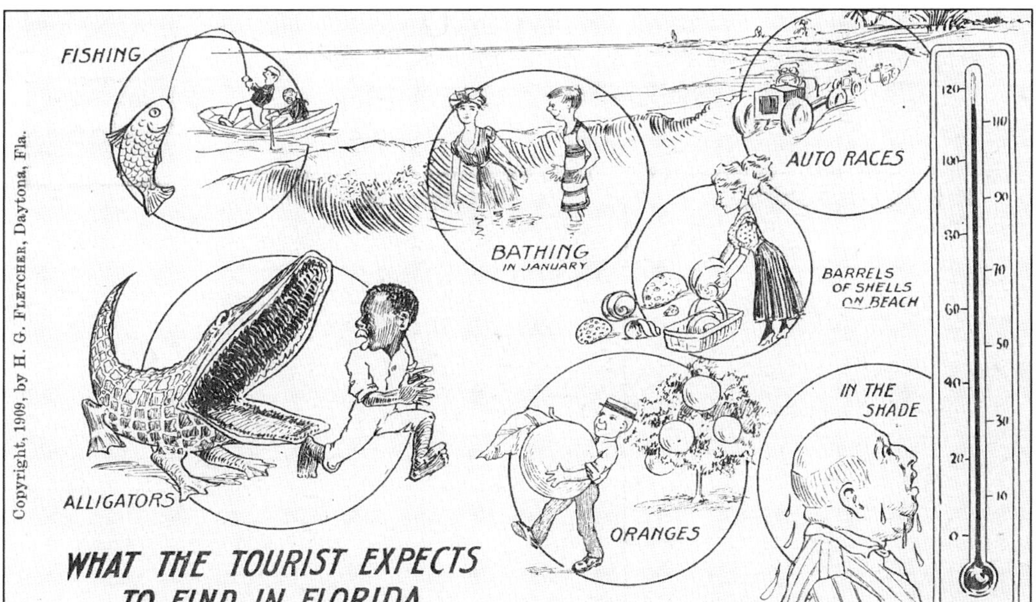

Postcard Promoting Florida Tourism. Tourism flourished in 1909, when this card was published. *Auto races* had brought thousands to the beaches of Ormond and Daytona, where they enjoyed bathing in January as well as collecting *barrels of shells on the beach*. Sportsmen found good *fishing* in rivers, lakes, and the ocean; some even made sport of shooting *alligators*. A special treat for winter visitors was the crop of *oranges* that reached perfection in the cool months, rather than in summer when the mercury soared to 100 degrees *in the shade*.

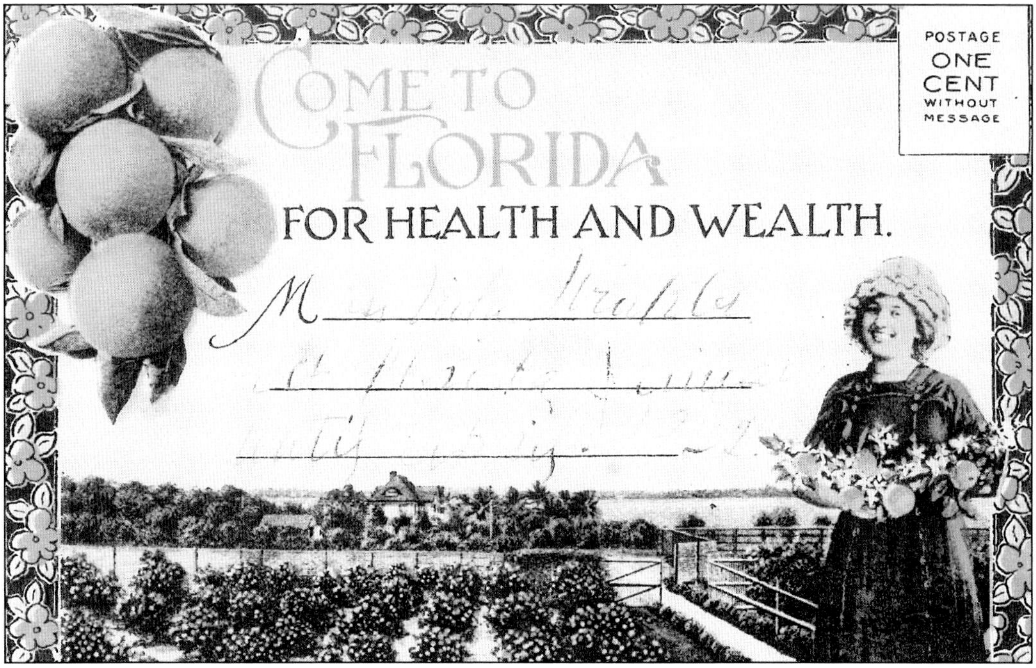

SOUVENIR POSTCARD FOLDER, C. 1922. Sending and collecting pictorial postal cards caught on in the United States about 1902. Cards were used for commercial advertising and to make social commentary, but the view card turned out to be the most popular type of postcard. Sets and souvenir folders offered a collection of scenes or pictures related to one theme. This folder included images of palm trees framing serene bays, orange trees loaded with fruit, and gardens full of exotic plants, all emphasizing the natural beauty of Florida. Accompanying descriptive text praised the climate: "In winter, when the northern states are frozen and blizzard-swept, Florida is warmed by the sun, and all winter her people may enjoy the finest climate in the world."

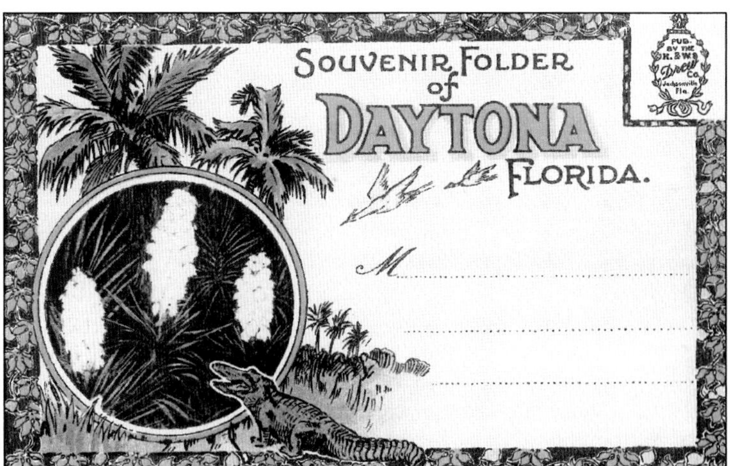

SOUVENIR POSTCARD FOLDER OF DAYTONA, C. 1922. Hotels, streets, historic sights, and natural attractions were the focus of this souvenir folder published in Florida by the H.&W.B. Drew Company of Jacksonville. The cover depicts palm trees, herons in flight, and an alligator around an inset of a Spanish Bayonet plant.

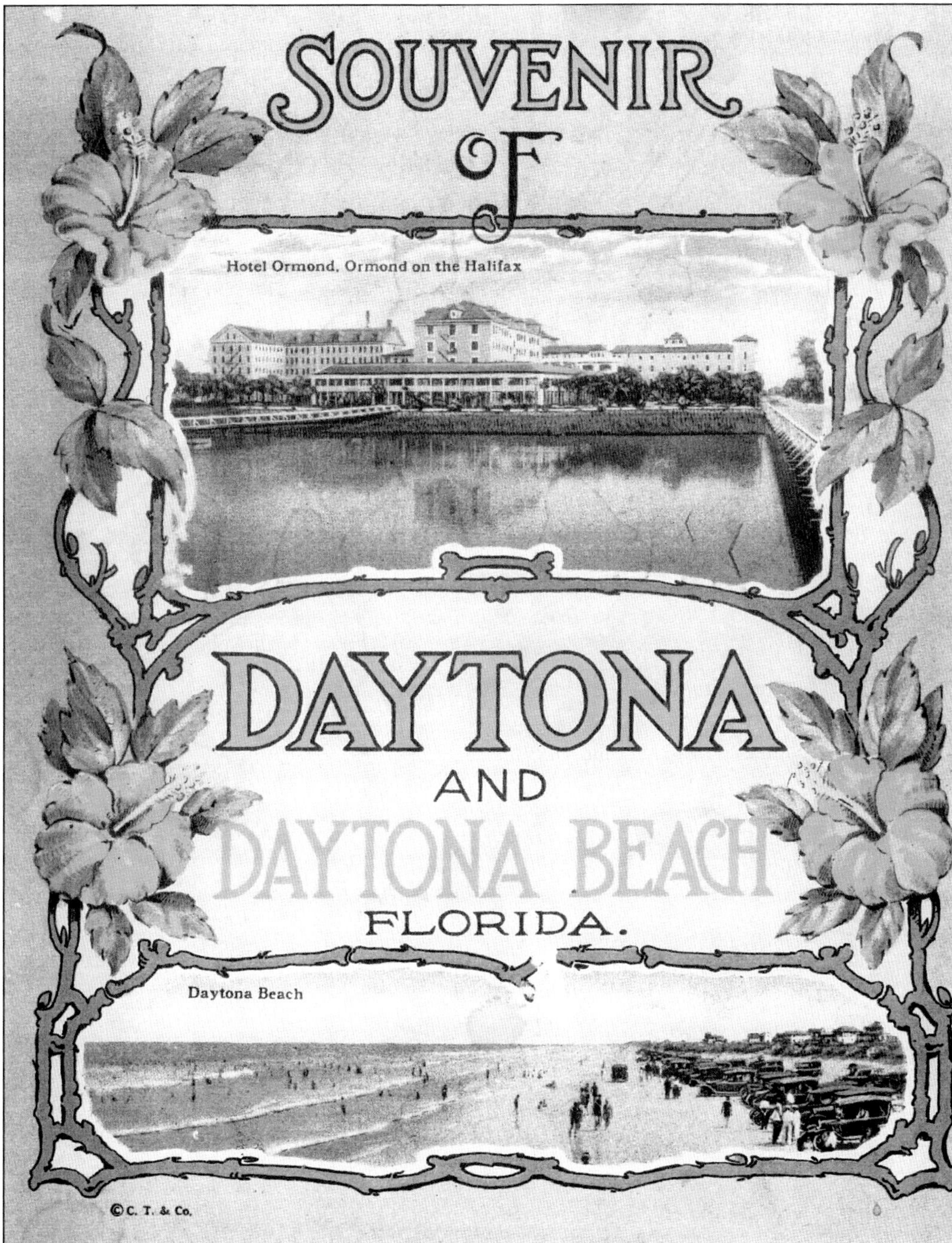

SOUVENIR POSTCARD BOOKLET, *c.* 1923. The Curt Teich Company produced this artistic souvenir booklet of Daytona and Daytona Beach that featured colorful pictures of hotels, points of interest, and scenic drives. The world-famous beach is on the cover along with the Ormond Hotel, which was the jewel of the Halifax River at one time, but was neither in Daytona nor Daytona Beach.

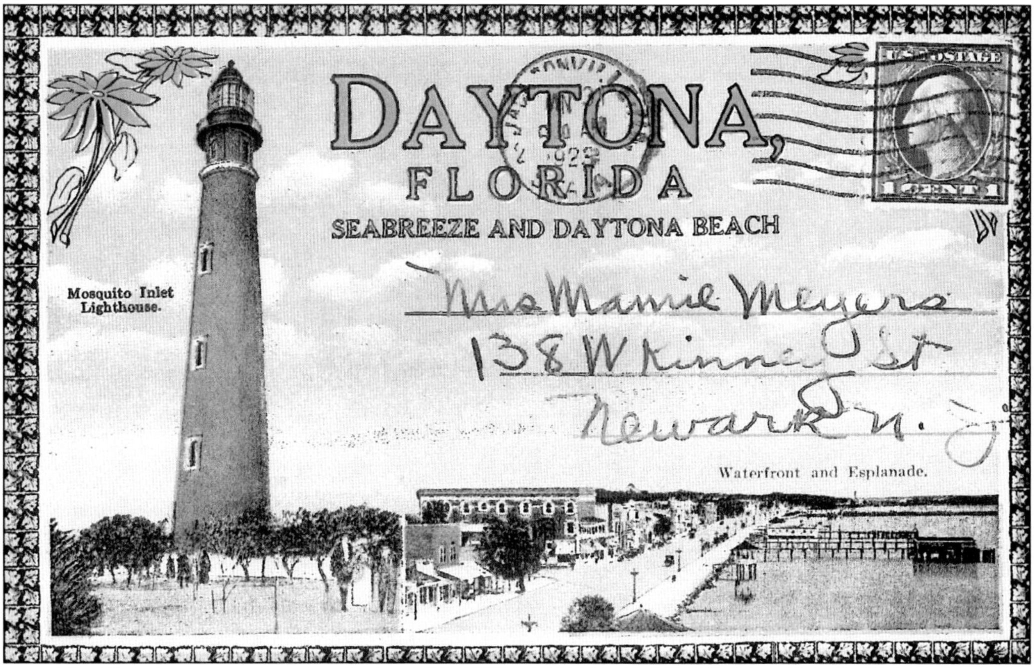

Souvenir Postcard Folder of Daytona, Seabreeze, and Daytona Beach, c. 1922. The Triple Cities of Daytona, Seabreeze, and Daytona Beach had all the charms of a resort community, as the words and pictures in this folder suggested. An exquisite climate, splendid automobile garages, the best artesian drinking water in the United States, and unsurpassed yachting, boating, and canoeing were just some of the reasons thousands came to the area each season.

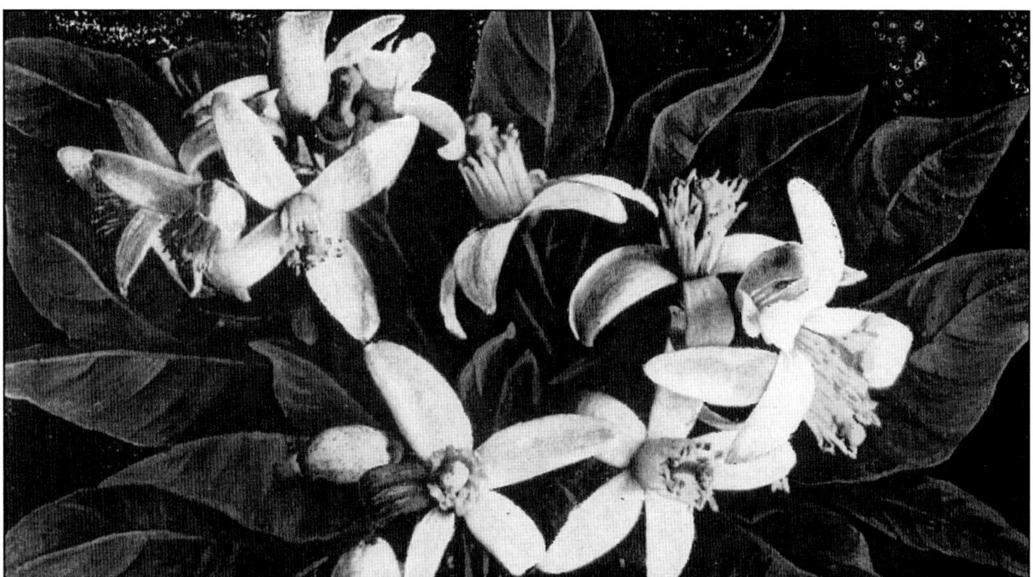

Orange Blossoms. Nothing symbolizes Florida so aptly as the orange blossom, which exudes an intoxicating fragrance matched only by the sweetness of the fruit. The orange blossom was adopted as the state flower in 1909.

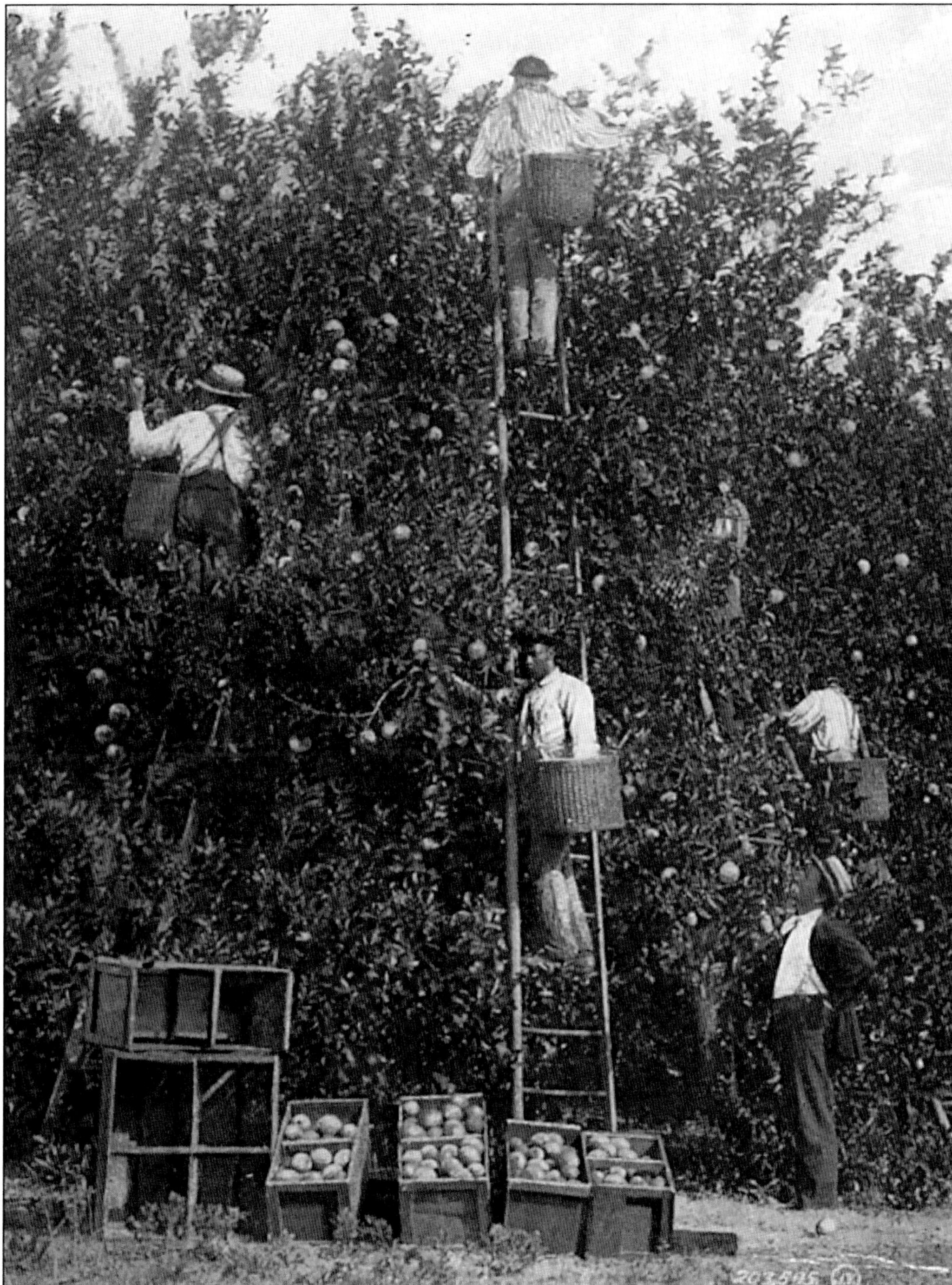

PICKING ORANGES. Many of Daytona's pioneer families engaged in orange growing either for a living or as an aside from their normal livelihood. The future of the industry north of St. Augustine was jeopardized by the freezes of 1894–1895, which not only severely damaged the fruit but also killed many of the trees. One of the major citrus growing areas in Florida was—and still is—farther south along the Indian River.

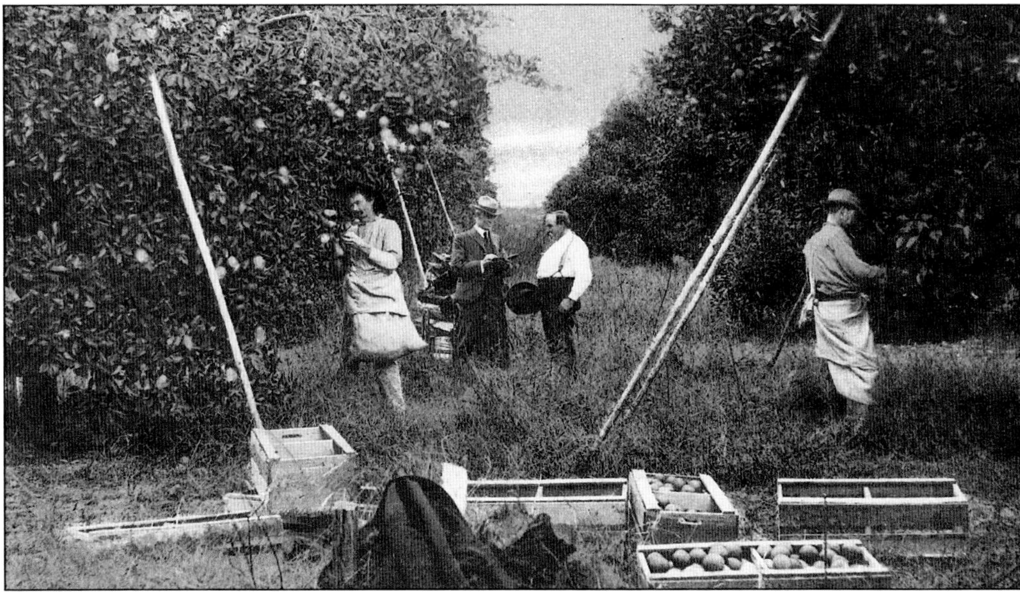

WORKING IN A GROVE. The average size of an orange grove in the early 1900s was about 5 acres. Fruit was picked by hand and boxed on site, as shown here.

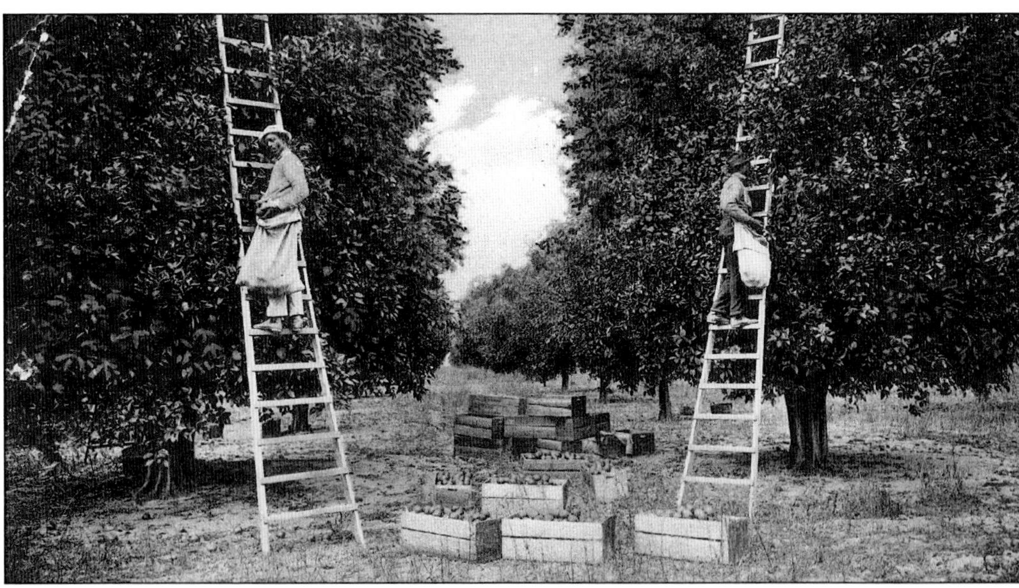

MATURE ORANGE TREES. Several historic freezes threatened orange crops in mid-Florida. They occurred in 1886, 1898, and 1899, but the most damaging were two in succession in December 1894 and February 1895. It took several years for surviving trees to recover and produce a crop.

At Santa Lucia Plantation, Ormond. Some of the area's most famous orange groves were open to turn-of-the-century visitors. One such orchard was Santa Lucia Plantation, which was next to the Ormond Hotel and owned by hotel co-founder John Anderson. Overall, citrus growing was so successful in Volusia County that locally grown oranges, including Anderson's, won awards at agricultural expositions in New Orleans and Jacksonville in the late 1880s. (Postcard courtesy Richard Dragoni.)

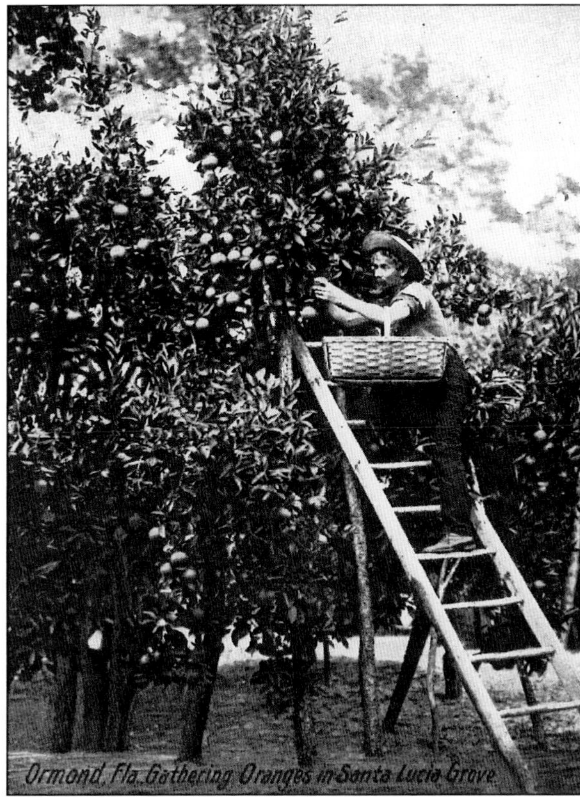

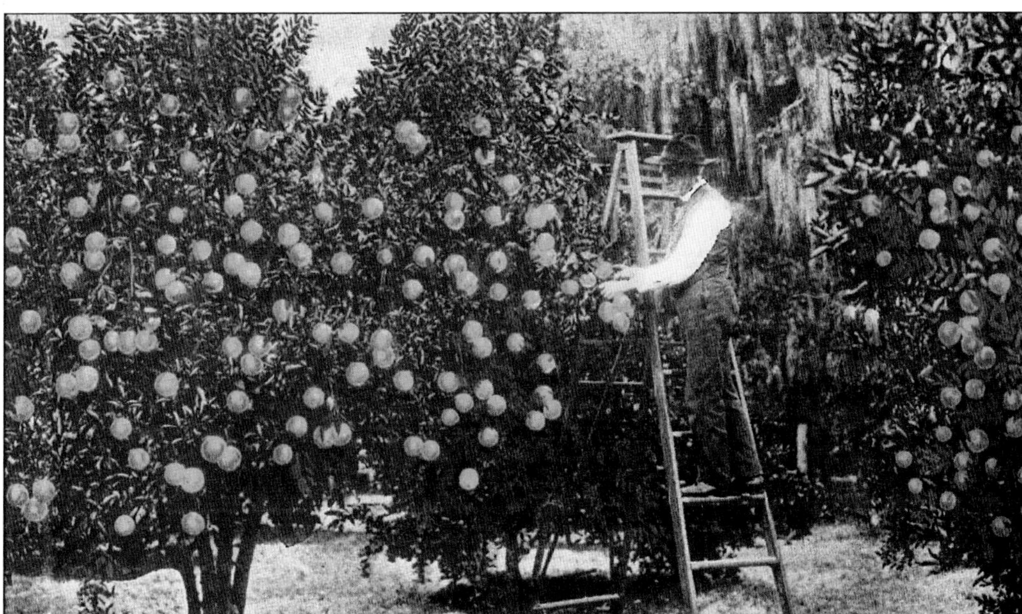

Orange Trees Laden With Fruit. Citrus groves were plentiful along the St. Johns and Halifax Rivers in the 1800s. In fact, Daytona was founded on a sugar plantation that also produced oranges in the 1700s.

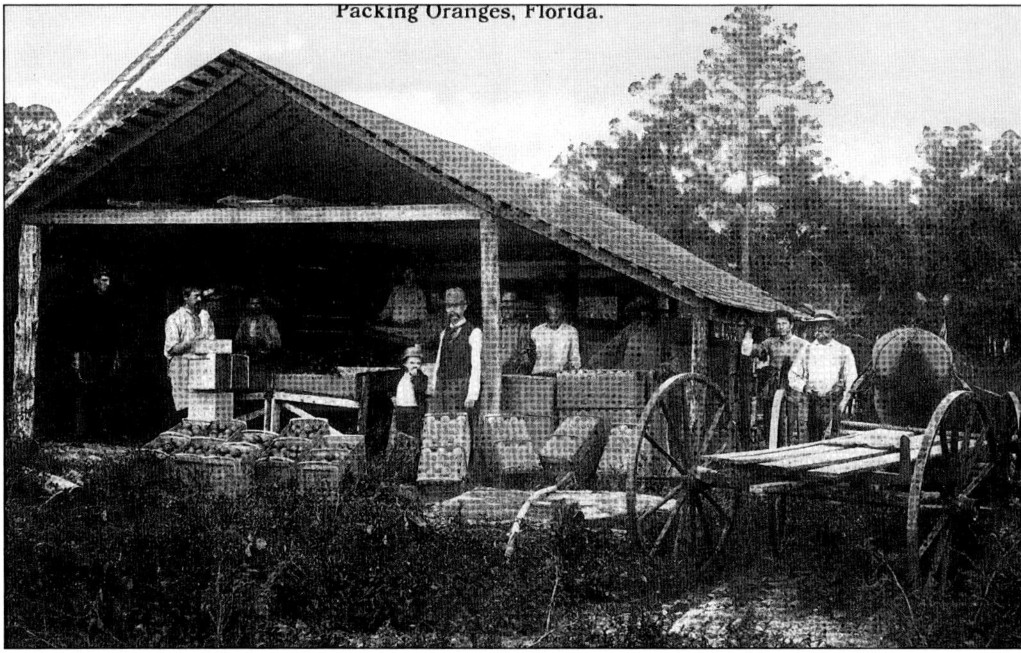

PACKING ORANGES. Fruit was collected at a packing shed and hauled by cart to a railroad depot or a steamboat landing for shipment to Jacksonville and Northern cities. Sidney Lanier offered readers of his guidebook, *Florida: Its Scenery, Climate and History*, advice on how to select a suitable orange: "You will at least produce an implication of your connoiseurship in the mind of the dealer if you ask for Indian River oranges, which many persons hold to be the typic fruit."

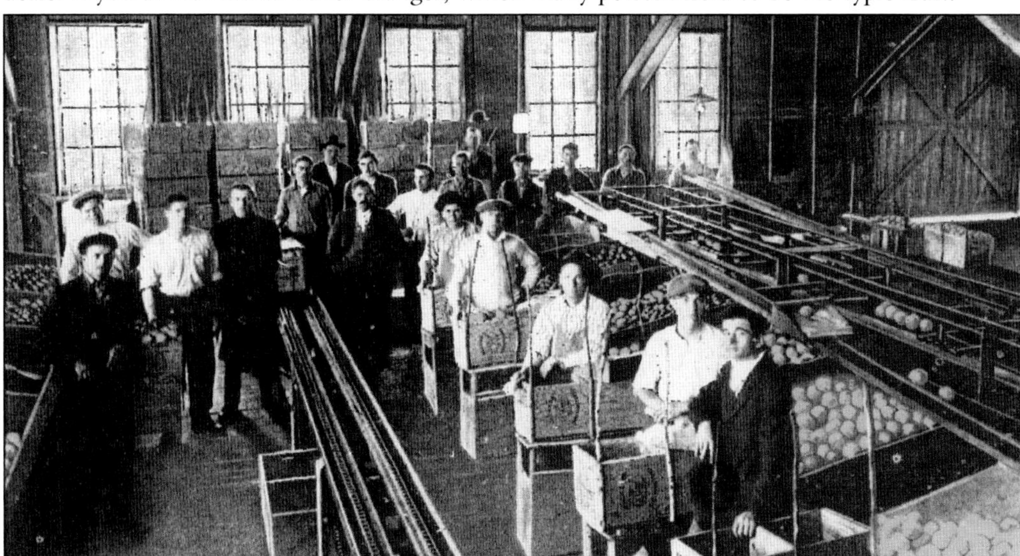

ORANGE PACKING HOUSE. Orange production increased in the early 1920s for several reasons. The land boom brought new farmers to the area; improved transportation got the fruit to market quicker; and mechanized packing techniques were devised. A Volusia County horticulturist of Chinese origin, Lue Gim Gong, is credited with developing hardier fruit with an extended tree life, capable of surviving adverse weather conditions. (Postcard courtesy Richard Dragoni.)

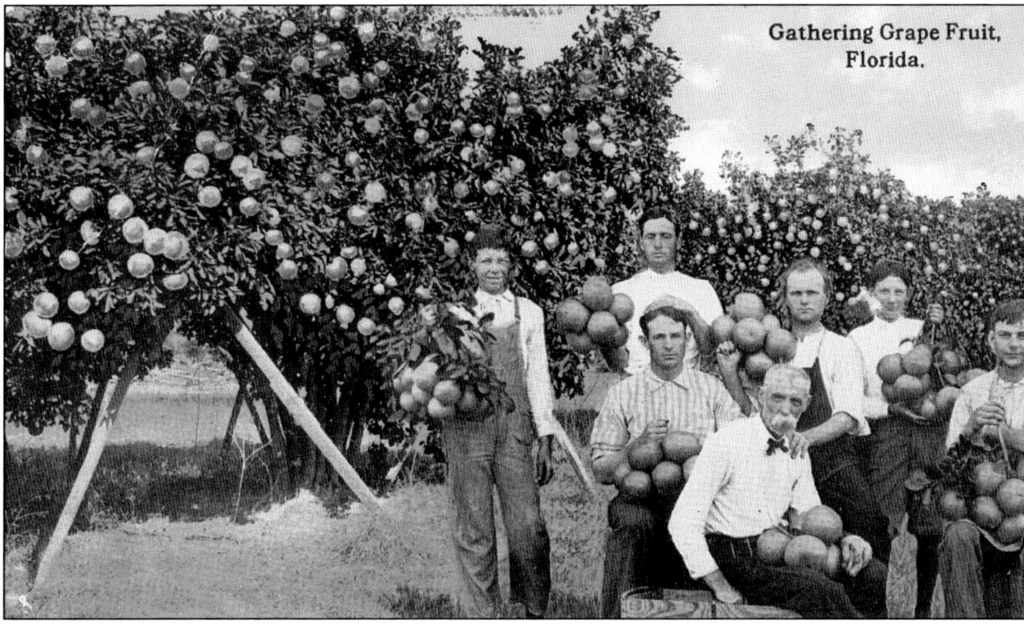

Grapefruit. Oranges weren't the only citrus fruit grown. The sender of this card wrote of having all the oranges, grapefruit, and tangerines he could eat growing right in his yard.

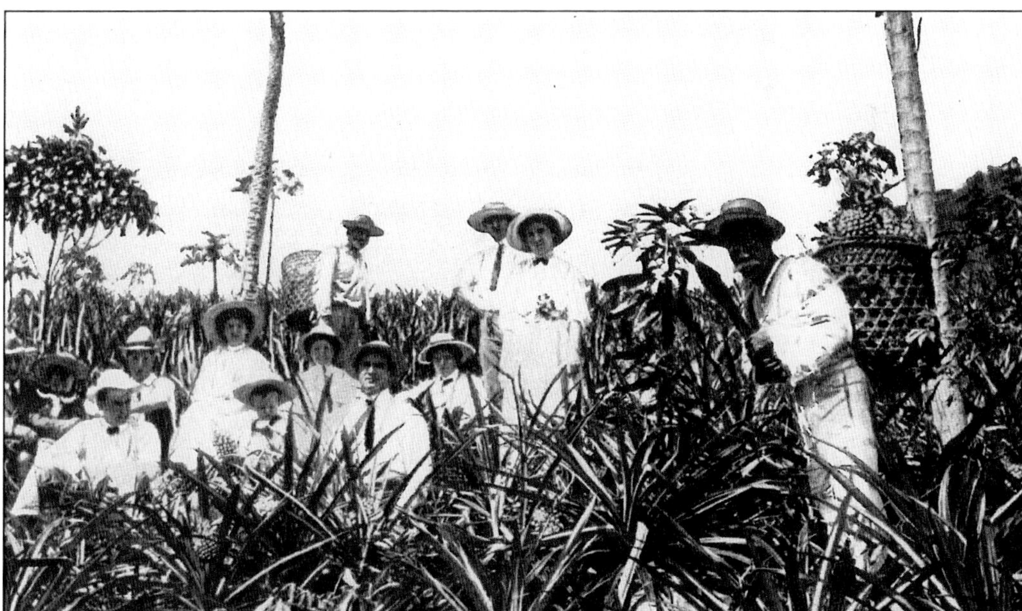

Pineapples. The pineapple industry, which was centered on the Indian River area south of New Smyrna, declined there after the first decade of the 1900s. There was a pinery in the Daytona area in the early days; however, pineapples are grown farther south today. (Postcard courtesy Richard Dragoni.)

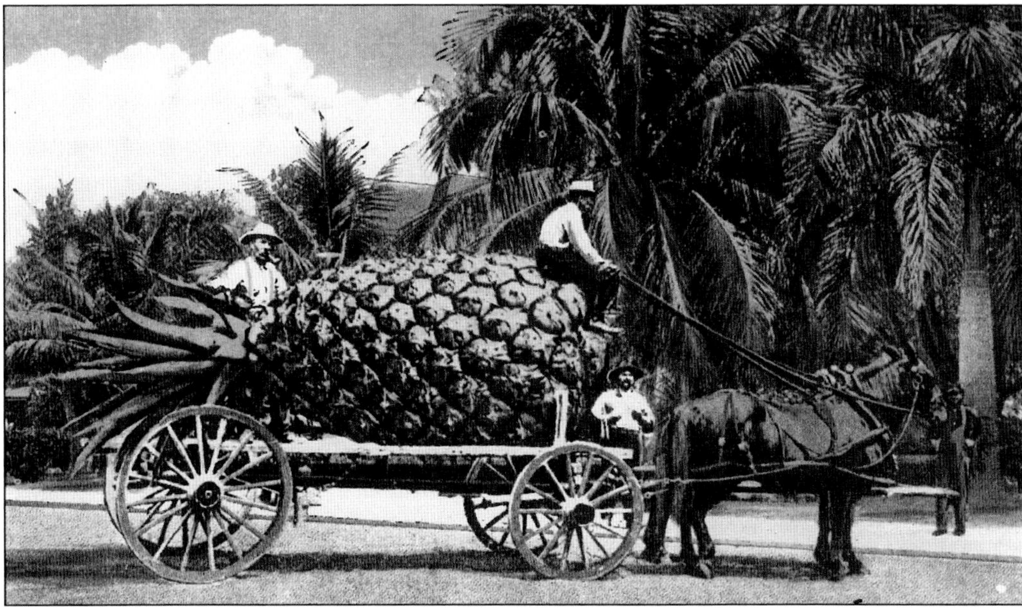

A Florida Pineapple. This humorous card defies description. Perhaps the crop is on its way from the Daytona Pinery to market or to the Sub-tropical Exposition in Jacksonville for exhibit. (Postcard courtesy Richard Dragoni.)

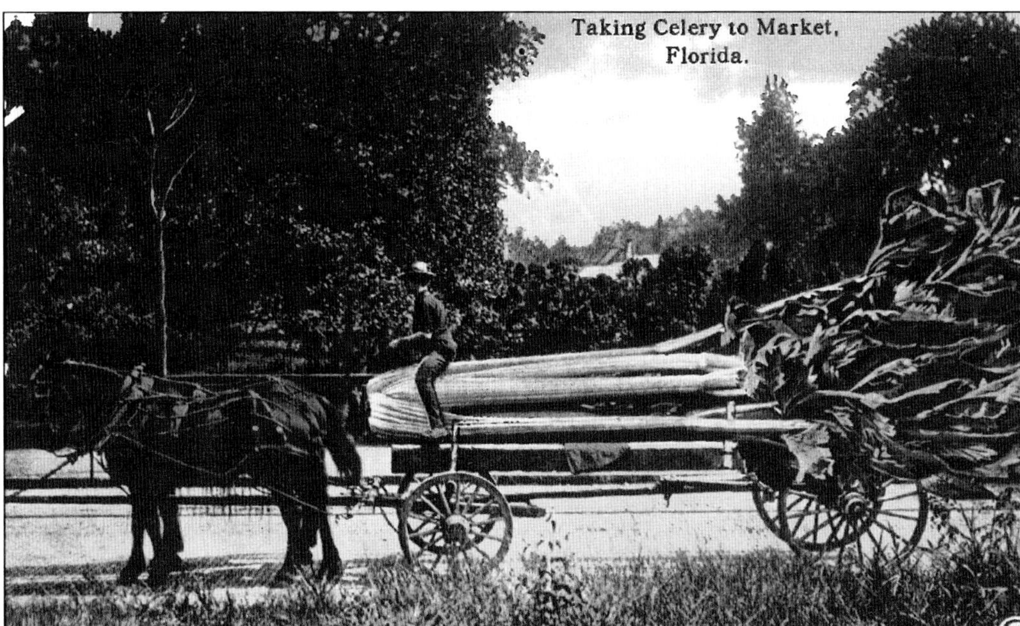

Florida Celery. Here is another example of what sandy soil and year-round sunshine can produce. Celery was grown in "large quantities" in some areas and yielded up to 1,000 crates per acre.

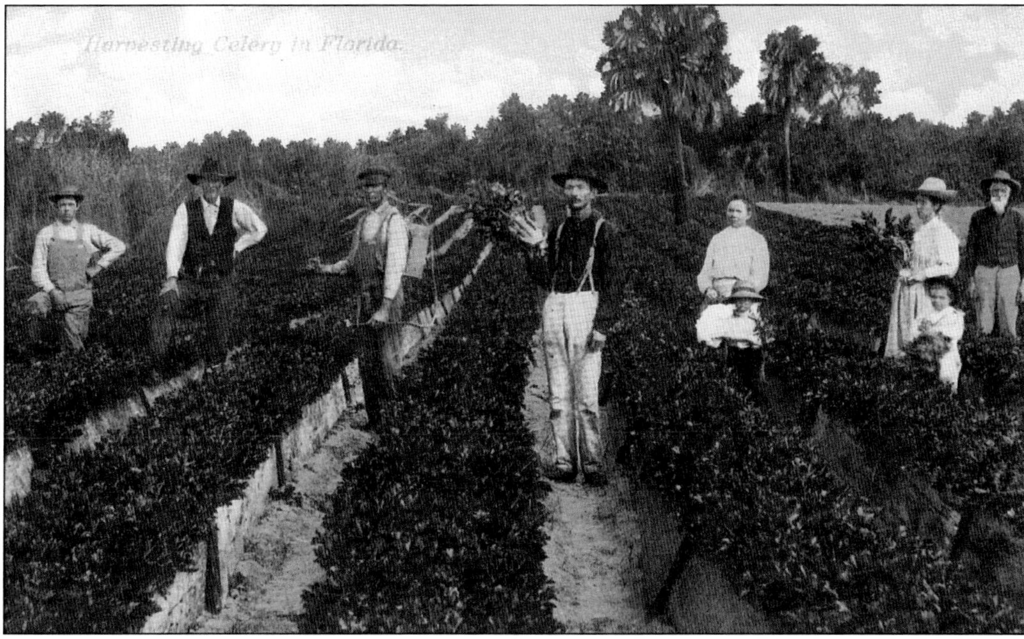

Harvesting Celery. Once the celery crop was harvested, lettuce could be planted on the same land. In the early 1920s, celery sold for up to $2.50 per crate, according to one promotional brochure. (Postcard courtesy Richard Dragoni.)

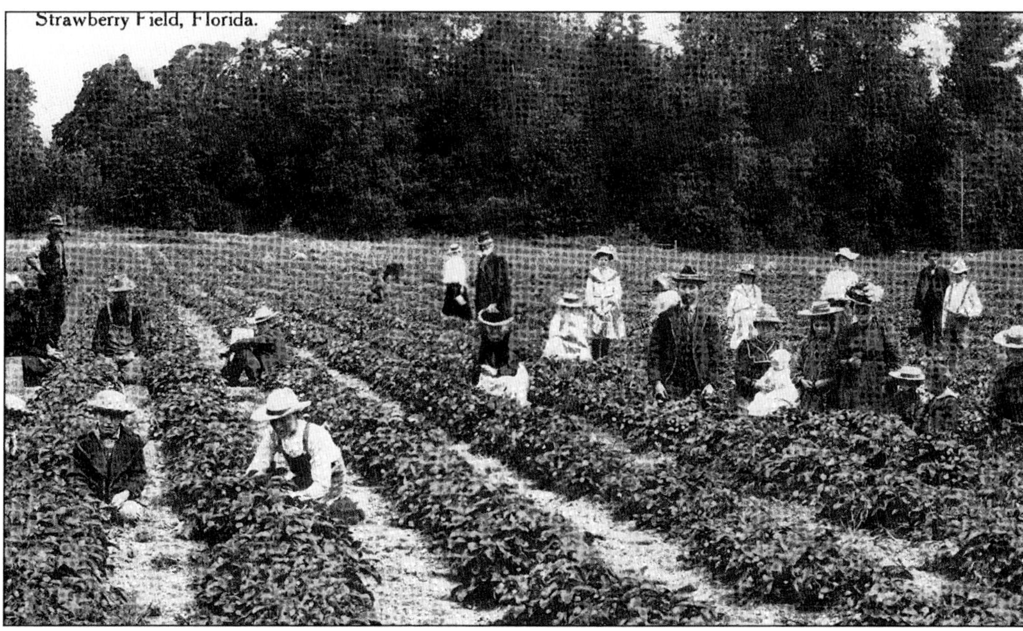

Strawberry Fields. Ripe berries were available for picking January through March at the strawberry patch west of Volusia Avenue in Daytona.

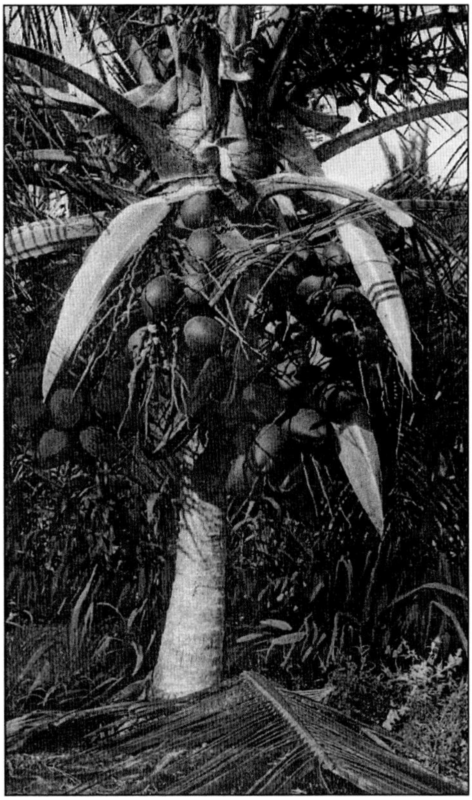

Coconut Palm Tree. Exotic fruit, colorful flowers, and indigenous plant life that conveyed a feel of the tropics were recurring subjects of early 20th-century postcards. The coconut palm was another unique tree that delighted first-time visitors. Associated primarily with South Florida, it was found as far north as Daytona.

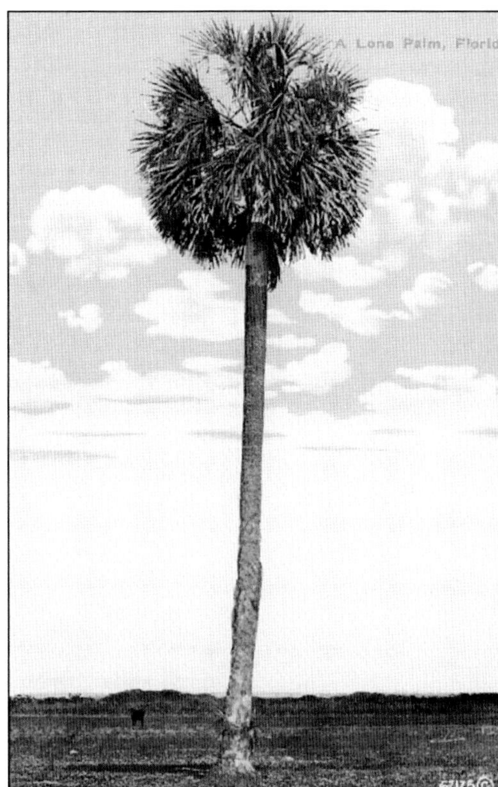

Sabal Palm. Another official state symbol, the sabal palm grows just about anywhere in Florida because it is highly adaptable to almost any type of soil. Also known as the cabbage palm, this versatile tree supplied building logs and roof thatching for pioneer dwellings as well as food for the table. Natives also made syrup from the berries, pounded the fronds into flour, and extracted salt from the trunk.

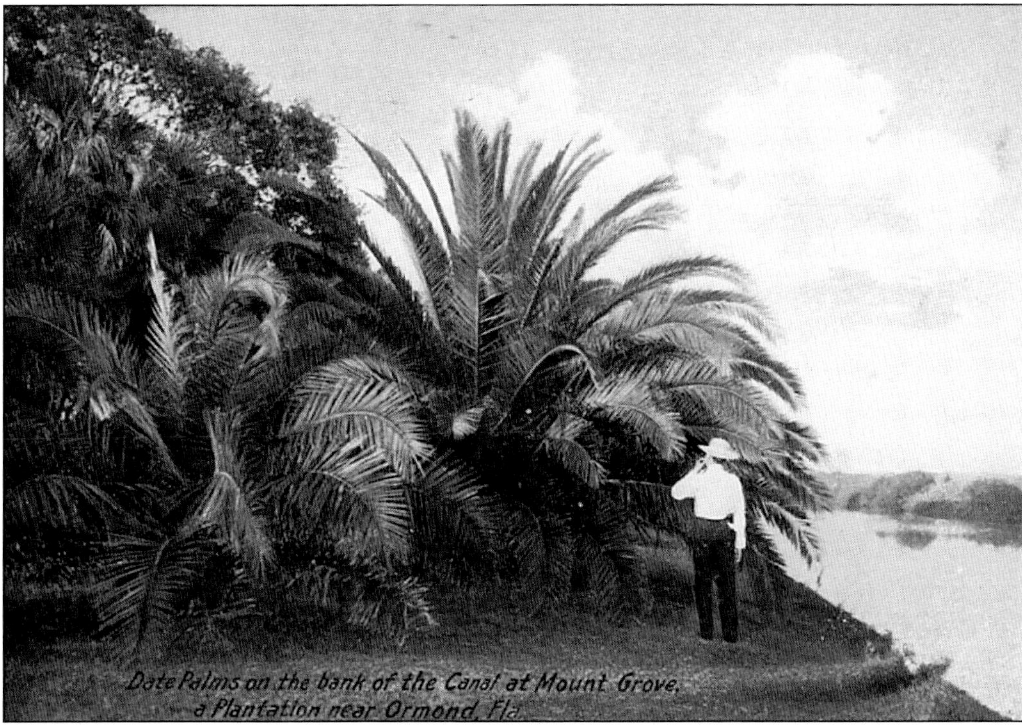

Date Palms. This is a date palm tree on a plantation near Ormond. Grace, the sender of this card, writes that she is going to have her picture taken under it, so it seems likely the folks back home in Massachusetts had never seen a date palm. Perhaps it was also a first for Grace.

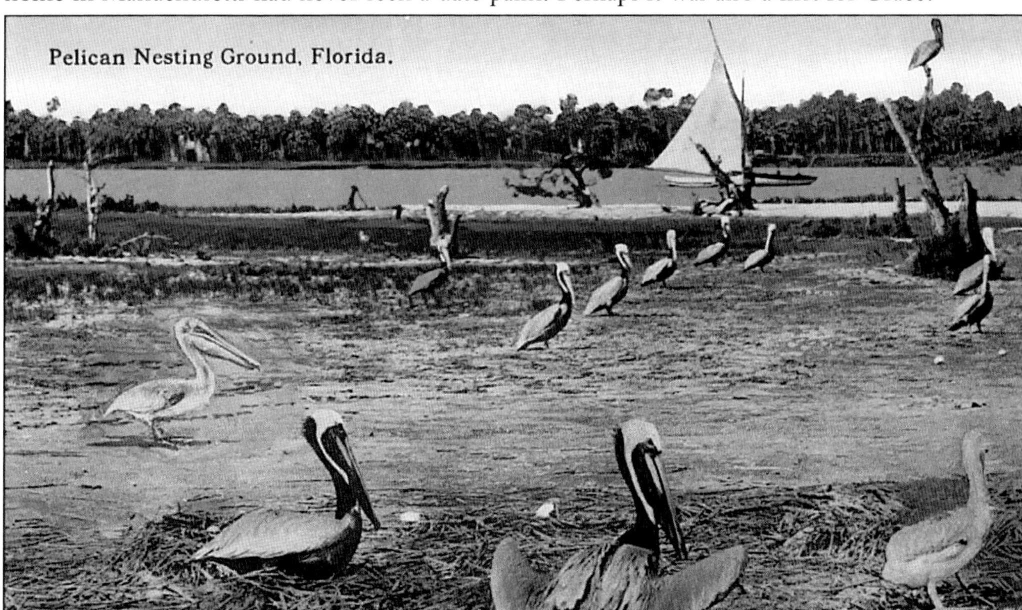

Pelicans. Brown pelicans fed in coastal waters and large inland lakes, but preferred mangrove islands for breeding and nesting, as shown here. They often were seen "fishing" along the beaches of the area.

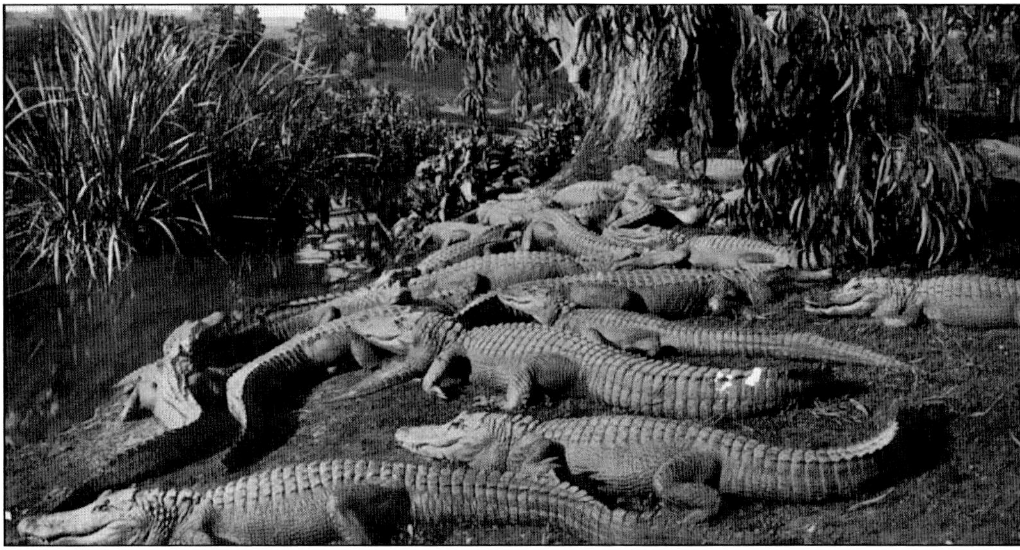

ALLIGATORS. Alligators thrilled 19th-century river travelers. In his book *Dixie, Southern Sketches and Scenes*, Julian Ralph recalled seeing 11 from the deck of a St. Johns River steamer in 1896: " One favored me with an exhibition of his pedestrianism by turning into the woods. He lifted his head and six-sevenths of his tail above the ground upon ungainly legs that stood apart from his body, almost like a spider's limbs. Then he walked as if he had not learned how."

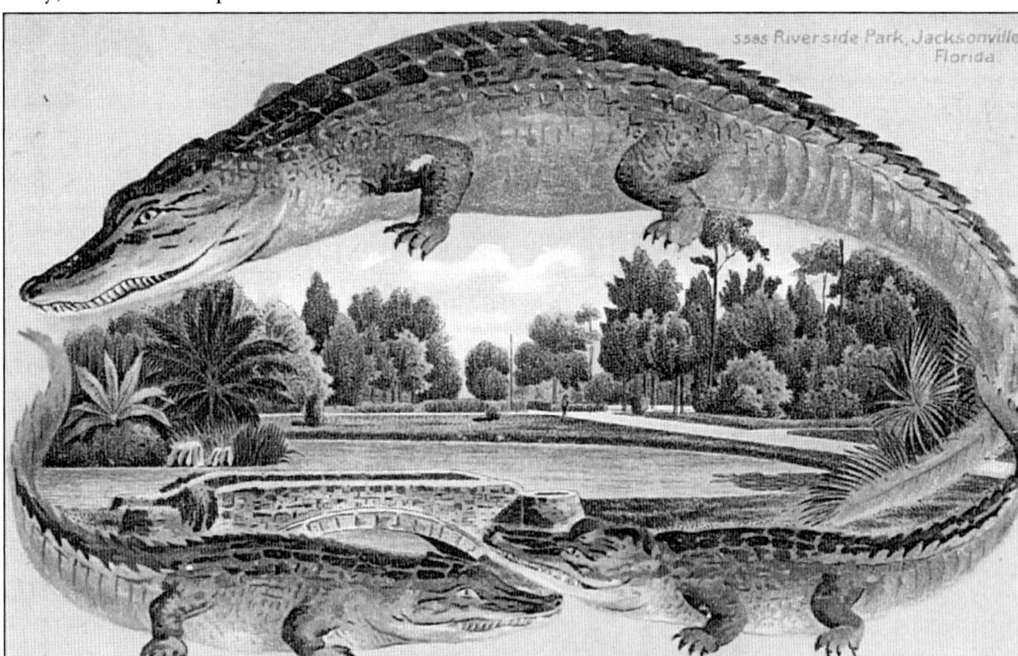

ALLIGATOR BORDER POSTCARD. The alligator was hunted by sportsmen, killed for commercial gain, and shot from steamboat decks. A symbol of Florida's wilderness, it was offered as a souvenir to tourists in a variety of forms. Its teeth were fashioned into jewelry; its hide became handbags; and its image was transferred to postcards and painted china. After years of being exploited, the alligator was placed on the endangered species list; today it is the official state reptile. (Postcard courtesy David Findlay.)

AN ALLIGATOR FARM. Tourists' fascination with alligators led to the creation of alligator farms, one of the first types of tourist attractions in eastern Florida. One of the oldest continuously operating alligator farms is in St. Augustine; it was established in 1893. (Postcard courtesy Richard Dragoni.)

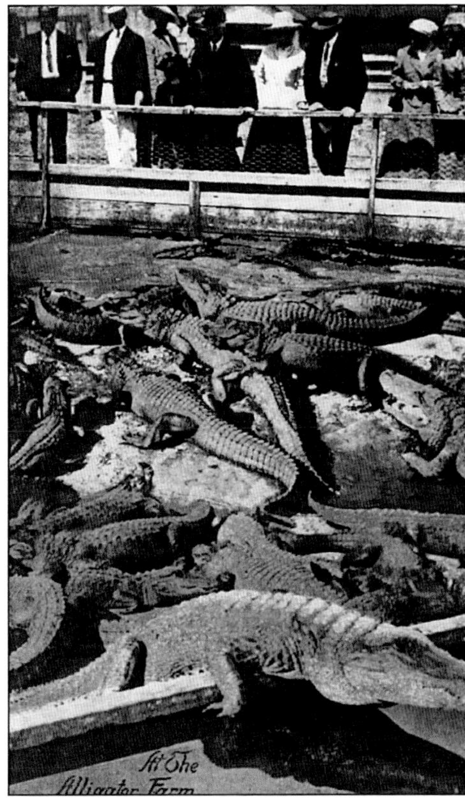

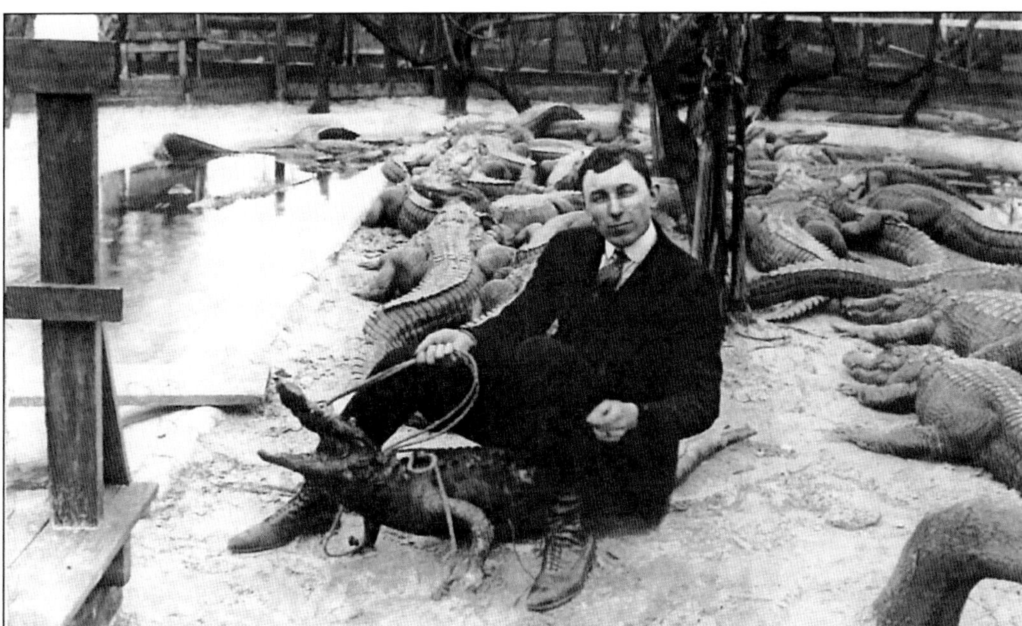

MAN POSING WITH AN ALLIGATOR. This picture was probably taken at an alligator farm. (Postcard courtesy Richard Dragoni.)

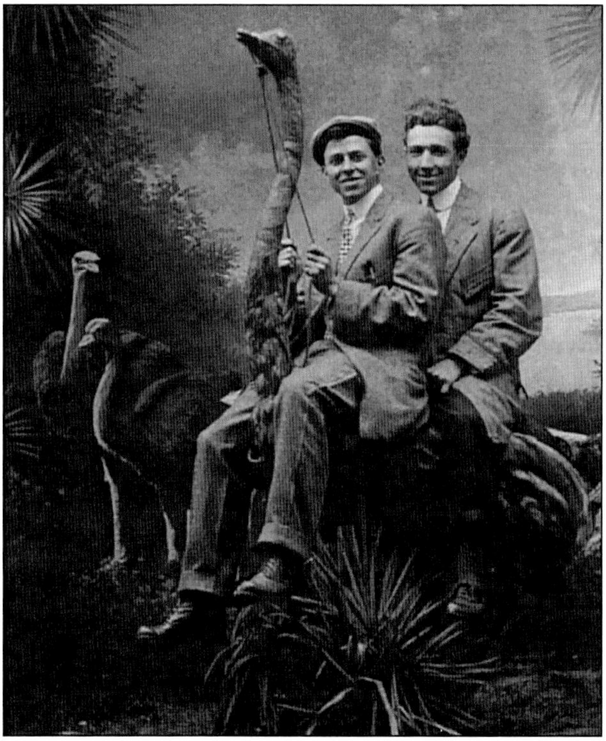

Two Men On An Ostrich. Studio cards showing tourists interacting with exotic animals were popular souvenir items. Ostriches were farmed in Jacksonville in the early 1900s.

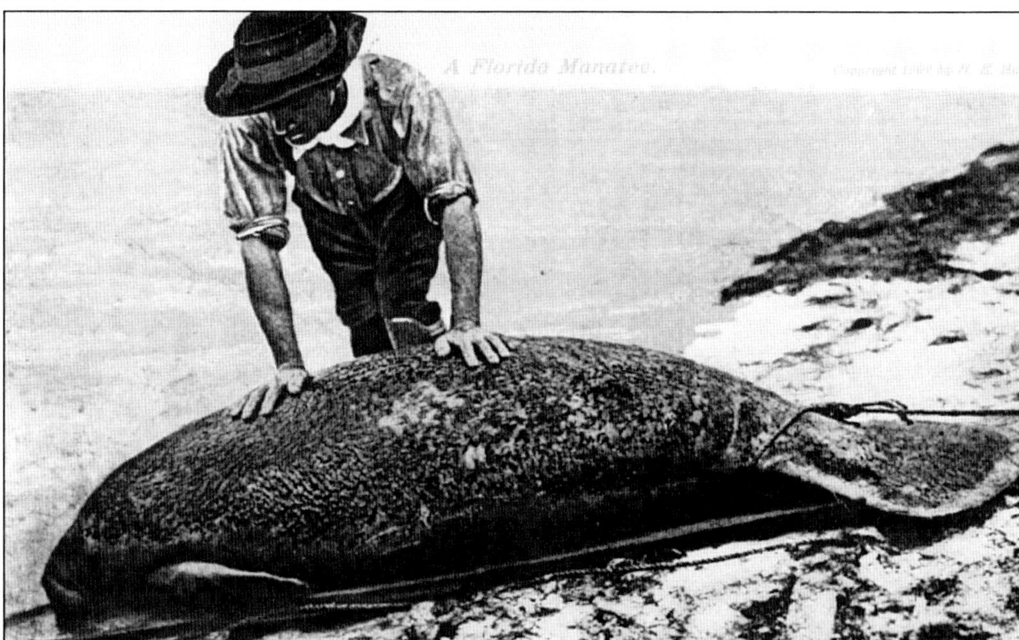

A Florida Manatee. The manatee is a type of sea cow that feeds on aquatic plants and migrates from ocean waters to warm rivers and springs during winter. Some made their way to Blue Spring in Volusia County every year by way of the St. Johns River. Protection of Florida's manatees dates to the 1890s; the nearly extinct creature was later adopted as the official state marine mammal. (Postcard courtesy Richard Dragoni.)

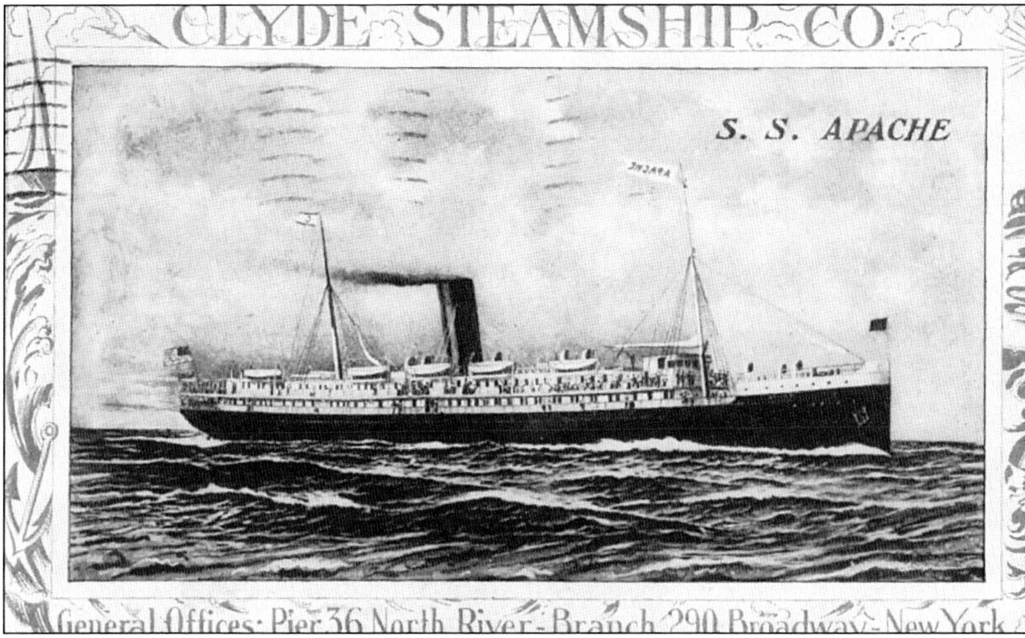

CLYDE STEAMSHIP COMPANY ADVERTISEMENT. The next series of cards offers insight into the development of three modes of transportation to the Land of Sunshine. Northern travelers came to Florida by steamship or railroad before the automobile and good roads simplified the touring lifestyle. Ocean travel down the East Coast in winter was not for the squeamish, however fashionable it may have been. The Clyde Line began service from New York and Boston to Jacksonville in 1886. The SS *Apache*, shown here, was launched in 1901.

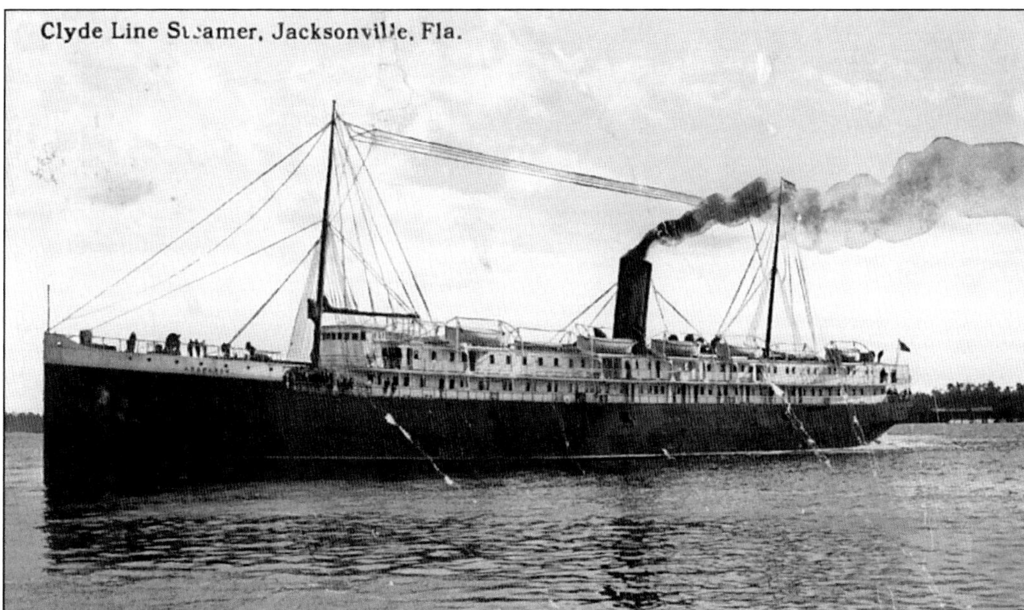

CLYDE LINE STEAMER. Most of the Clyde steamers bound for South Carolina, Georgia, and Florida were named after Indian tribes. This is the *Arapahoe*, sister ship to the *Apache*. In 1901, the Clyde Line initiated tri-weekly trips from New York to South Carolina and Florida ports.

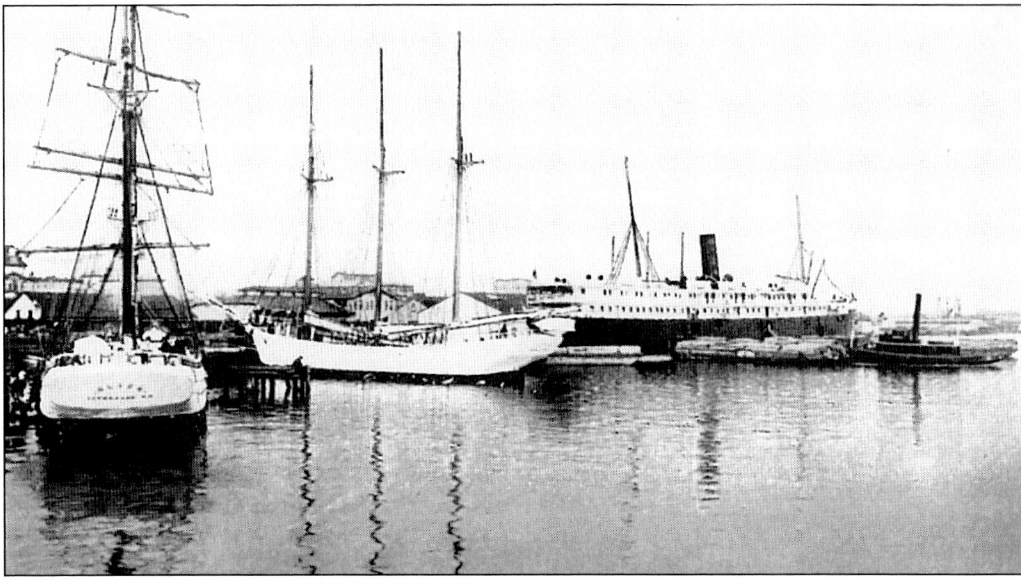

JACKSONVILLE WATERFRONT, C. 1904. After the Civil War, Jacksonville thrived as a commercial center and became a major seaport as well as the embarking point of steamers carrying freight and passengers on the St. Johns River. (Postcard courtesy Richard Dragoni.)

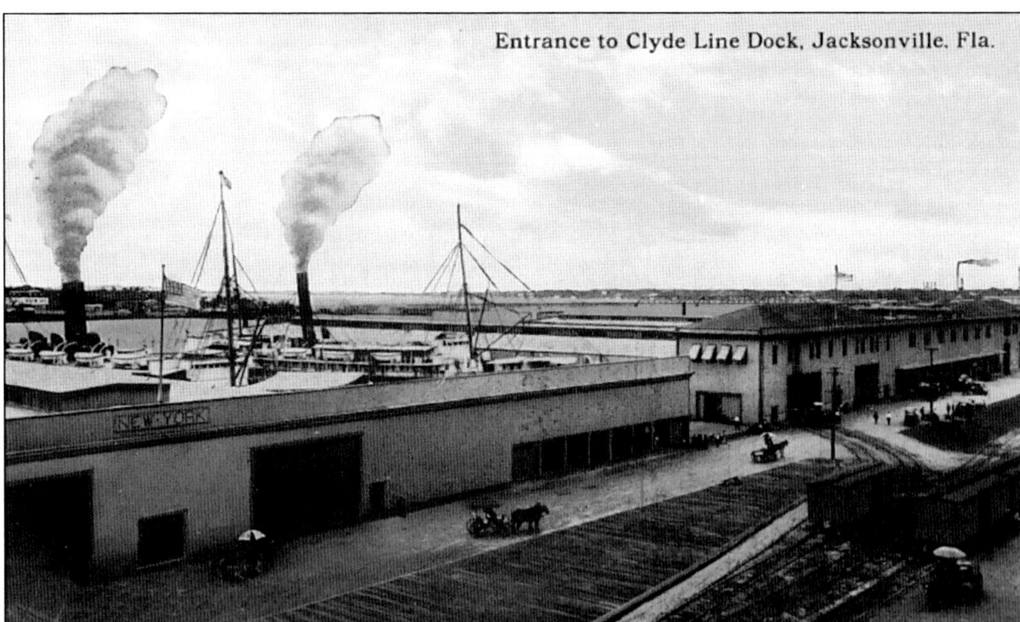

CLYDE LINE NEW YORK DOCK, JACKSONVILLE. The Clyde Steamship Company's warehouses were built between Washington and Market Streets about 1911. Smokestacks of two New York-bound ships are shown on the waterfront, but up to six ships could dock there at one time.

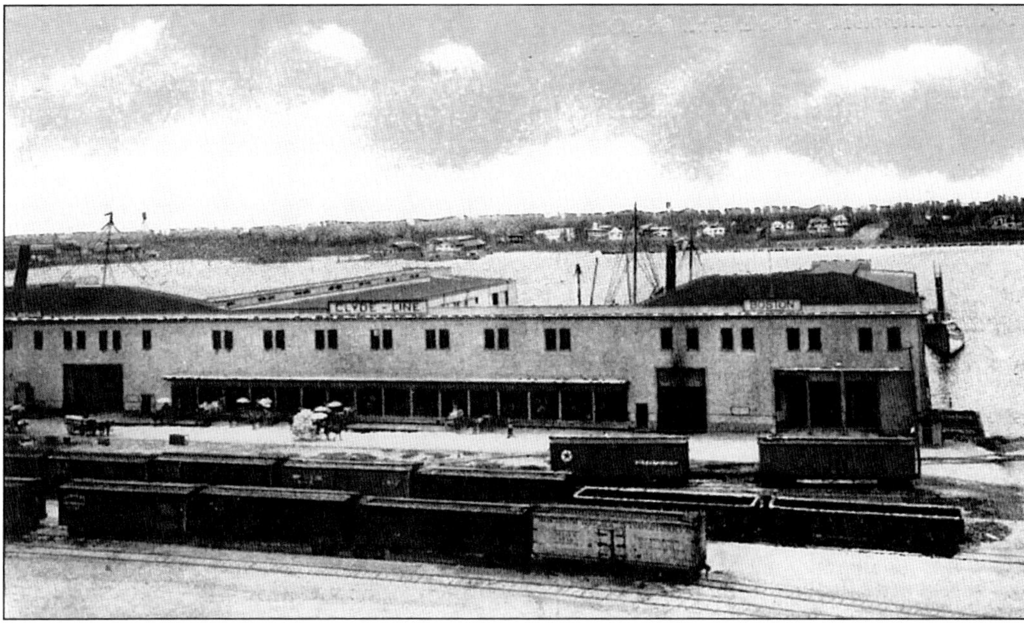

Clyde Line Boston Dock, Jacksonville. The Clyde Line's Boston facility was next to its New York docks. (Postcard courtesy Richard Dragoni.)

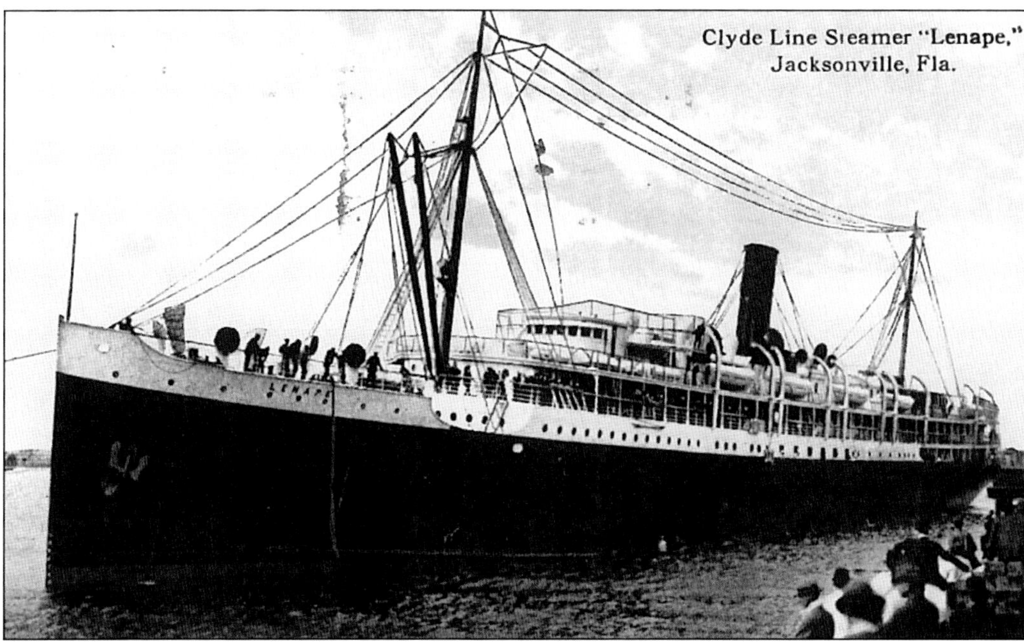

Clyde Line Steamer *Lenape*. The *Lenape*, one of the largest ships in the Clyde fleet, made its first trip to Jacksonville around 1913. At that time, many winter visitors shipped their automobiles south from New York, then drove part or all of the way home in spring. (Postcard courtesy Richard Dragoni.)

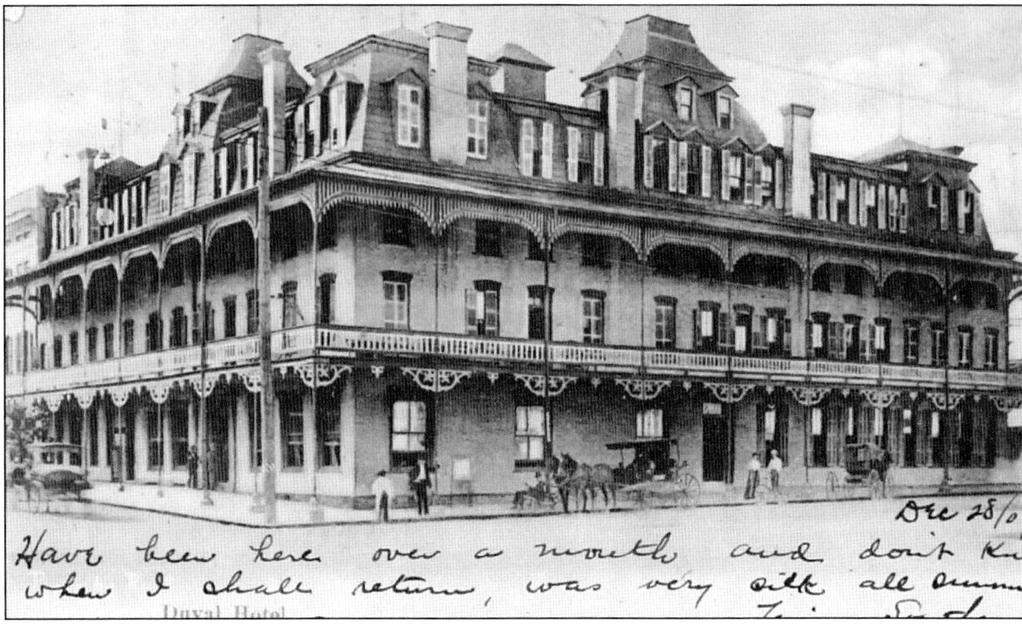

Duval Hotel, Jacksonville, c. 1906–1907. Jacksonville had a number of hotels in the early 1900s, some of which had been rebuilt after the 1901 fire that destroyed most of the city. The wooden Duval, at Hogan and Forsyth Streets, survived that devastation.

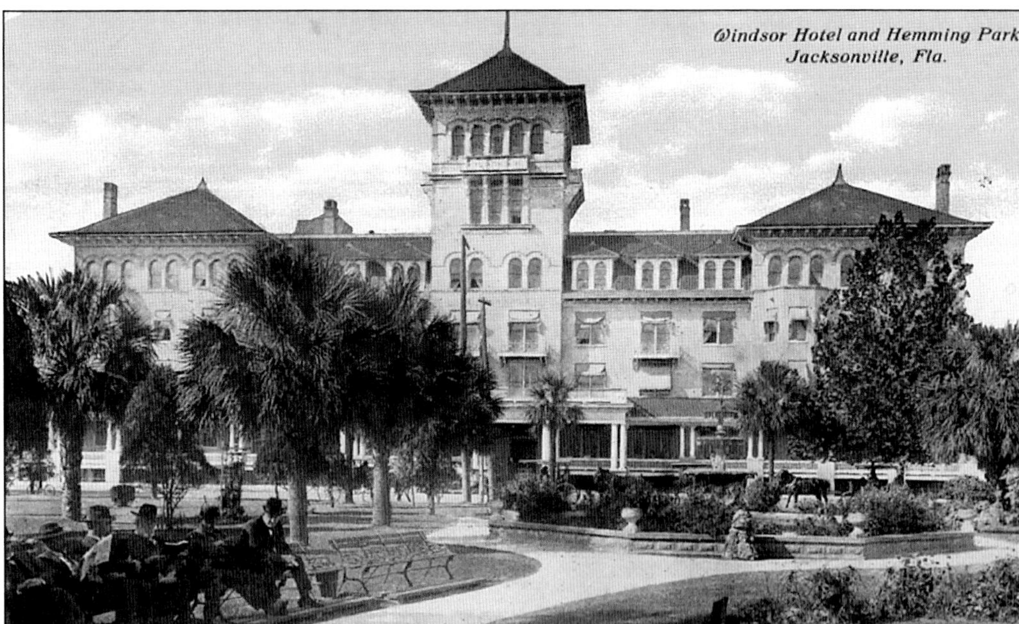

Windsor Hotel And Hemming Park, Jacksonville, c. 1909. The Windsor was one of Jacksonville's finest turn-of-the-century establishments. The 1875 building burned in 1901, and a larger hotel opened for business less than a year later. Fronting Hogan Street and facing Hemming Park, the Windsor occupied an entire city block.

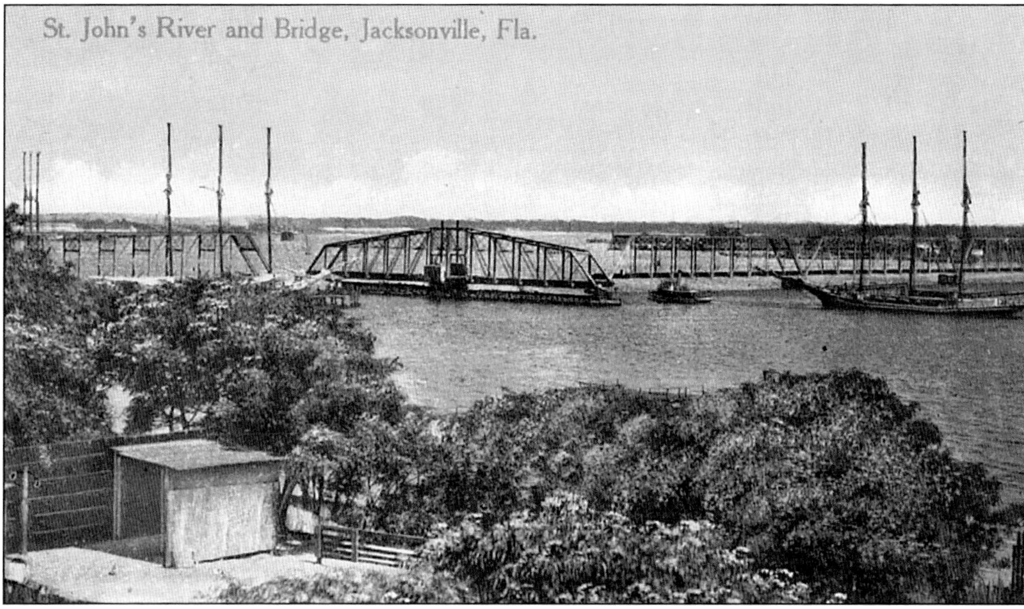

ST. JOHNS RIVER BRIDGE. In 1890, Henry Flagler completed the South's first steel railroad bridge in Jacksonville. Before then, southbound travelers got off the train in the city, rode a ferry across the river, and boarded another train to continue on. While providing a more convenient through-route for passengers, the new bridge also allowed the wealthy to take private Pullman cars farther south, rather than leave them in Jacksonville, as Henry Flagler had done on an 1885 trip to Florida.

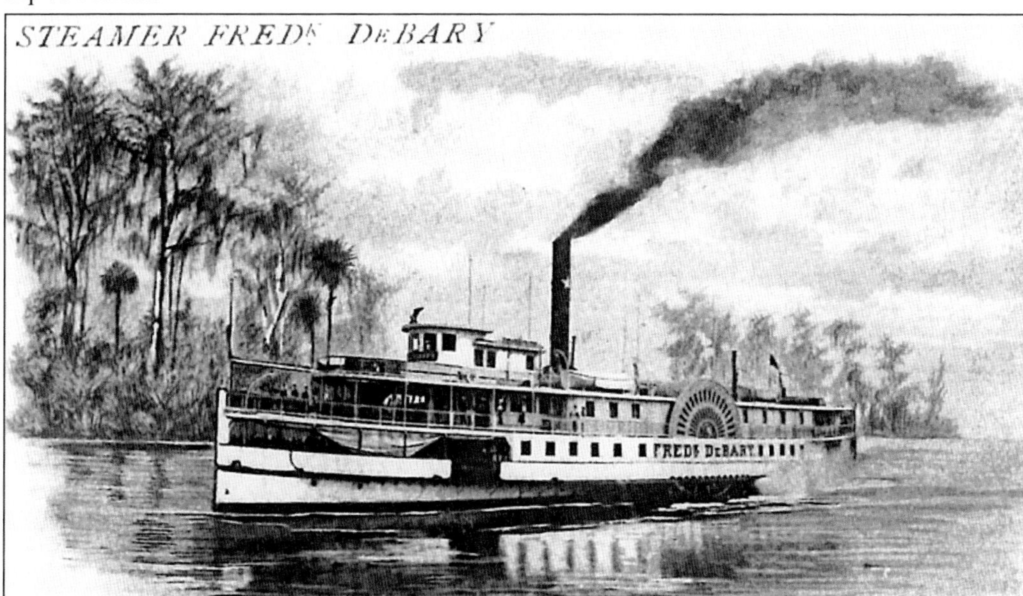

CLYDE ST. JOHNS RIVER LINE ADVERTISEMENT CARD. From Jacksonville, a number of steamers plied south on the St. Johns River. This one was named after the steamboat line owner, Count Samuel Frederick de Bary, founder of a plantation near Enterprise on Lake Monroe. The town of DeBary (spelling altered) bears his name. (Postcard courtesy Richard Dragoni.)

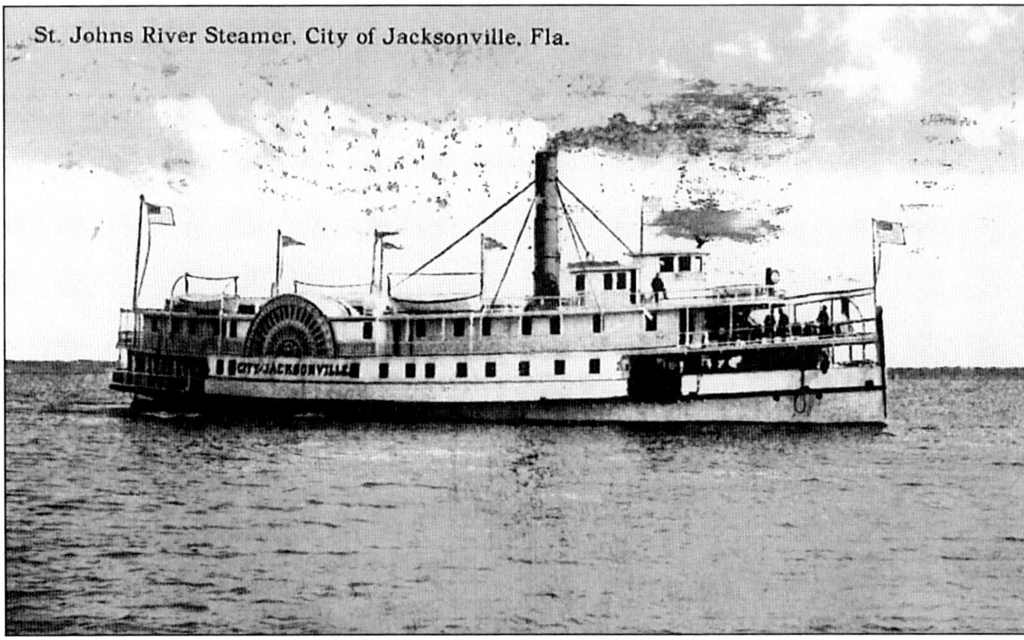

Clyde Steamer *City of Jacksonville*. Built at a northern boat yard in the early 1880s, the *City of Jacksonville* became one of the most reliable passenger and freight vessels to travel the St. Johns River between Jacksonville and Sanford. In the late 19th century the fare, including meals and berth, was $3.75. (Postcard courtesy Richard Dragoni.)

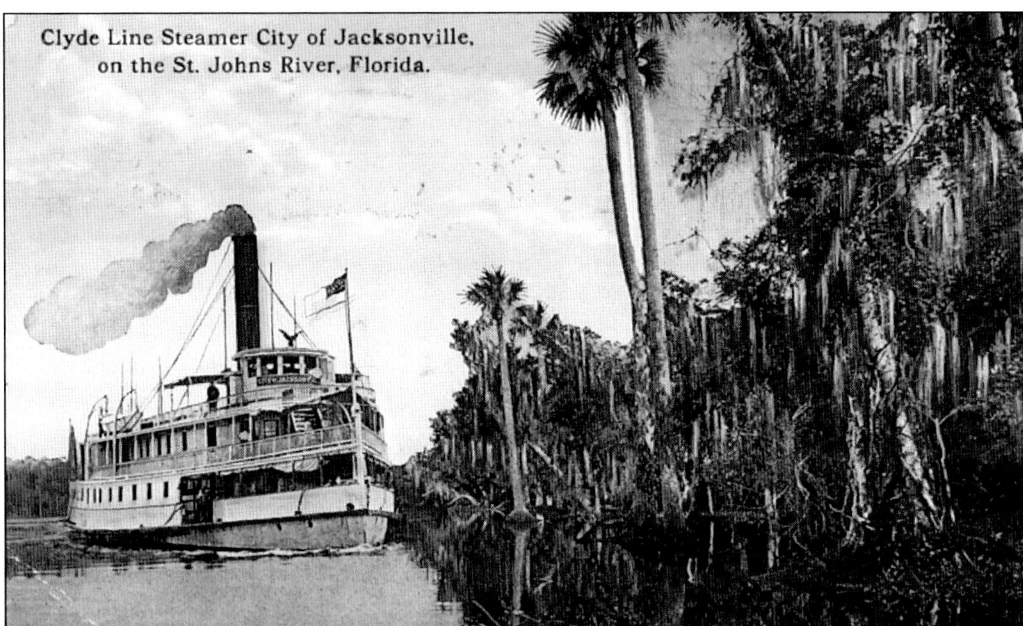

***City of Jacksonville*.** For many years the *City of Jacksonville* made the round trip to Sanford three times a week, stopping at several landings along the way to connect passengers with Ocklawaha River steamers bound for Silver Spring, or with railroad lines to eastern towns.

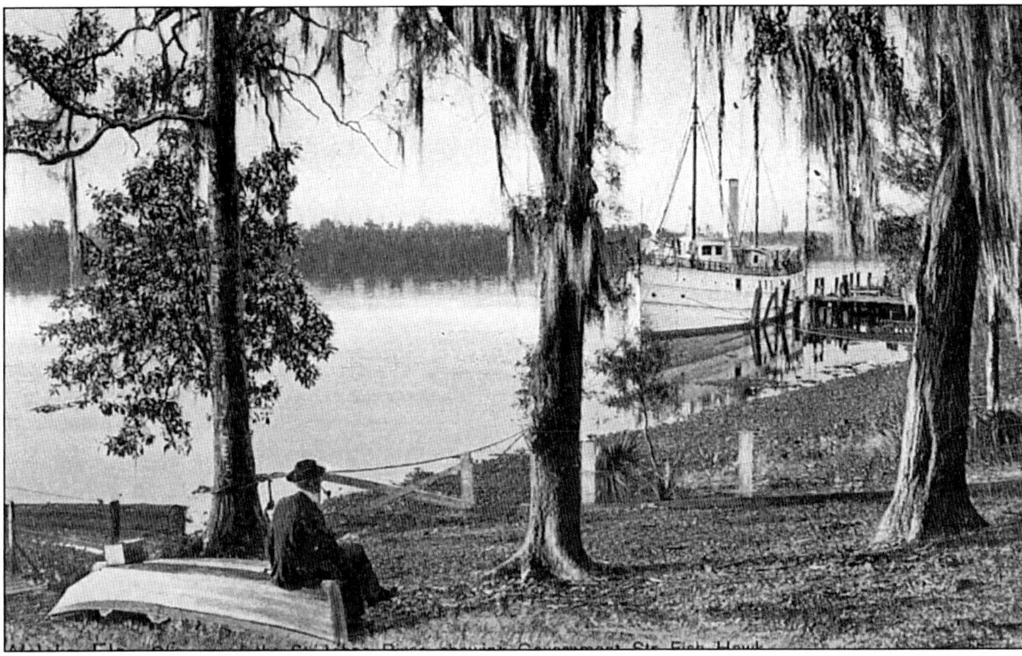

Steamboat Landing on the St. Johns River. Welaka was one of many small steamboat landings on the St. Johns River. It had the distinction of being near the confluence of the St. Johns and Ocklawaha Rivers. Welaka was an Indian name for the St. Johns River. (Postcard courtesy David Findlay.)

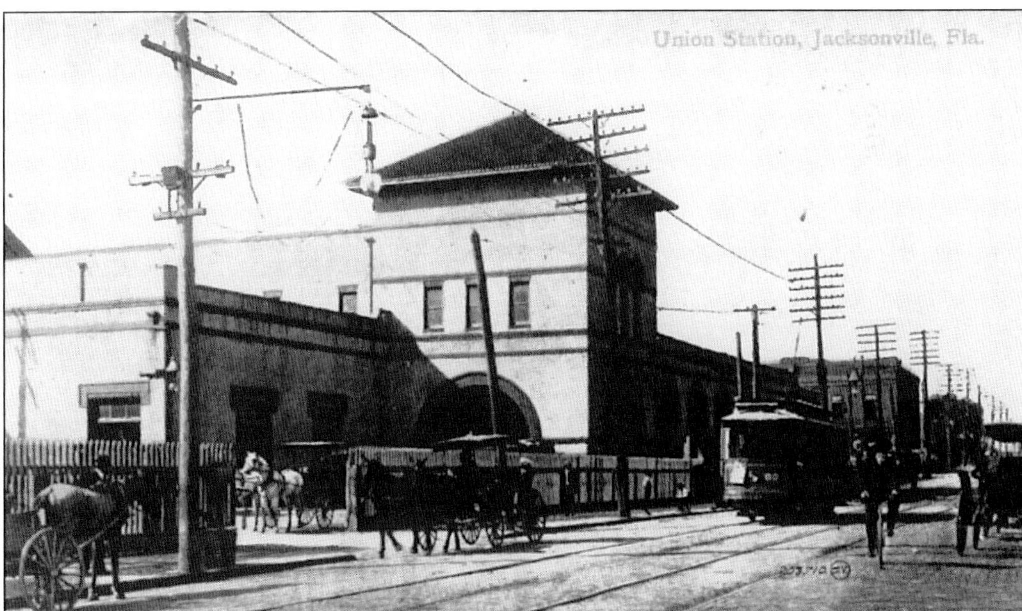

Union Station, Jacksonville. By the late 1880s, most Southern rails had been converted to a uniform gauge already used by the Northern railroad companies. This enabled trains from New York to come straight through to Jacksonville's Union Station. (Postcard courtesy Richard Dragoni.)

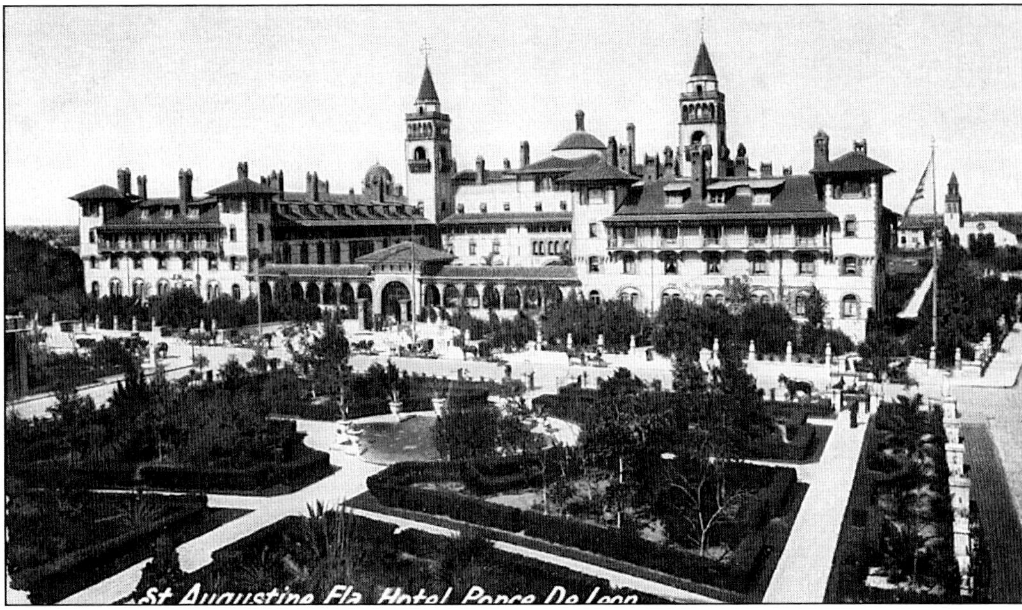

PONCE DE LEON HOTEL, ST. AUGUSTINE. Henry Flagler's first luxury hotel opened in January 1888, marking the beginning of his plan to establish Florida's east coast as the American Riviera. The opening coincided with that of the Ormond Hotel on the Halifax River in Ormond, which Flagler would later purchase. Clearly, the Ponce de Leon was intended for the well-to-do. Julian Ralph, author of *Dixie, or Southern Scenes and Sketches*, observed that a stay at the Ponce de Leon was like being at a royal palace, but a modest man could "hobnob with millionaires" for about $5 a day.

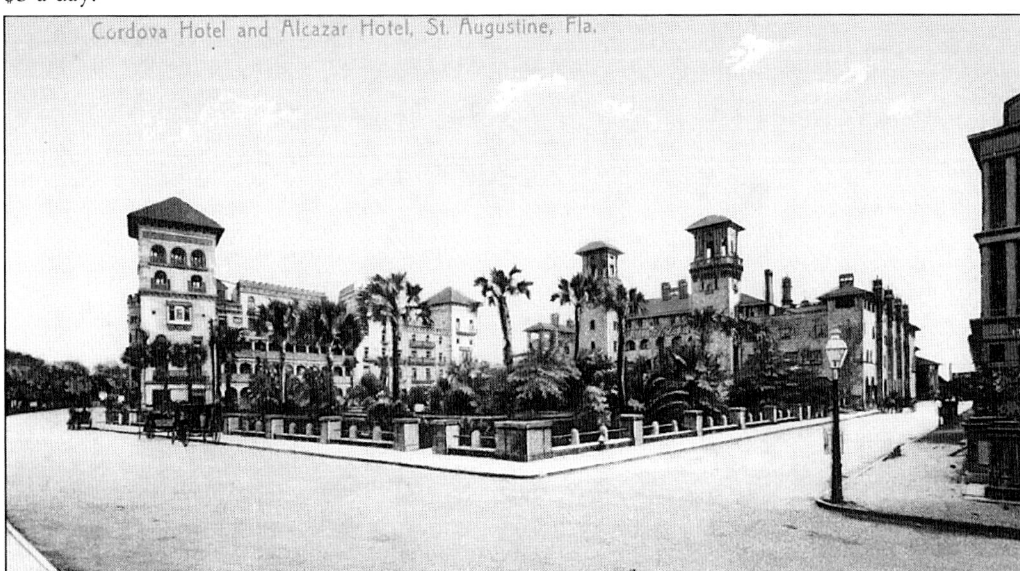

CORDOVA AND ALCAZAR HOTELS, ST. AUGUSTINE. Construction of the Alcazar, another Flagler establishment, was begun before completion of the Ponce de Leon. In 1889 Flagler purchased the nearby Casa Monica Hotel, renamed it the Cordova, and later joined it with the Alcazar. Note how the architecture of the three hotels harmonizes with the area's Spanish heritage.

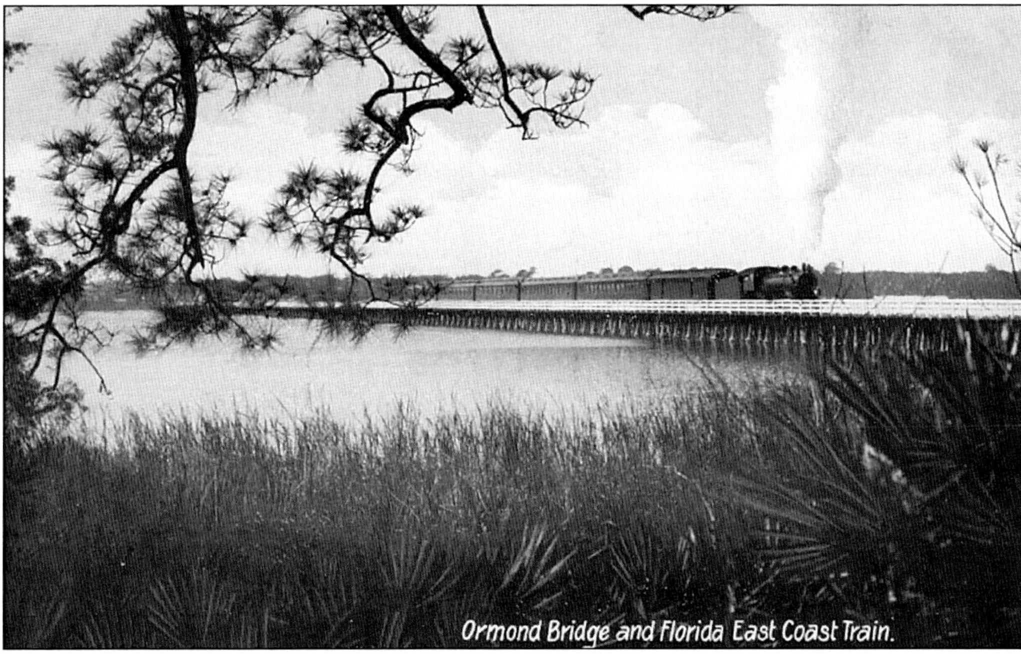

Ormond Bridge And Florida East Coast Railway. Tourism in the Halifax River region was boosted with the coming of Henry Flagler's Florida East Coast Railway. About the time he purchased the Ormond Hotel, Flagler built a wooden railroad bridge across the river to deposit passengers at its doors. The train backed over the river to return to the mainland.

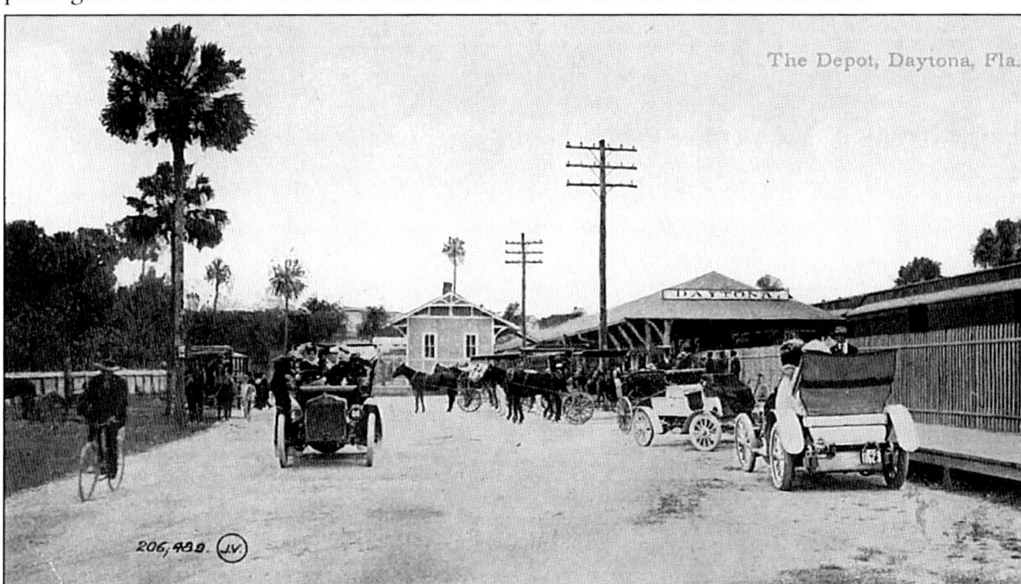

Railroad Depot, Daytona. In 1886 the St. Johns and Halifax River Railroad arrived from Palatka, marking Daytona's first direct rail link with another town. A station was built near First Avenue (now Seagrave) and Volusia Avenue (now International Speedway Boulevard). To facilitate shipping, a spur line was placed down Orange Avenue to the Halifax River, where a depot and commercial loading dock were built. Henry Flagler purchased the railroad, making it part of his Florida East Coast Railway System. (Postcard courtesy David Findlay.)

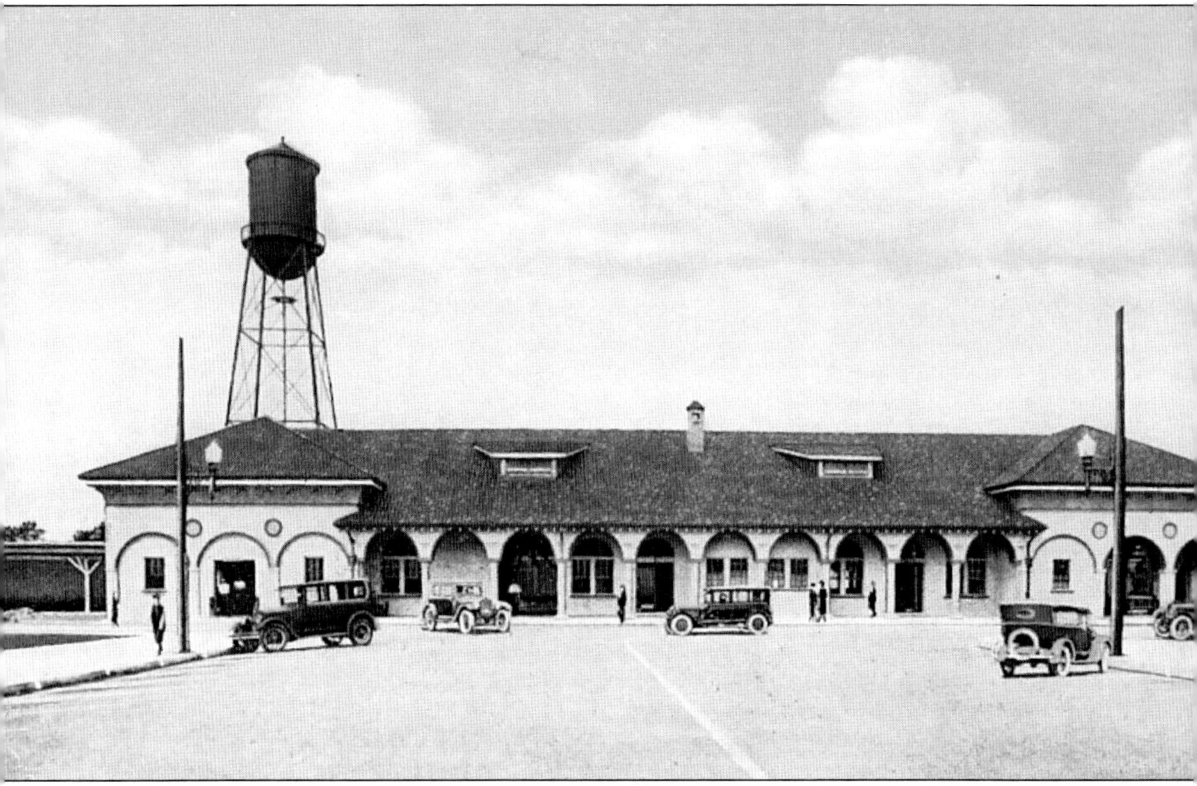

Florida East Coast Railway Station, Daytona. About 1889 Henry Flagler extended his railroad line south towards New Smyrna, laying the tracks through Daytona just west of Ridgewood Avenue. Pictured here is the main Daytona railroad station as it was in the mid-1920s.

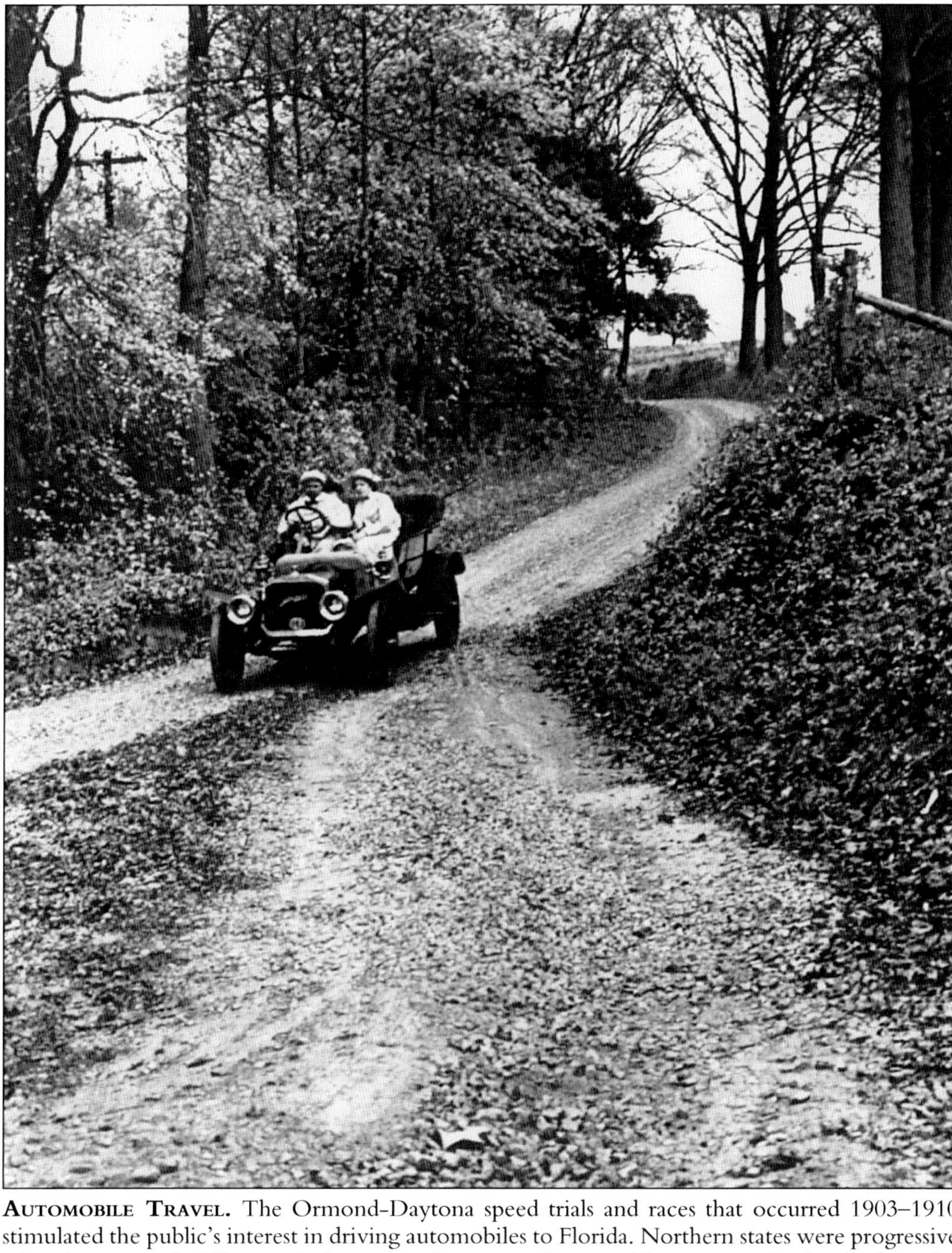

AUTOMOBILE TRAVEL. The Ormond-Daytona speed trials and races that occurred 1903–1910 stimulated the public's interest in driving automobiles to Florida. Northern states were progressive when it came to building roads; however, there were few passable routes to the South along the lower eastern seaboard. Ironically, once an automobile made it to the Halifax River region, one of the best roads to Daytona was the beach! (Photograph courtesy AAA.)

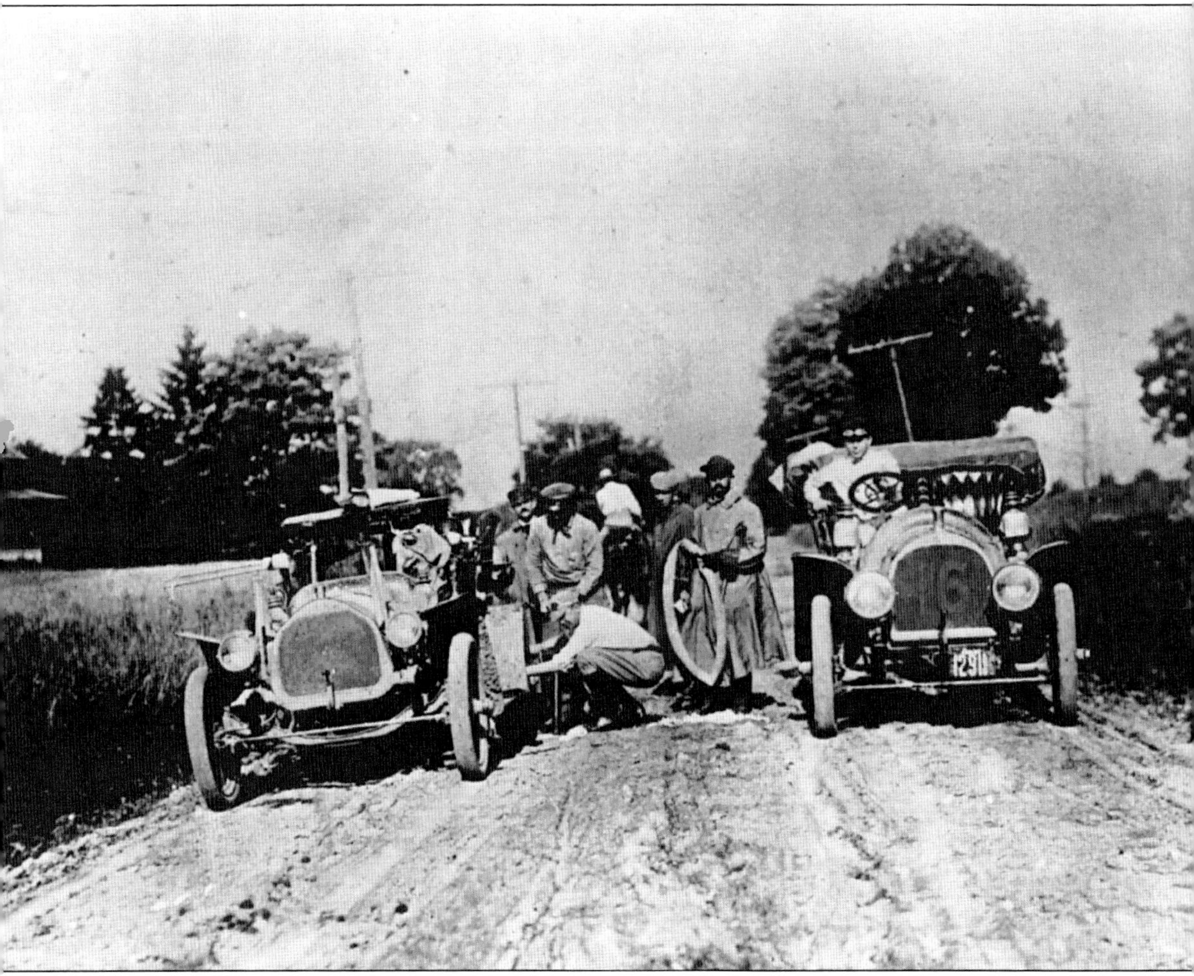

THE PERILS OF BAD ROADS. Road surfaces differed from state to state, as some motorists learned the hard way. Another hindrance to motor travel was the lack of maps, road signs, and bridges, as well as roadside assistance. In 1907, motorist Ralph Owen drove from New York to Daytona in 17 days, making one of the earliest recorded through trips. Southern automobile travel received a great deal of publicity in 1911 when the Glidden Tour went from New York to Jacksonville to test the reliability of roads between the two points. (Photograph courtesy AAA.)

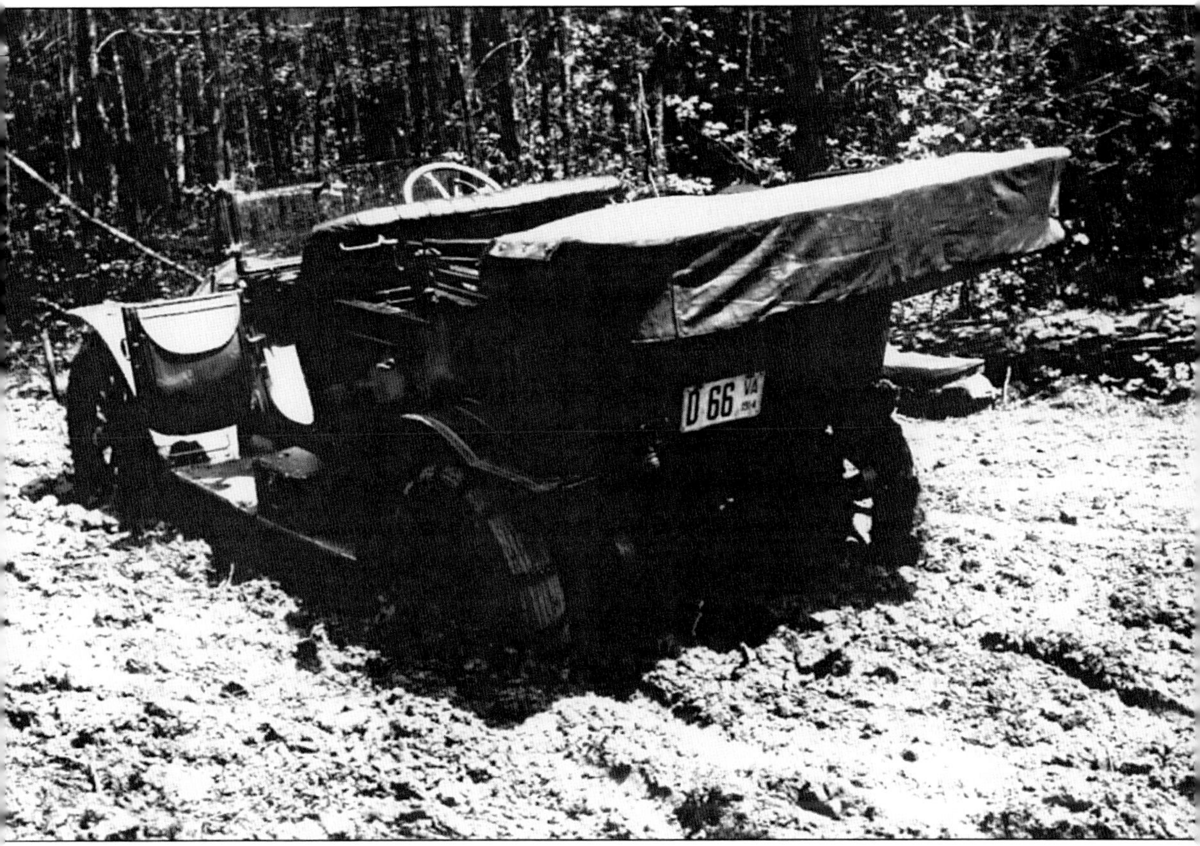

MOTORING THROUGH THE SOUTH. In Georgia and North and South Carolina, sand and clay roads provided smooth driving, but only when dry. Florida's early roads were surfaced with a hodgepodge of materials, including shell, vitrified brick, pine straw, and sawdust. The sandy soil in Florida's open country was sufficient when wet, but the beach sand was superior, as the racing set discovered in 1903. Some of the earliest guidebooks recommended the beach in routing descriptions. (Photograph courtesy AAA.)

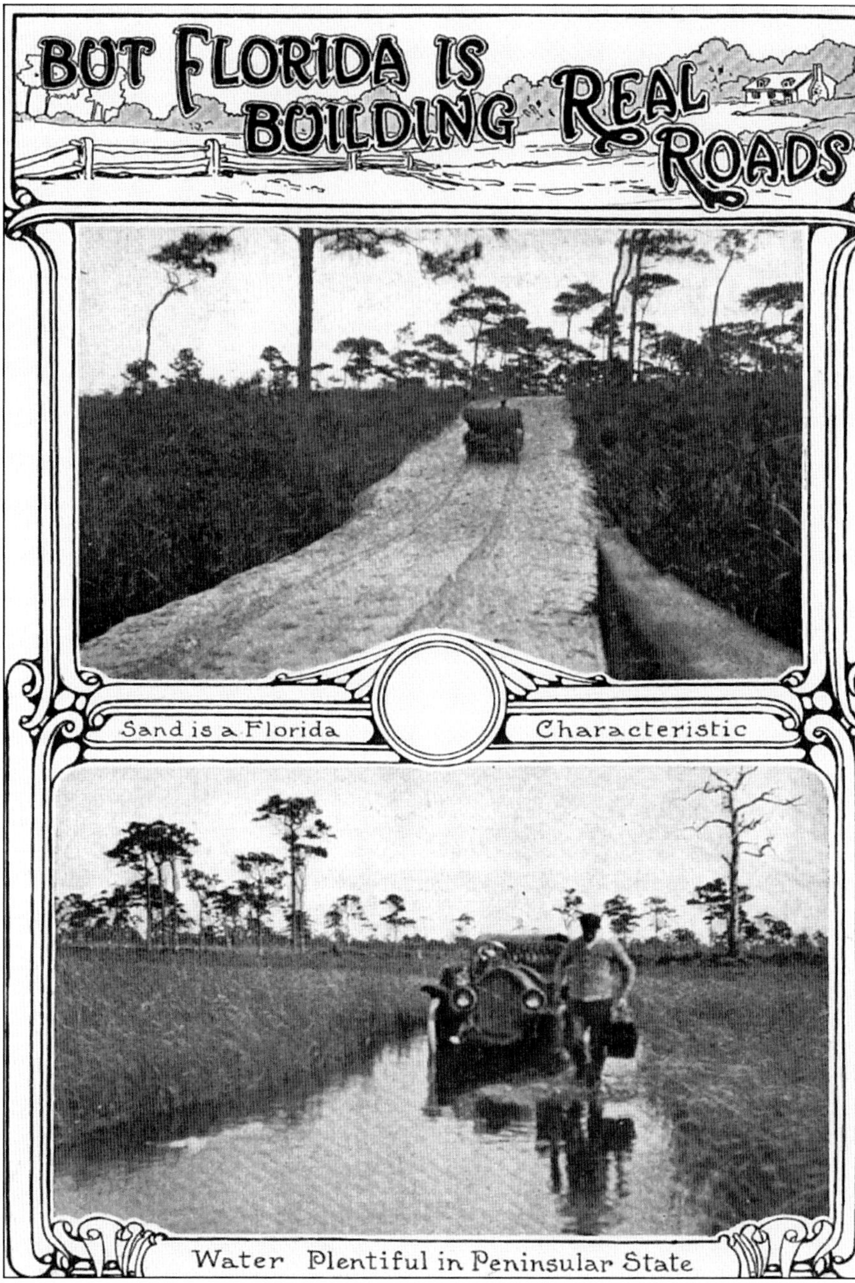

Good Roads In Florida. In 1910 a team of motorists blazed a trail 386 miles, from Jacksonville to Miami, traveling up and down sand knolls, dodging trees, pushing through grass, fording streams, and riding ferries. At one point they encountered a new road being filled with tree limbs, rocks, and clods of earth. They skirted a blazing forest fire, stampeded cattle, and made a "Spanish windlass" to haul the car out of a mire. The last 80 miles of the journey took them over excellent roads to their final destination, a feat accomplished in 33 hours of traveling time that spanned seven days. This account appeared in a 1910 edition of *American Motorist* magazine, but an intrastate road network was still a few years away. (Photograph courtesy AAA.)

Two

Street Scenes in the Triple Cities

Before formal roads were built or railroad tracks laid, the Halifax River was the primary highway to the Daytona settlement. For this reason, commerce and transportation centered on Beach Street. This section features the business and residential avenues of Daytona as well as the main arteries of Seabreeze and Daytona Beach in their formative years.

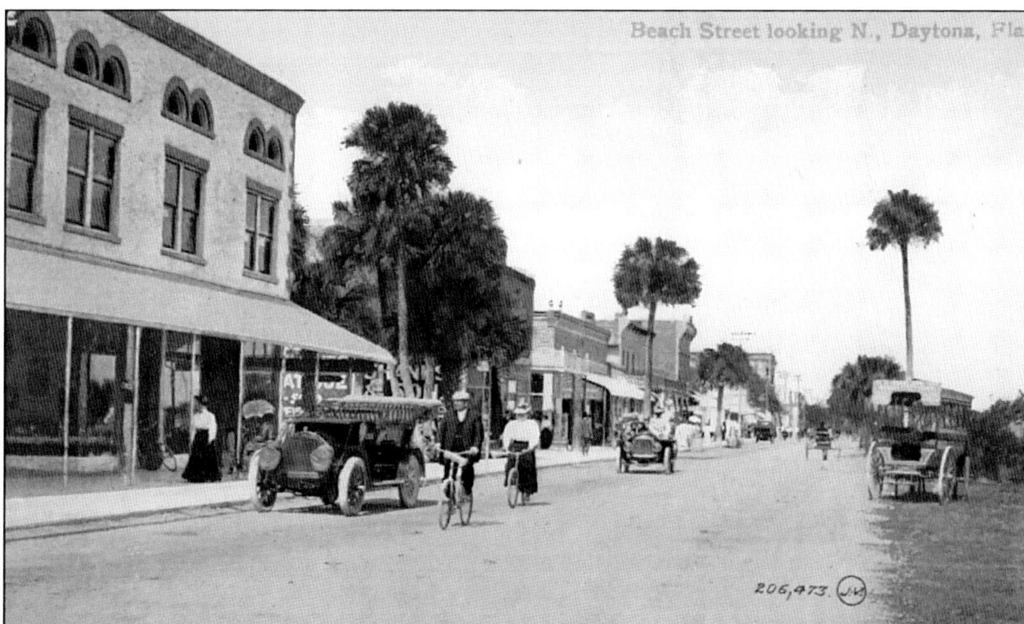

South Beach Street Near Orange Avenue, *c.* 1909. This postcard shows a busy section of South Beach Street just north of Orange Avenue. The property with the palm trees behind the automobile in the foreground became the site of the Merchant's Bank building in 1911. Advertising partially hidden on the side of the next building was for J.A. Shanks & Son, Confectioners, who offered candy and ice cream.

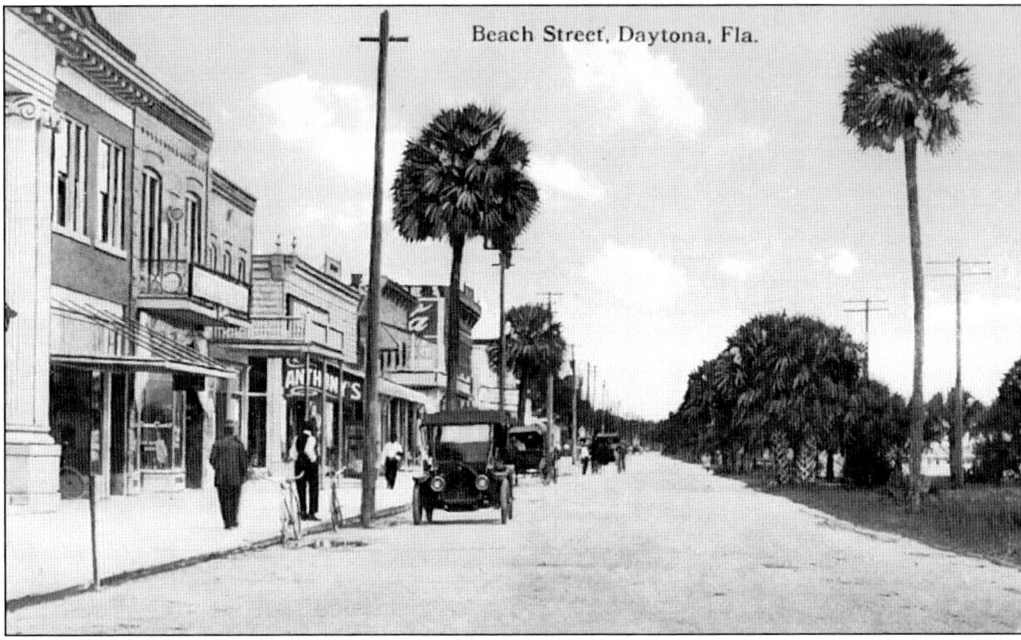

SOUTH BEACH STREET NEAR IVY LANE, c. 1912. The columns supporting the entrance to the Merchants Bank building can be seen at the far left. Anthony's, one of the town's leading clothiers, was located at the corner of Ivy Lane, although the narrow street is hardly discernible in this picture. Anthony's also operated in Palm Beach.

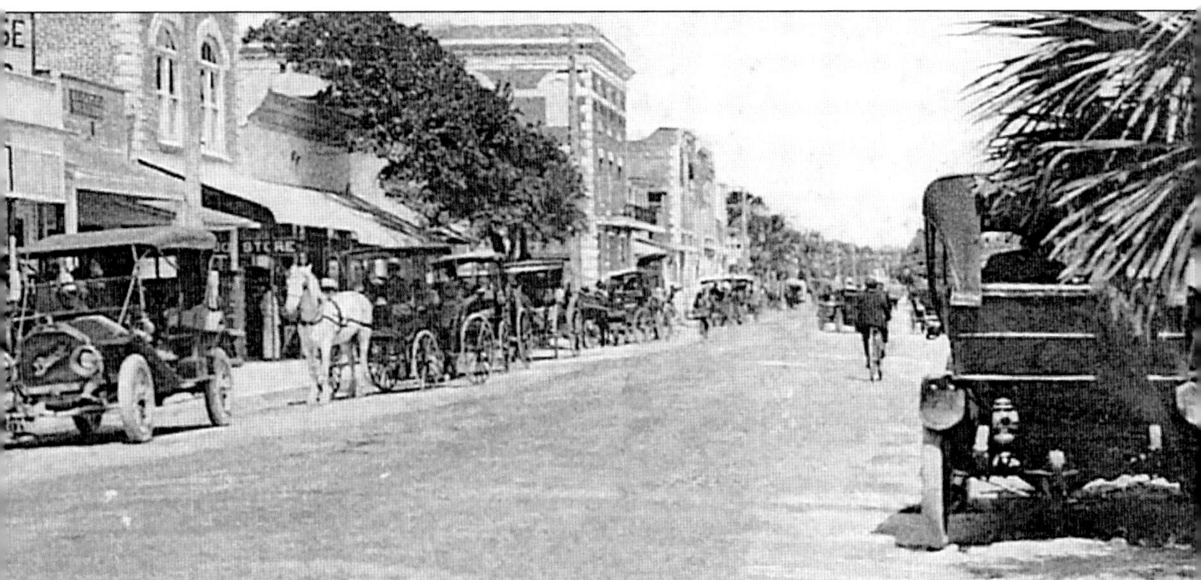

EAST AND WEST SIDES OF SOUTH BEACH STREET, c. 1912. Beach Street hugged the Halifax River for a distance of about 2 miles. This panorama card puts into perspective the proximity of the town's commercial district to the river. The lady shading herself under the palmettos (right) looks north towards the corner of Magnolia Avenue, where the post office was located. A Buick automobile (left) is parked in front of Gardiner's Art Shop. Mr. Gardiner was a successful portrait and scenic photographer whose work was sold in shops throughout the country. The impressive

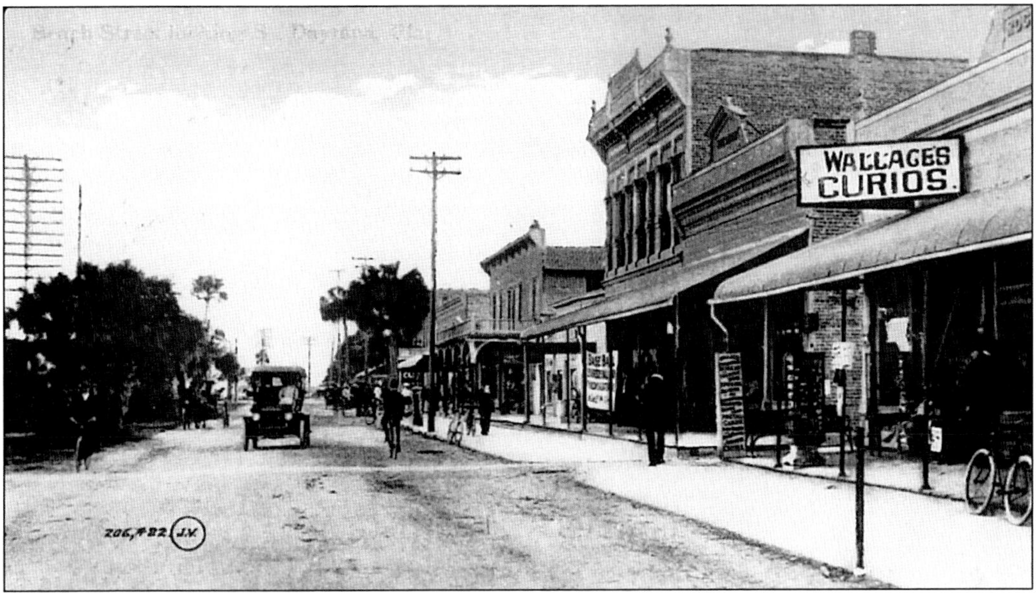

South Beach Street, Looking South, Midway Between Magnolia And Orange Avenues. Wallace's Curios, established in 1901, sold souvenirs such as postcards, china, and spoons, according to the free-standing sign in front of the shop. A banner stretched across the posts in front of the next store announced the coming of a baseball game. Baseball debuted in Daytona about 1914 with the construction of a field on the landfill that became City Island; the local team was called the Islanders. (Postcard courtesy Richard Dragoni.)

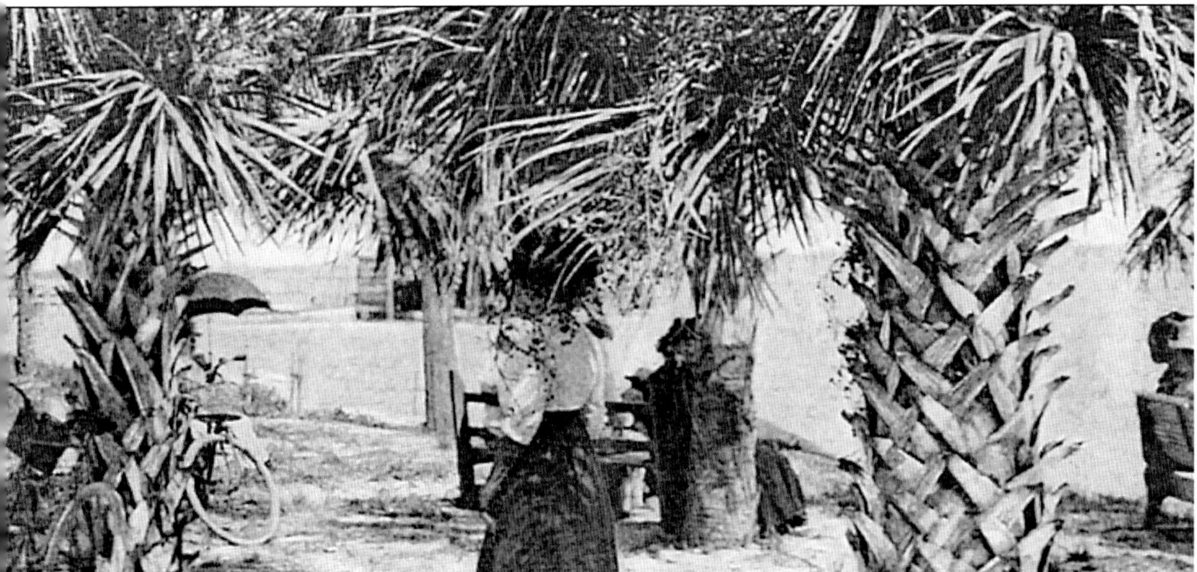

three-story building farther north housed the Peck-Hendricks Company, which offered dry goods at "prices as low as New York department stores." Anything from trunks to carriage trimmings, from cotton duck to pantesote awning cloth, was available along with notions, shoes, and ready-to-wear garments. Note the people resting on benches at the river's edge. (Postcard courtesy David Findlay.)

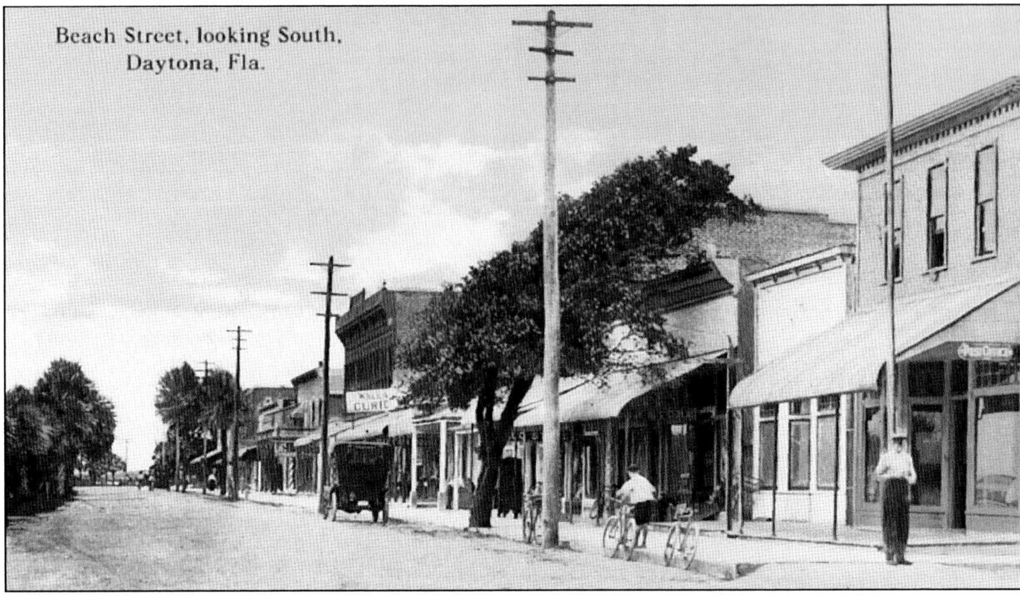

South Beach Street, Looking South From Magnolia Avenue. The building with the awning on the corner was the post office. Shoppers also could find a variety of services and merchandise in this block: Two doors south of the post office was Our Store, a grocery owned by H.S. Miller, followed by Clark's Drug Store and Wallace's Curios. The striped pole farther down the street marked the location of tonsorialist G.H. Hooper's shop.

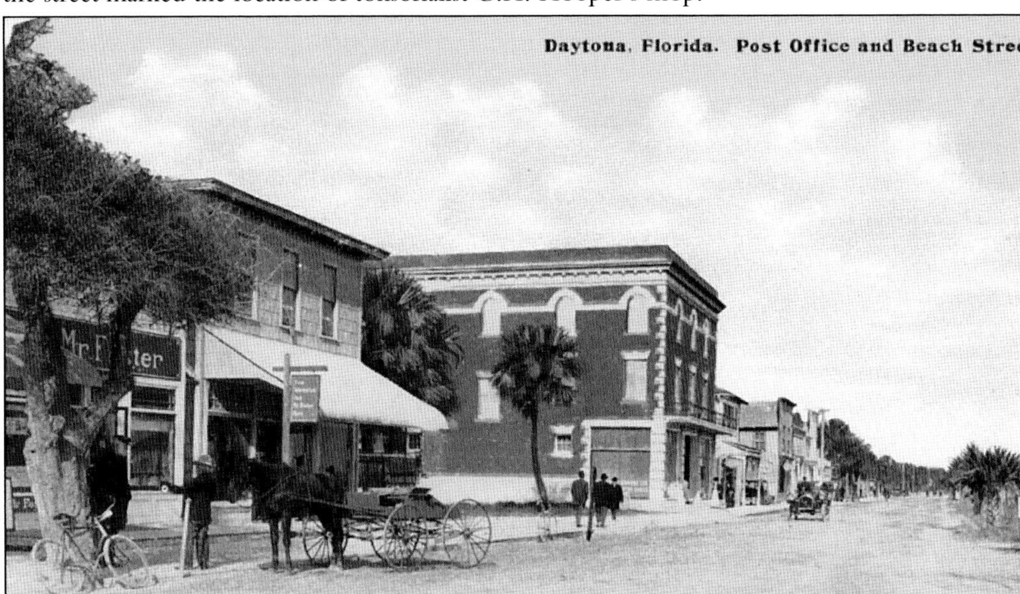

Post Office, Corner South Beach Street And Magnolia Avenue. The caption on the back of this 1912 card described the post office as a second-class office that handled a "vast amount of mail matter for the size of the town." Door-to-door delivery service started in 1911. Foster's Information Bureau occupied the building just south of the post office, as evidenced by the street sign behind the horse and buggy which reads: "Free information, ask Mr. Foster here." The Peck-Hendricks building is also shown again.

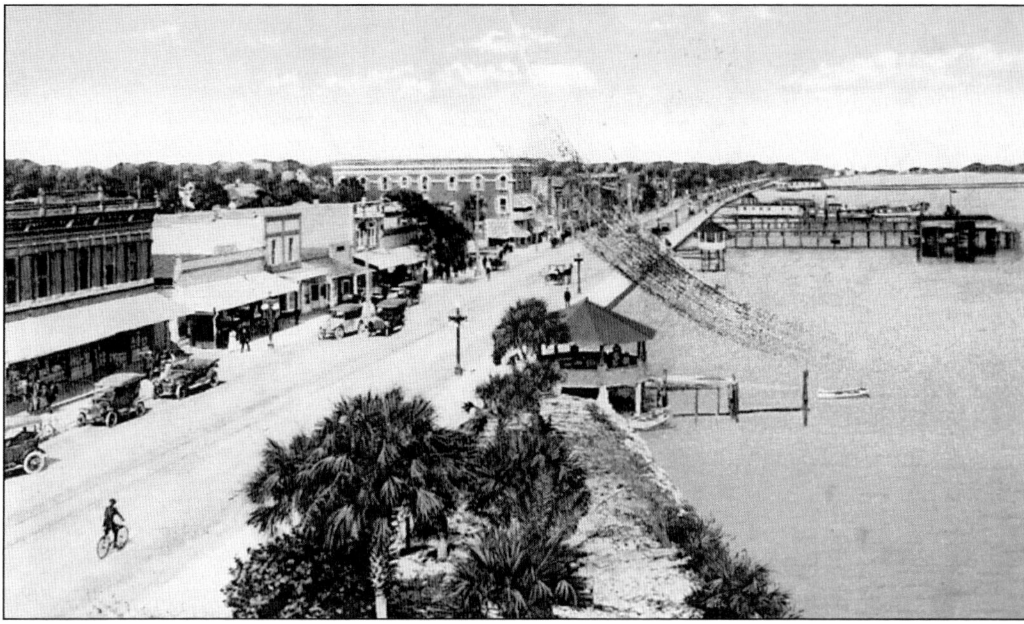

Esplanade Along South Beach Street. Improvements to South Beach Street can be seen in this 1919 postcard. The sidewalk with lampposts skirting the river was donated to the town in 1914 by one of its most generous citizens, Charles G. Burgoyne. This "esplanade" extended north from Orange Avenue to Bay Street, in front of Burgoyne's mansion.

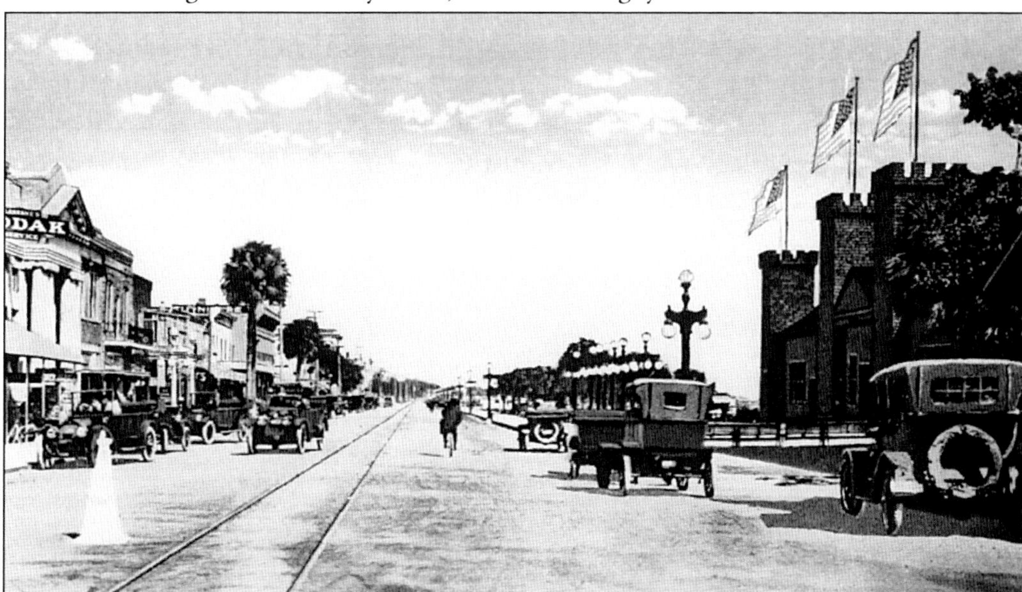

South Beach Street At Orange Avenue. This was one of Daytona's busiest intersections. In addition to the railroad depot and Casino Burgoyne, there were banking and commercial establishments in the area. Note the Merchant's Bank building, left, next to the "Kodak" sign marking the shop of R.H. LeSesne, one of Daytona's foremost photographers. The rails down the middle of the street supported the Central of Florida Railway's electric streetcars, which began operating about 1914–1915.

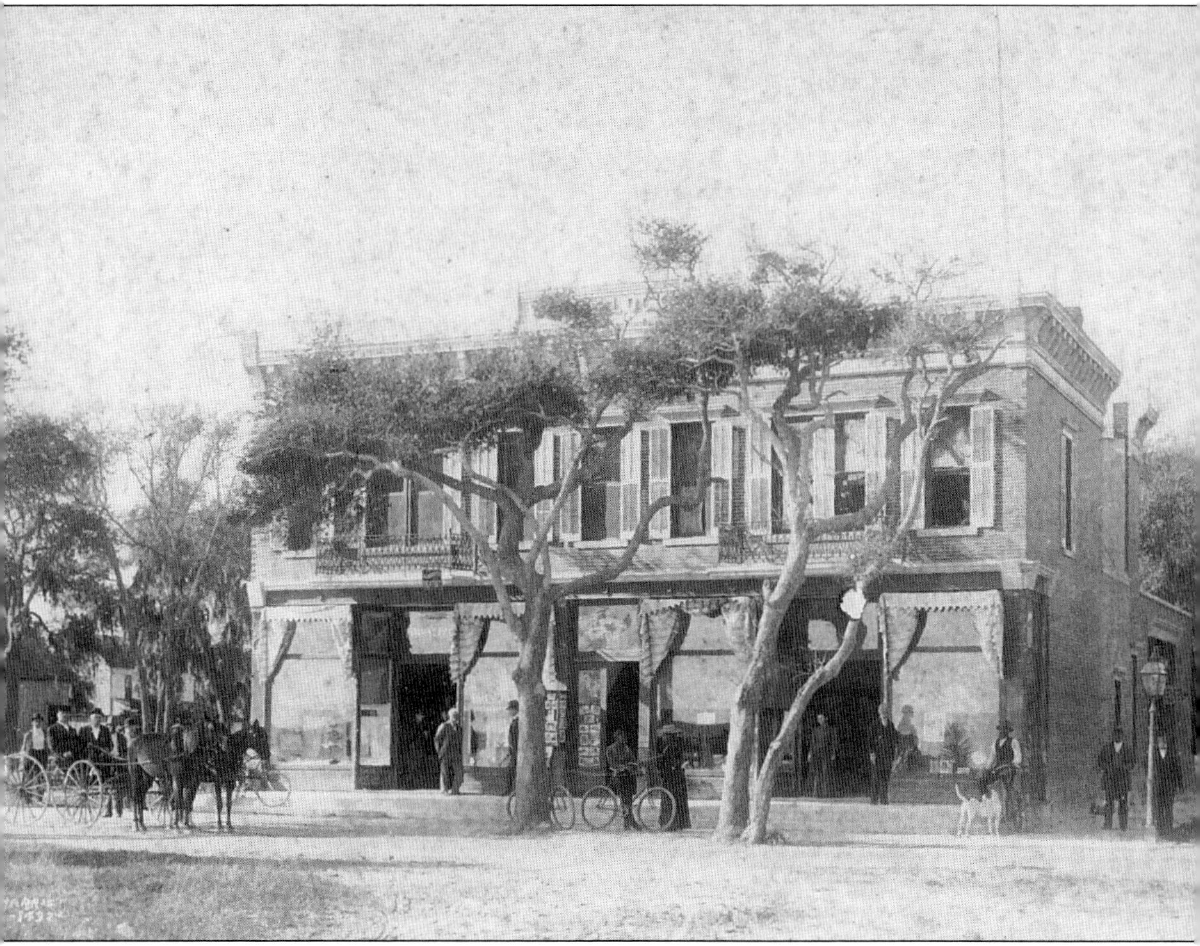

CORNER OF SOUTH BEACH STREET AND ORANGE AVENUE, C. 1900. The studio of Edward G. Harris, who is the assumed photographer of this picture signed "Harris," was in this building, along with F.T. Peck's dry goods store and the dental office of Dr. T.H. Houghton. Actually, the building was called the Peck Block. The Harris business was later taken over by another respected photographer of Daytona scenes, W.L. Coursen. (Photograph courtesy Shear family.)

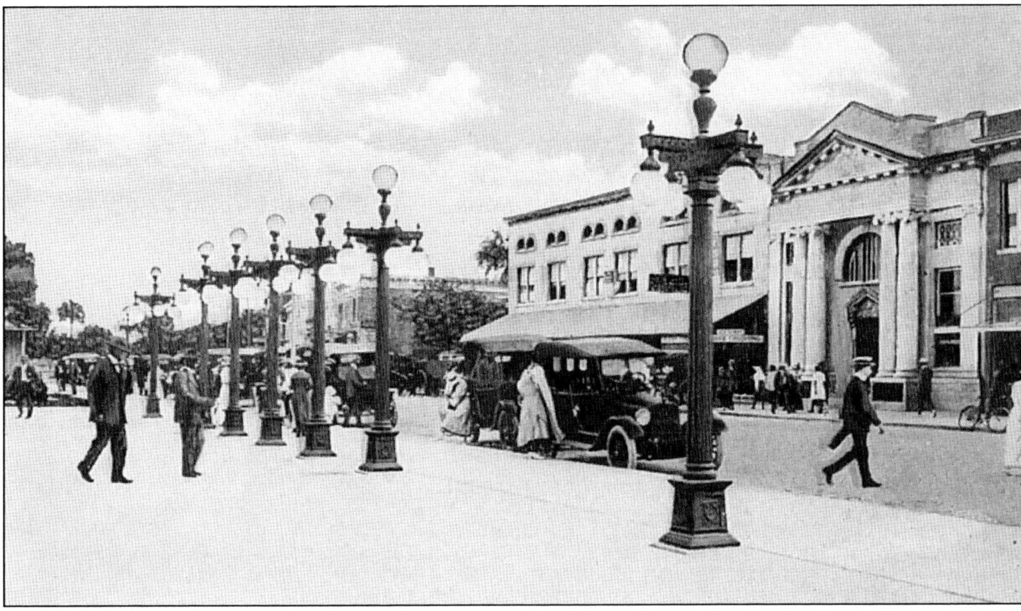

South Beach Street and Orange Avenue. This is an excellent depiction of the stately Merchant's Bank building, as seen from the esplanade in front of Casino Burgoyne. After the bank failed in the late 1920s, the building changed hands several times, then became the home of the Halifax Historical Museum.

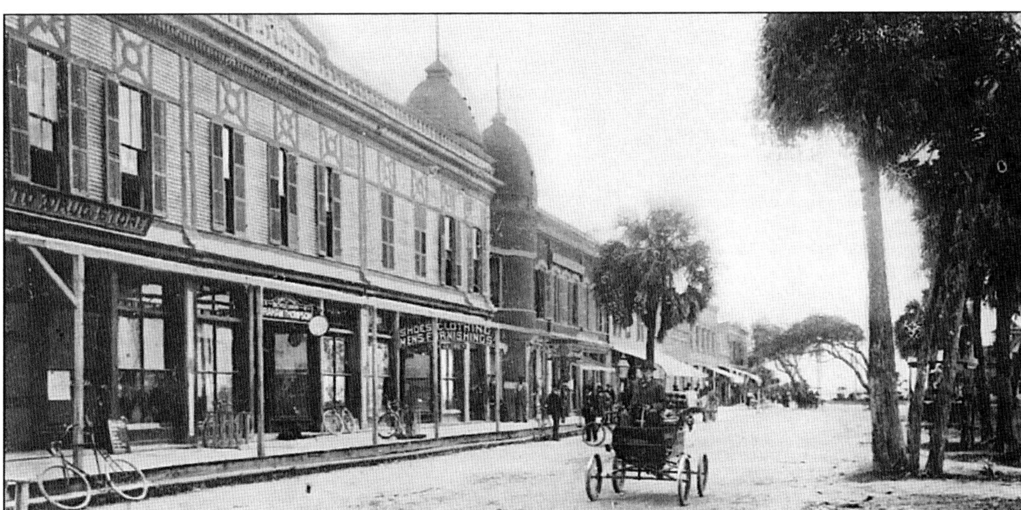

South Beach Street, South of Orange Avenue. The building in the foreground often was referred to as the Atlantic Block, as the lettering atop the second story indicates. It was occupied by a men's furnishings store, a drugstore operated by Mr. Huston, and Graham Thompson's bicycle shop. An opera house was on the second floor of the building. Note the horseless carriage in the street.

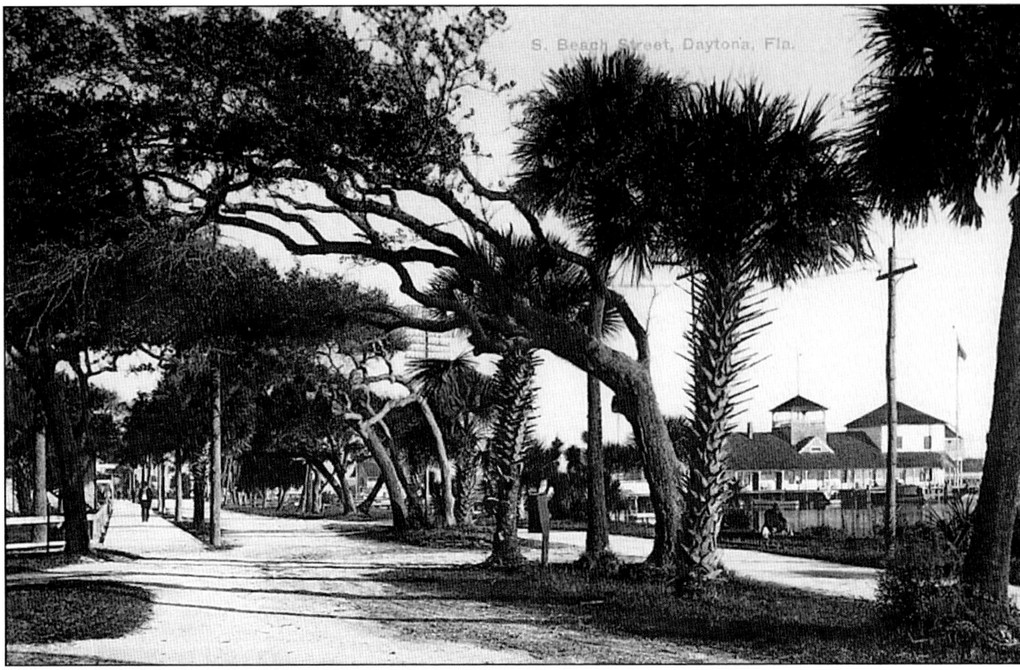

SOUTH BEACH STREET, LOOKING NORTH FROM LOOMIS AVENUE. The Halifax River Yacht Club was just south of Orange Avenue.

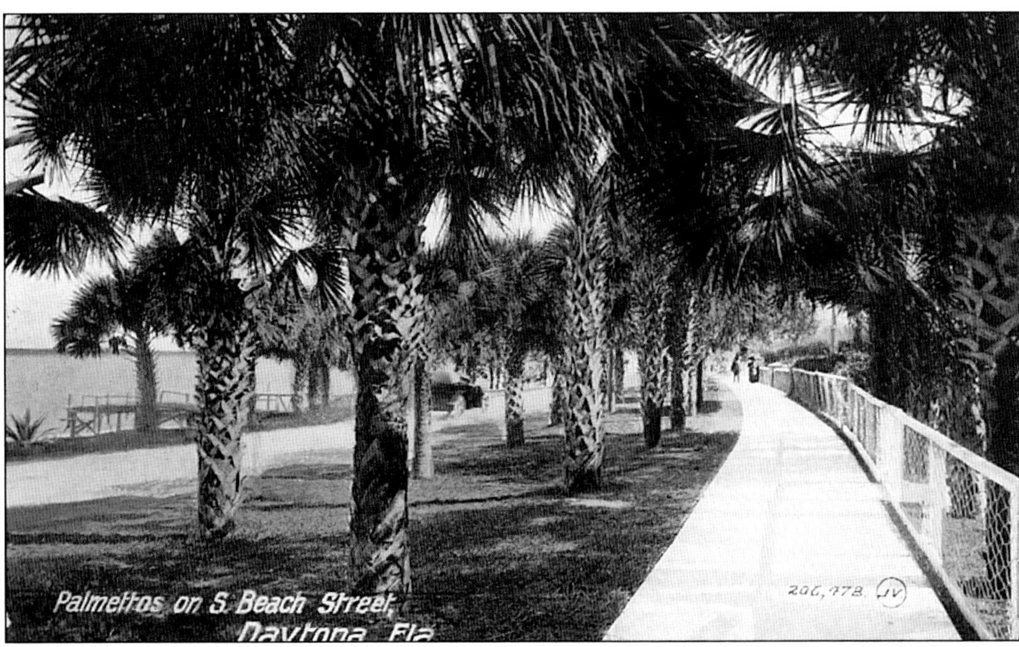

LOOKING SOUTH ON SOUTH BEACH STREET. This is how South Beach Street looked prior to 1909, just south of the Halifax River Yacht Club.

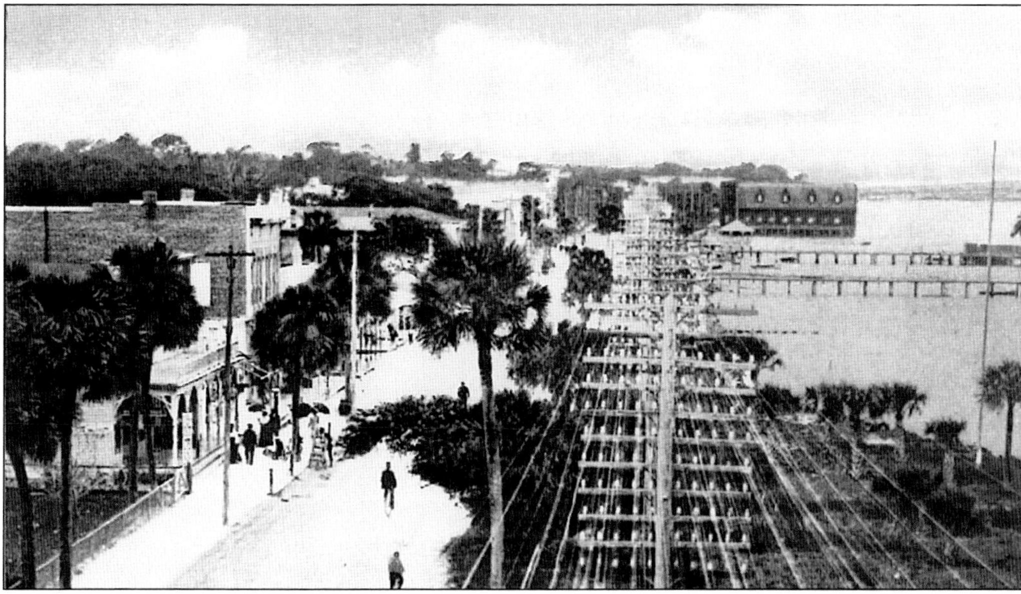

North Beach Street Near Volusia Avenue, Daytona. Beach Street was divided into north and south segments by Volusia Avenue, which intersected the block depicted in this card. In the distance was the boathouse where Charles G. Burgoyne kept his yacht *Sweetheart*, opposite his mansion at Bay Street. This postcard pre-dates 1911, when the boathouse was removed. Burgoyne's interest in yachting and his affiliation with the Halifax River Yacht Club earned him the nickname "Commodore." (Postcard courtesy Richard Dragoni.)

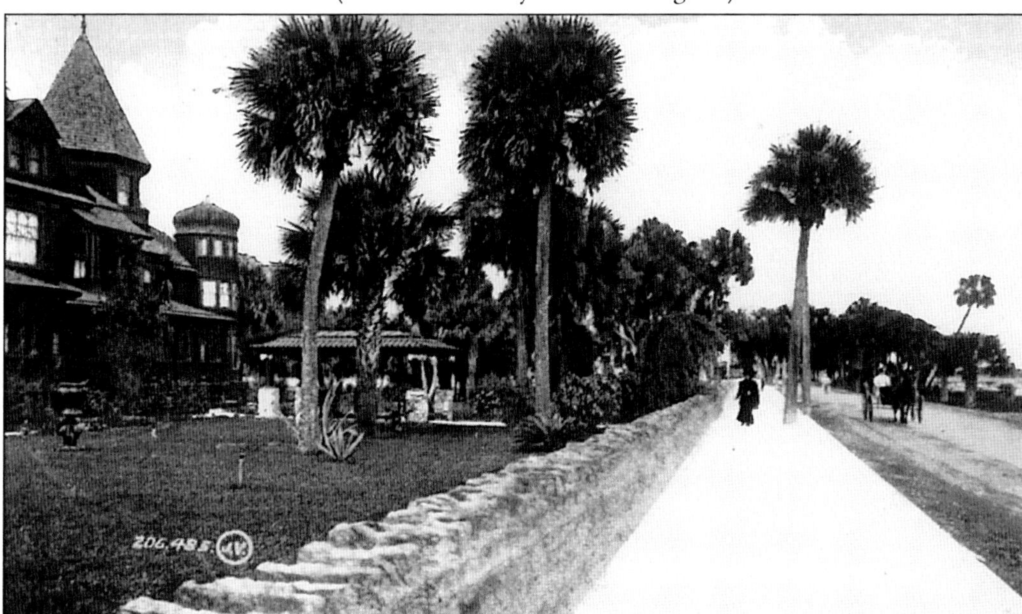

Burgoyne Residence. The Burgoyne estate occupied almost an entire block of North Beach Street between Volusia Avenue and Bay Street. It included a stable and servants' quarters, and was surrounded by a rock wall. Locals referred to Commodore Burgoyne's home as the "castle." This was the second home built by Burgoyne, the first being located on the peninsula. (Postcard courtesy Richard Dragoni.)

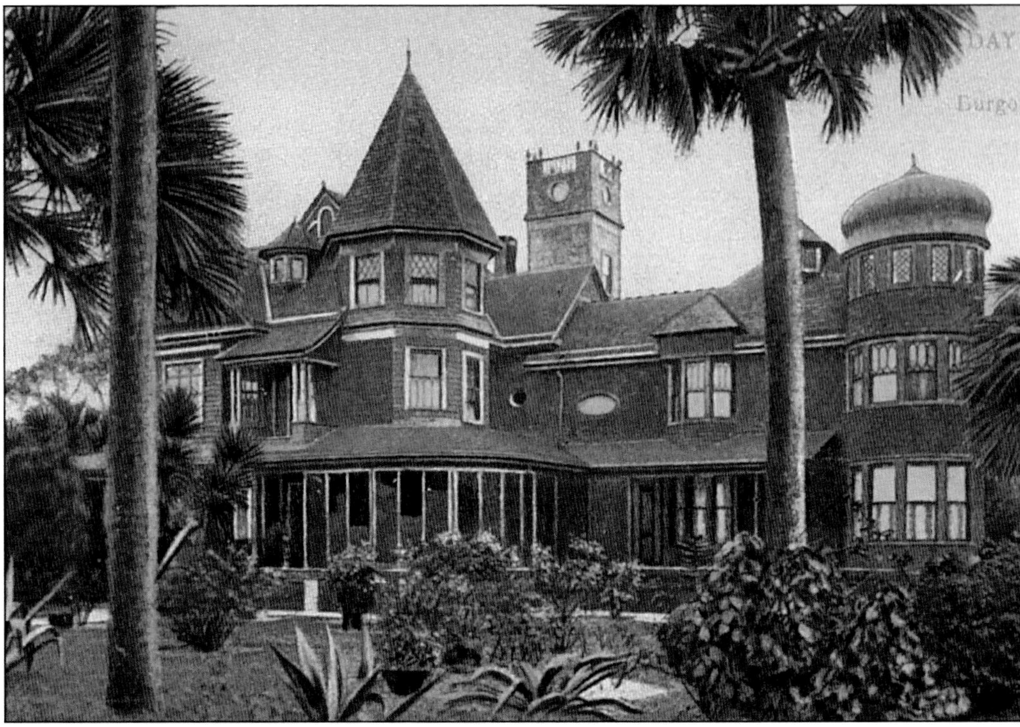

BURGOYNE MANSION ON NORTH BEACH STREET. The Burgoynes hosted musical events in their mansion and gave an annual party for local children on the grounds of the estate. Charles G. Burgoyne died in 1916, leaving a legacy of community service and philanthropic deeds. His wife, who some say turned reclusive after Burgoyne's death, sold the property to a developer in the 1940s.

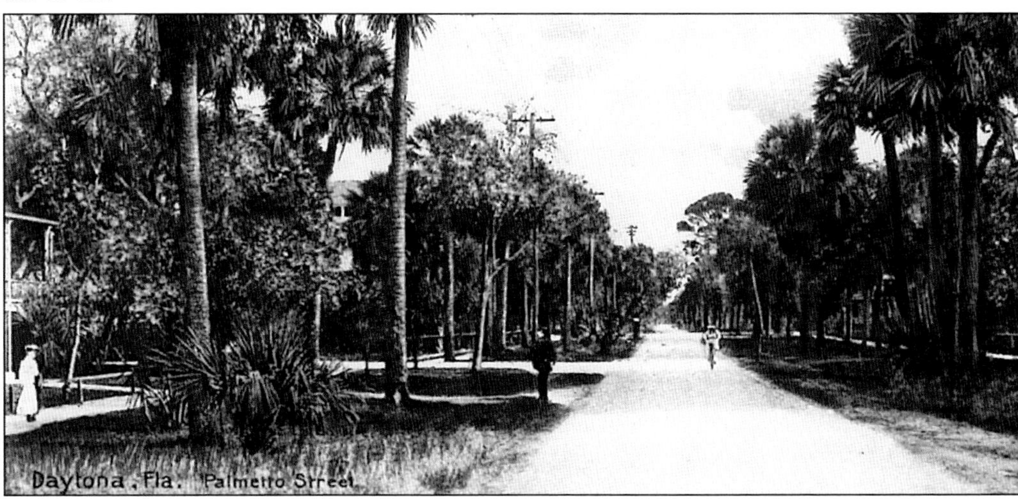

PALMETTO AVENUE, DAYTONA. Palmetto Avenue, originally named Canal Street, paralleled Beach Street one block west of the river. The first school building was erected on Palmetto in 1874, as were many church buildings. In 1900 the first St. Paul's Catholic Church went up on the corner of Myrtle Avenue; the First Congregational Church held services near Volusia Avenue; and the First Baptist Church settled permanently north of Volusia Avenue. (Postcard courtesy Richard Dragoni.)

METHODIST EPISCOPAL CHURCH ON PALMETTO AVENUE. At the southwest corner of Bay and Palmetto was the church of the Methodist Episcopal congregation, later known as the First United Methodist Church.

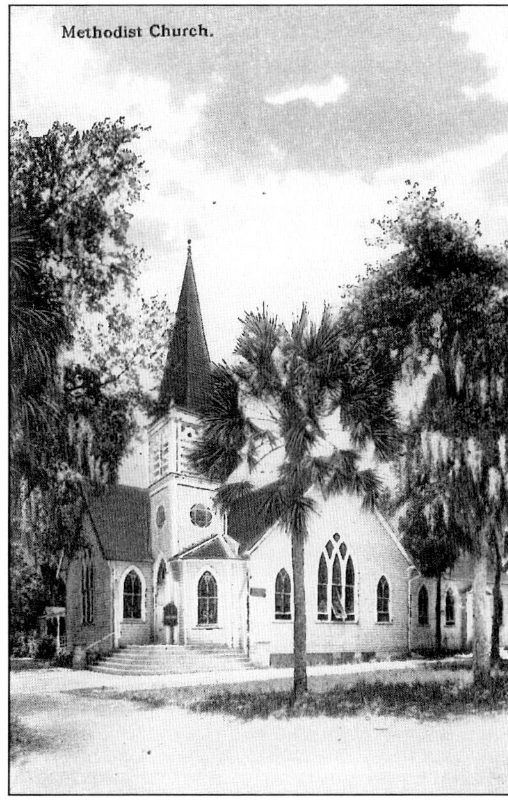

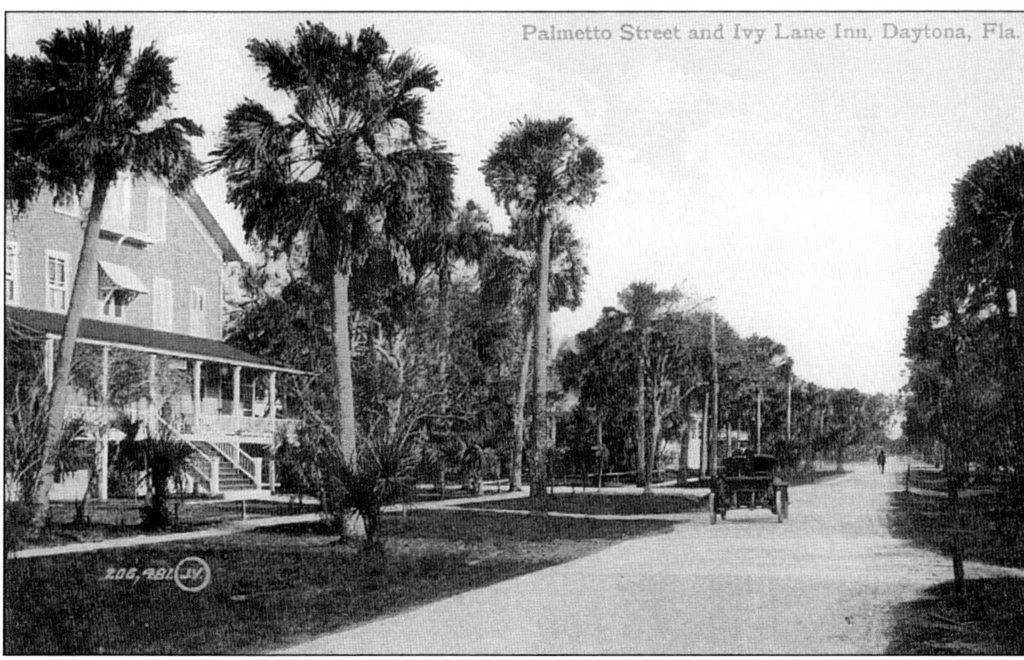

PALMETTO AVENUE, LOOKING SOUTH FROM IVY LANE. The Ivy Lane Inn faced west at the corner of Palmetto Avenue and Ivy Lane. According to advertisements, it was "a high grade house catering to the most particular people." (Postcard courtesy David Findlay.)

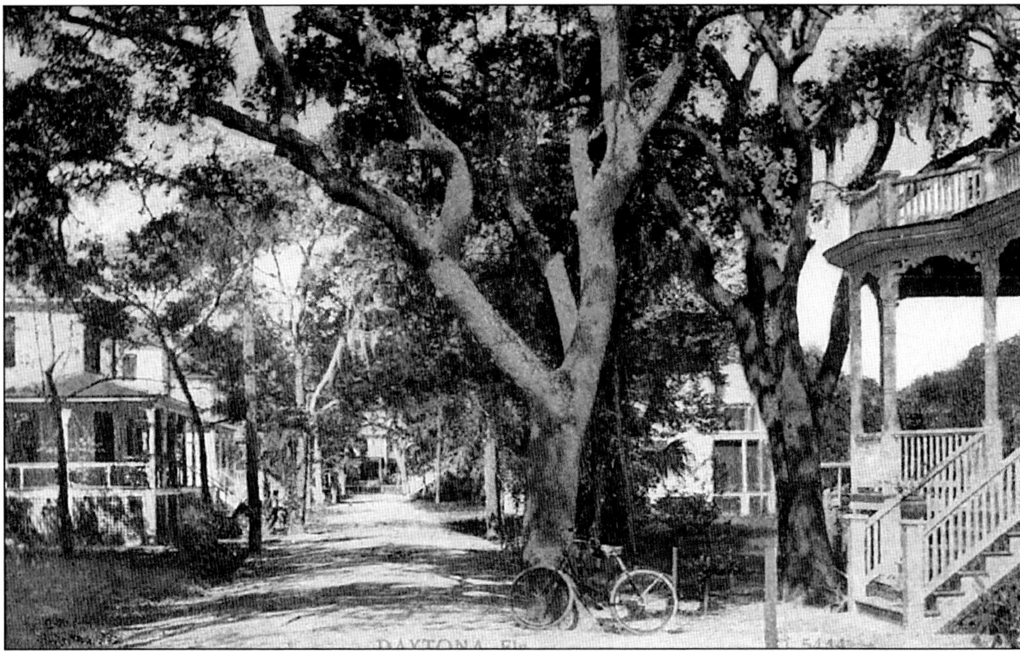

Ivy Lane, *c.* 1905–1910. One of the narrowest and shortest streets in Daytona was sandwiched between Orange and Magnolia Avenues and ran east to west one block from South Beach Street to Palmetto Avenue.

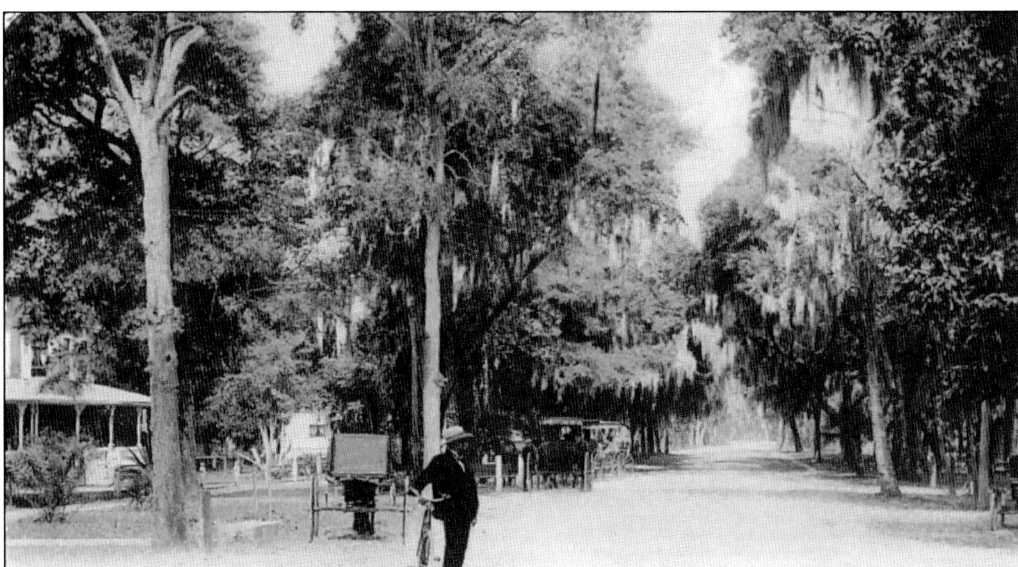

Ridgewood Avenue, Daytona, *c.* 1904. A 1908 brochure titled "Sub-Tropical Florida" gave a description of Daytona that seems appropriate for this postcard: "Built right into a forest of oaks, palmettos and glossy magnolias, all the most charming features of a park have been preserved, and the residences beneath them appear to be incidental to the park-like appearance, rather than the main feature." The carriages midway down the street suggest that the Ridgewood Hotel was on the left.

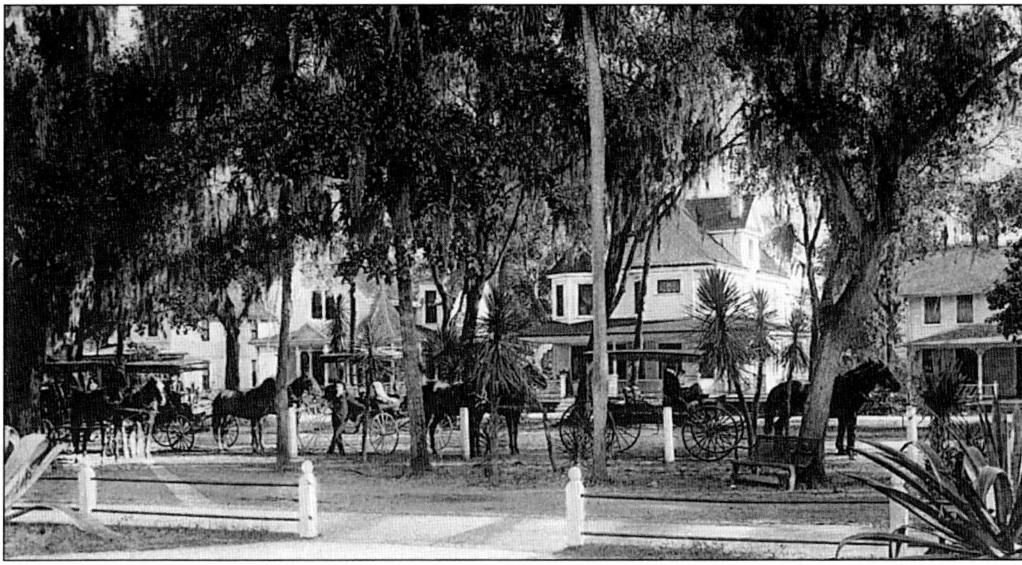

Ridgewood Avenue, c. 1905. Several Ridgewood Avenue residences are shown here, probably just across the street from the Ridgewood Hotel, where horse-drawn livery wait for hotel guests in the shade of the magnificent oak trees draped with Spanish moss. When a Vermont businessman purchased the Ridgewood Hotel in 1911, his hometown newspaper proudly reported to Burlington society that eight millionaires lived in close proximity to the hotel.

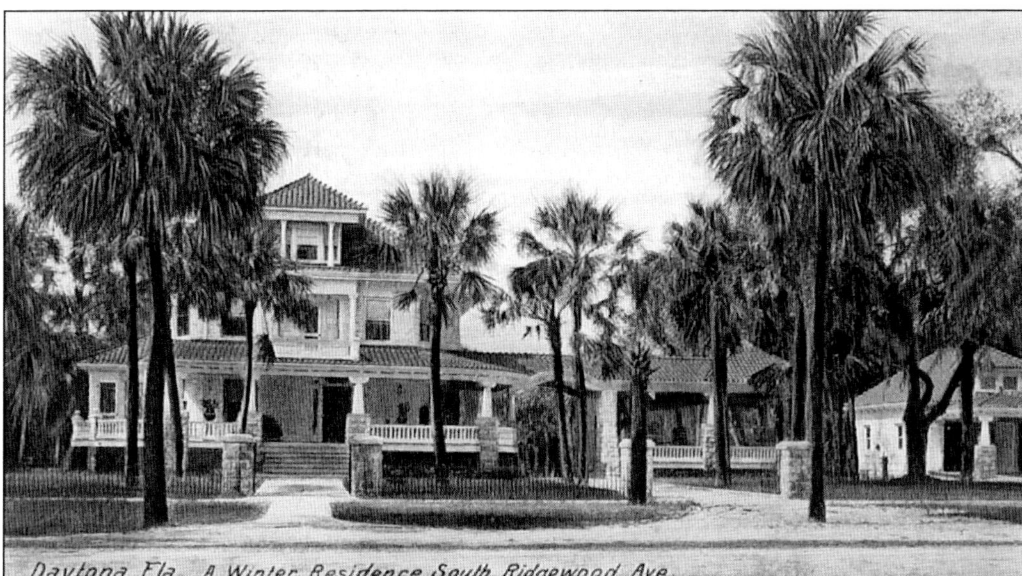

A Winter Residence on Ridgewood Avenue. This is the type of home that wealthy winter residents might have owned. The senders of this January 1909 postcard were scouting for a place to stay next season; they wrote: "Here is another winter home for our folks. This has been rented this season for $5,000, furnished and with use of two autos. It is built of snow white stone from Miami, with red tile roof. Very beautiful in its green setting." (Postcard courtesy David Findlay.)

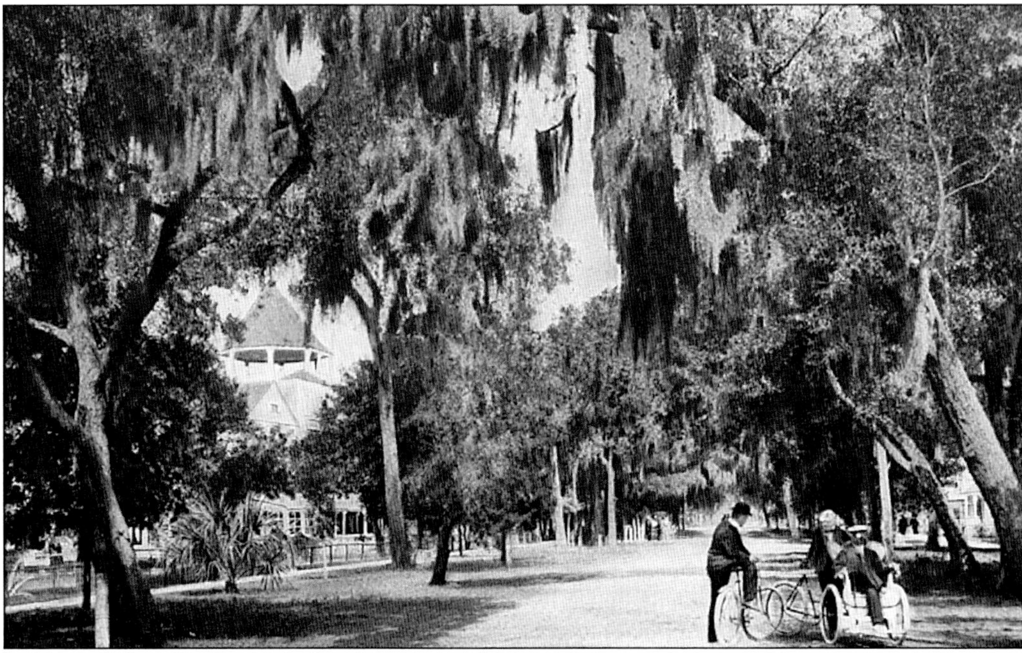

Ridgewood Avenue and the Ridgewood Hotel. The cupola of the Ridgewood Hotel can be seen in the clearing to the left. Miles, the sender of this card, said on March 23, 1909, that he "just arrived to take in the auto races." In addition to sanctioned speed trials, he also may have witnessed a most unusual spectacle said to have occurred that March when a Buick automobile sped along the beach with an airplane. Speaking of speed, note that the cyclists in this picture seem to be in no hurry.

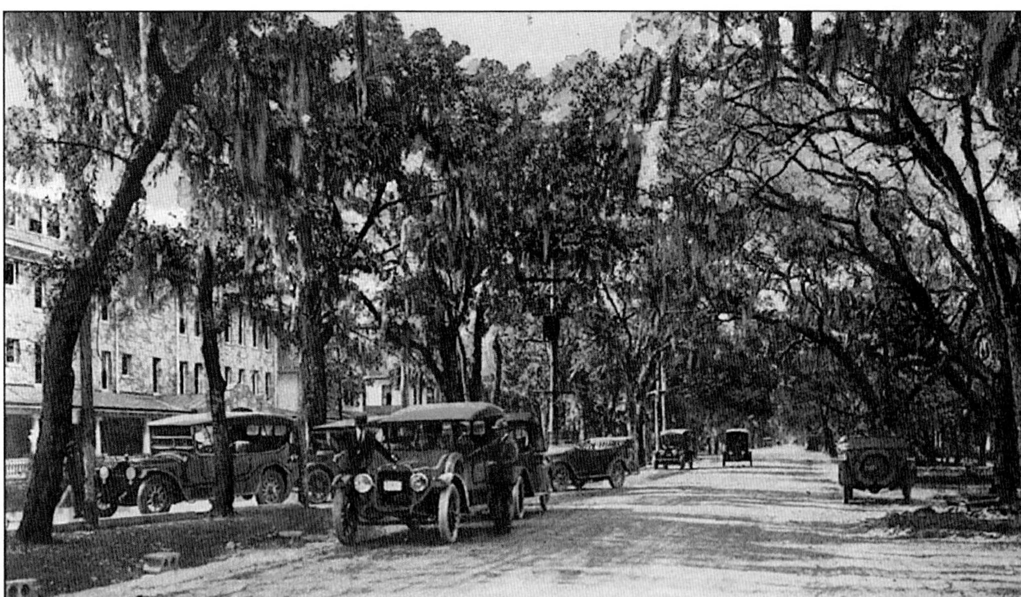

Ridgewood Avenue, Looking North Past the Ridgewood Hotel. After 1911 the Ridgewood Hotel got a facelift, and motor cars lined up along Ridgewood Avenue in place of buggies. Sadly, many of the beautiful oak trees were later removed to widen the street.

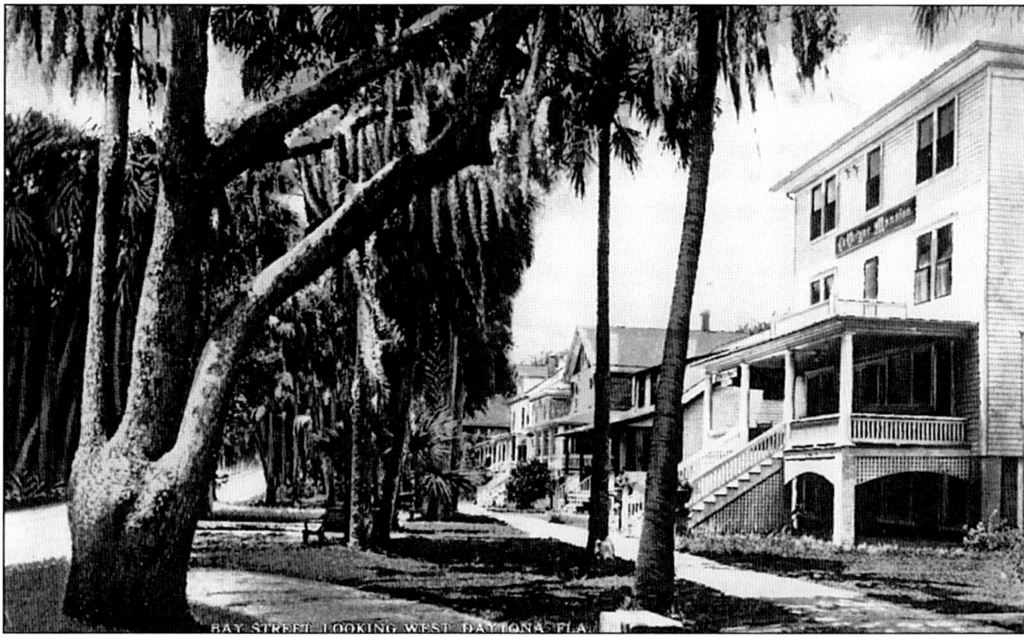

Bay Street, Looking West, Daytona. Bay Street formed part of the northern boundary of town as platted by Romanus Hodgman in 1871 for Mathias Day. The homes pictured here, including one named LaVergne Mansion in the foreground, were just across the street from the Burgoyne estate, which occupied most of the south side of the first block of Bay. (Postcard courtesy Richard Dragoni.)

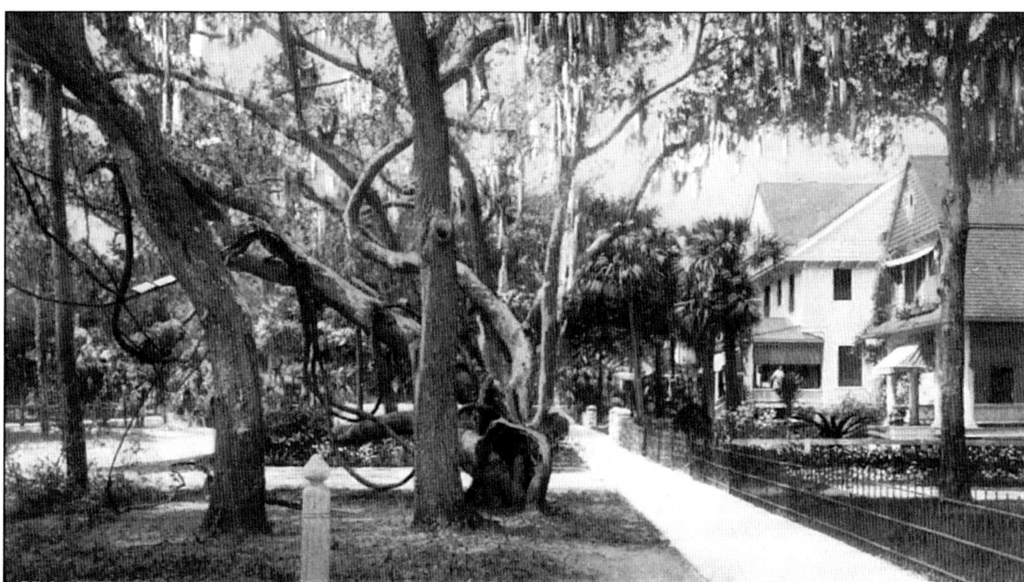

Magnolia Avenue, Daytona. Magnolia Avenue ran west from the Halifax River. The photogenic "crooked branch tree" shown here was the true subject of this postcard and similar others published in the early 1900s.

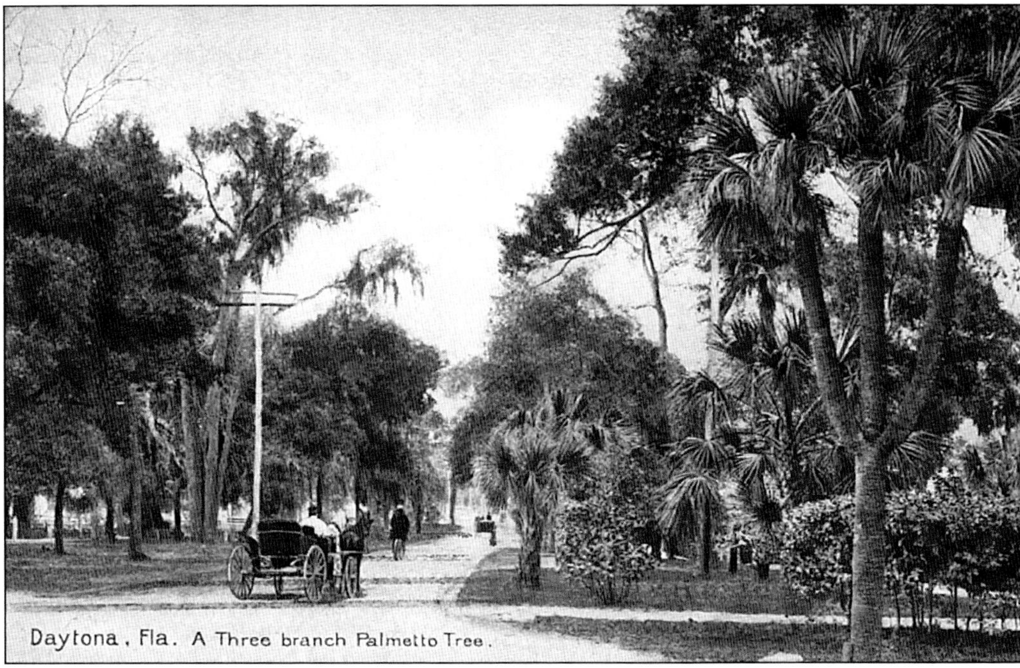

VOLUSIA AVENUE, DAYTONA. Another curious tree that captured the fancy of photographers stood on the northwest corner of Volusia and Ridgewood Avenues; this three-branch palmetto starred in quite a few postcards of the day, probably because the variety typically grows one very straight trunk.

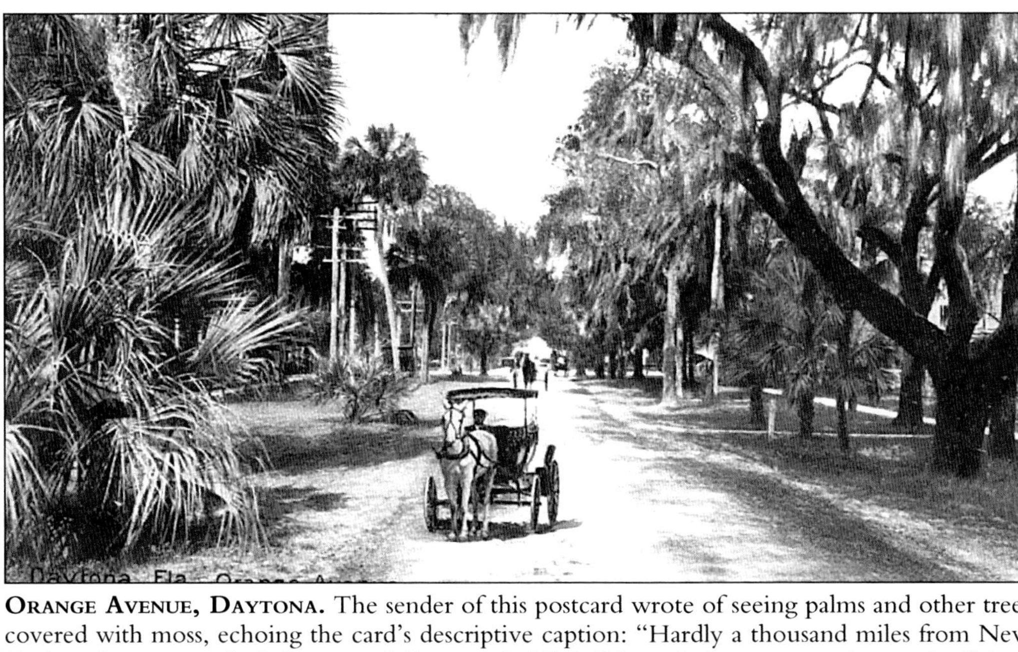

ORANGE AVENUE, DAYTONA. The sender of this postcard wrote of seeing palms and other trees covered with moss, echoing the card's descriptive caption: "Hardly a thousand miles from New York and one may find the most delicate and delightful tropical scenery and may dwell in a climate which neither Hawaii nor southern Italy can excel."

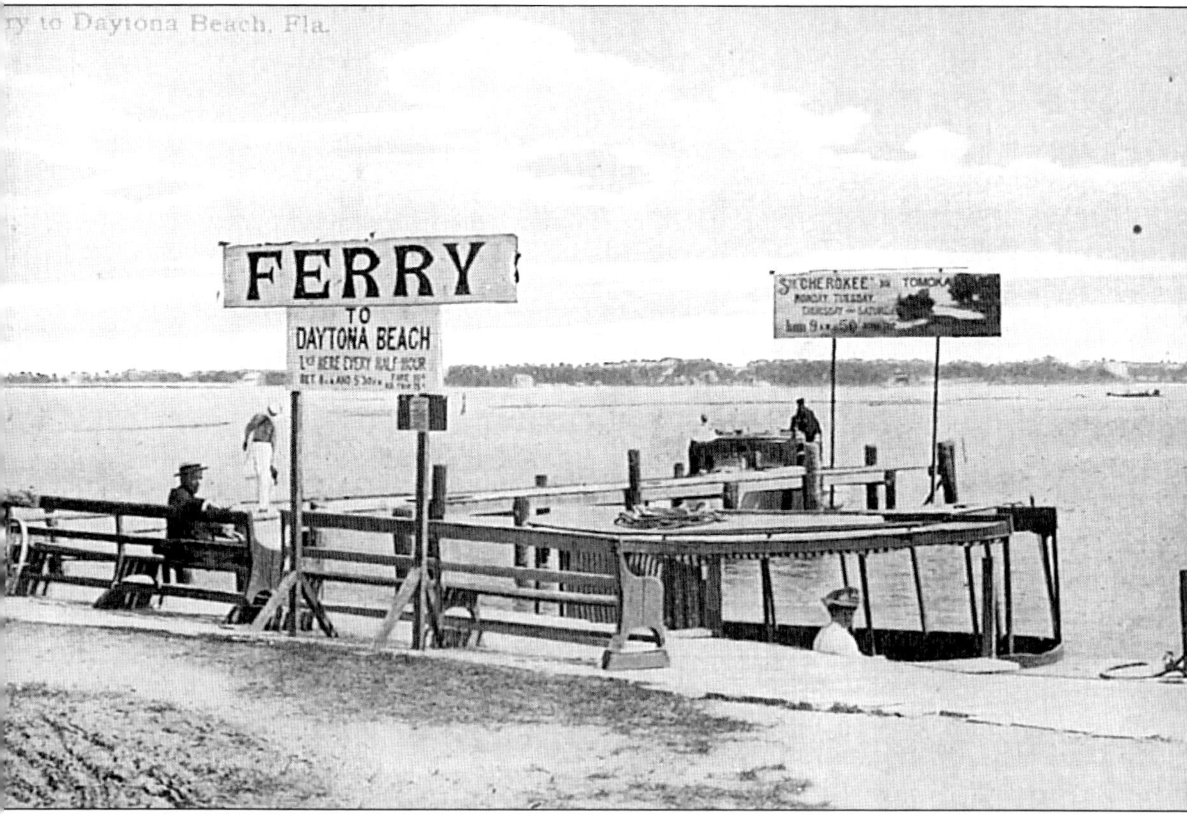

FERRY TO DAYTONA BEACH, *c.* 1912–1915. Before Daytona's bridges were built in the late 1880s, ferries carried passengers across the Halifax River to the peninsula. They departed from a landing off Beach Street at Volusia Avenue between 8 a.m. and 5 p.m.; according to the sign, the fare was 10¢ one way to the Main Street landing in Daytona Beach, and 15¢ round trip. The ferry boats were named *Yankee Doodle* and *Dixie,* according to the published recollections of local resident Lawson Diggett. Note that this also was the landing for the excursion steamer *Cherokee,* bound for the Tomoka River. (Postcard courtesy David Findlay.)

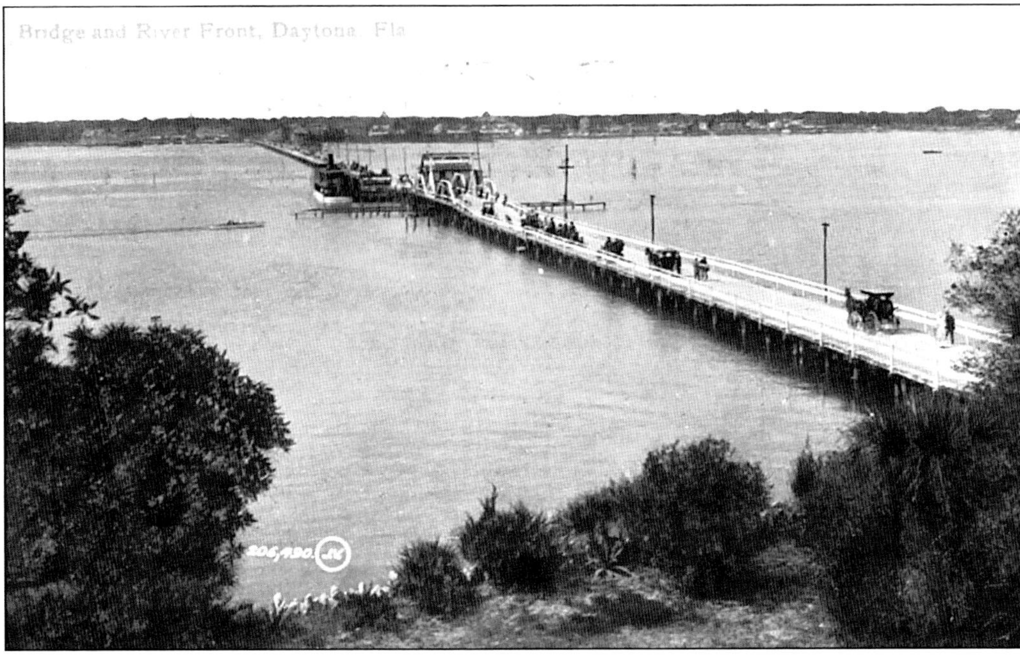

SOUTH BRIDGE, DAYTONA, c. 1909. The wooden South Bridge was one of Daytona's earliest Halifax River crossings. This postcard was mailed February 15, 1909, just one day after St. Valentine's Day and a historic event that occurred on the peninsula. The sender tells the story: "I drove in an auto over this bridge to dine at the Clarendon at Seabreeze. The inn burned at 5 a.m. two days later; it had 250 guests, but no lives were lost."

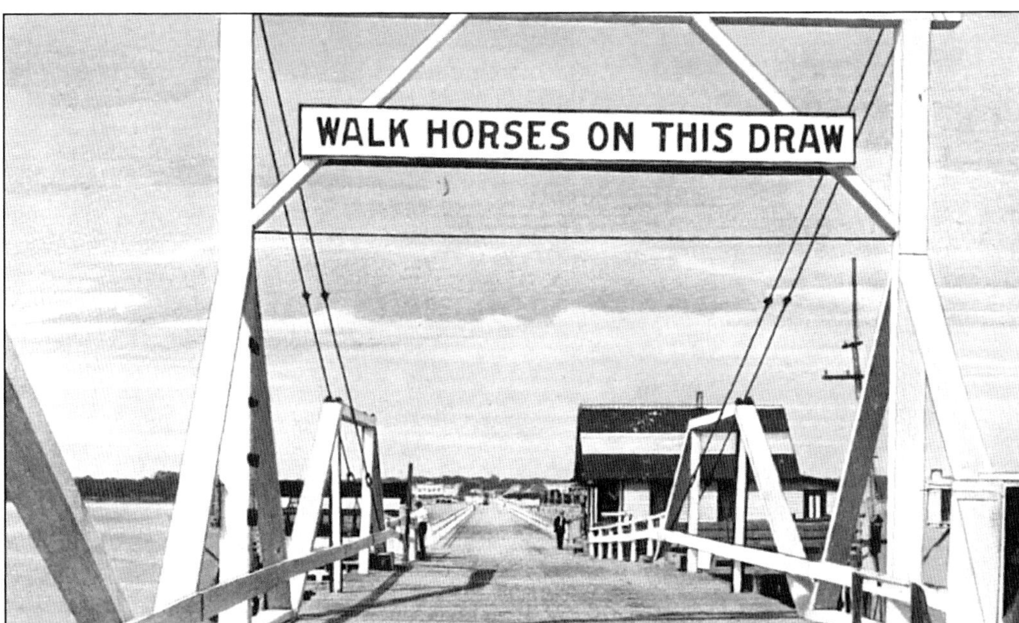

SOUTH BRIDGE, LOOKING EAST FROM GOODALL TO DAYTONA. Goodall was the former name of part of the area that became Daytona Beach. Built in 1888, the South Bridge was destroyed by a storm in 1910, but was soon replaced. The newest span is called Memorial Bridge.

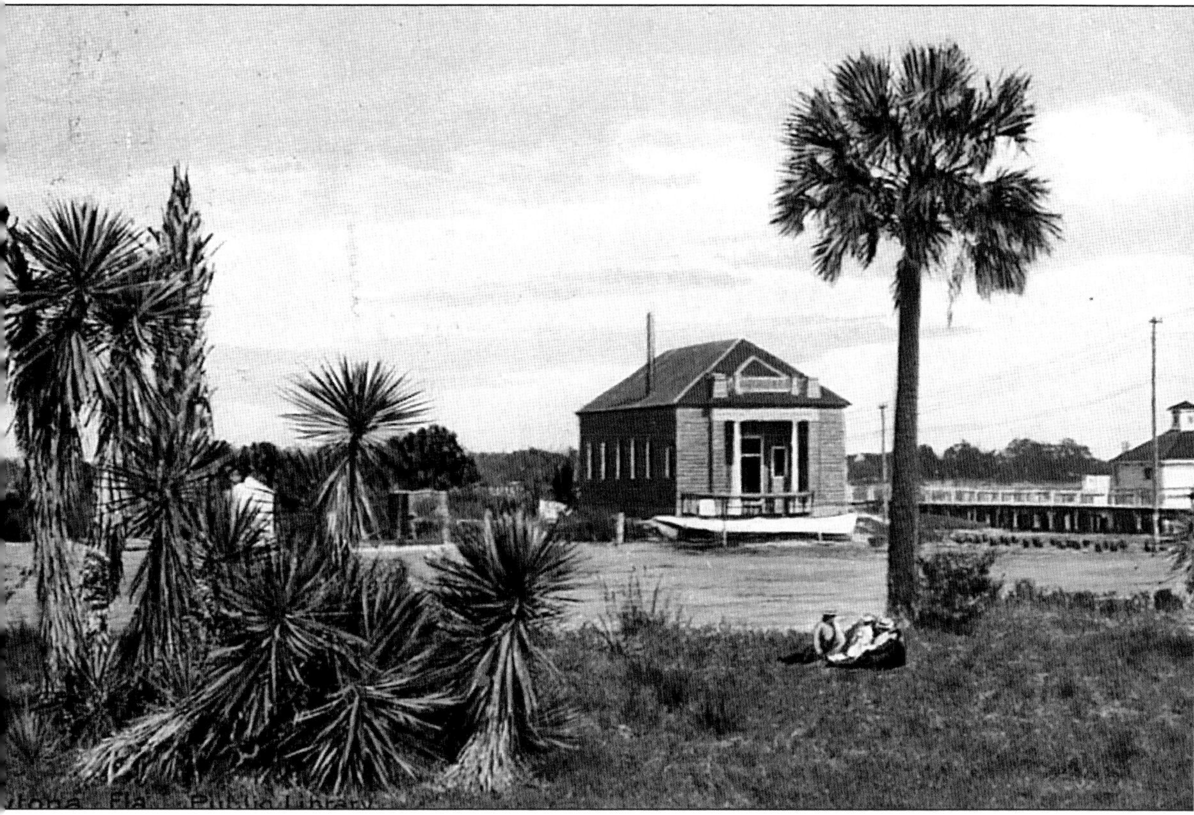

South Bridge and Library. The two-room, cement block library was built prior to 1910 on a landfill that became City Island. James M. Gamble, president of the Daytona Reading Room Association, funded the construction. It is said the building's high windows were attributed to Mr. Gamble's belief that one who came to read did not need the diversion of scenery. The Reading Room got its start in the late 1800s.

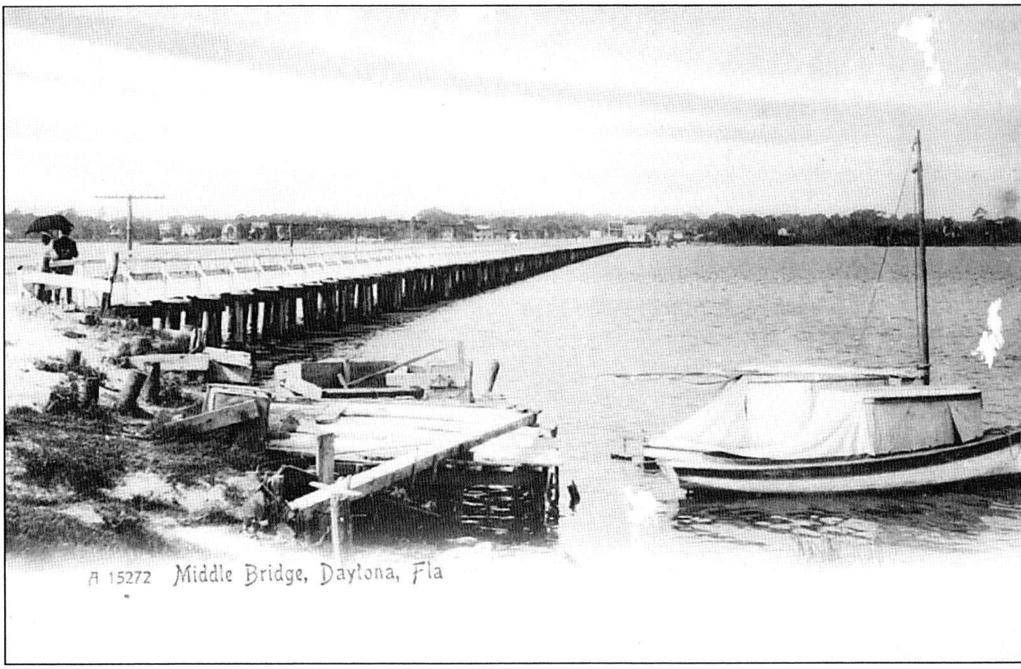

Middle Bridge. This may be the Central Bridge, going from Fairview Avenue in Daytona to Seabreeze Avenue in Daytona Beach.

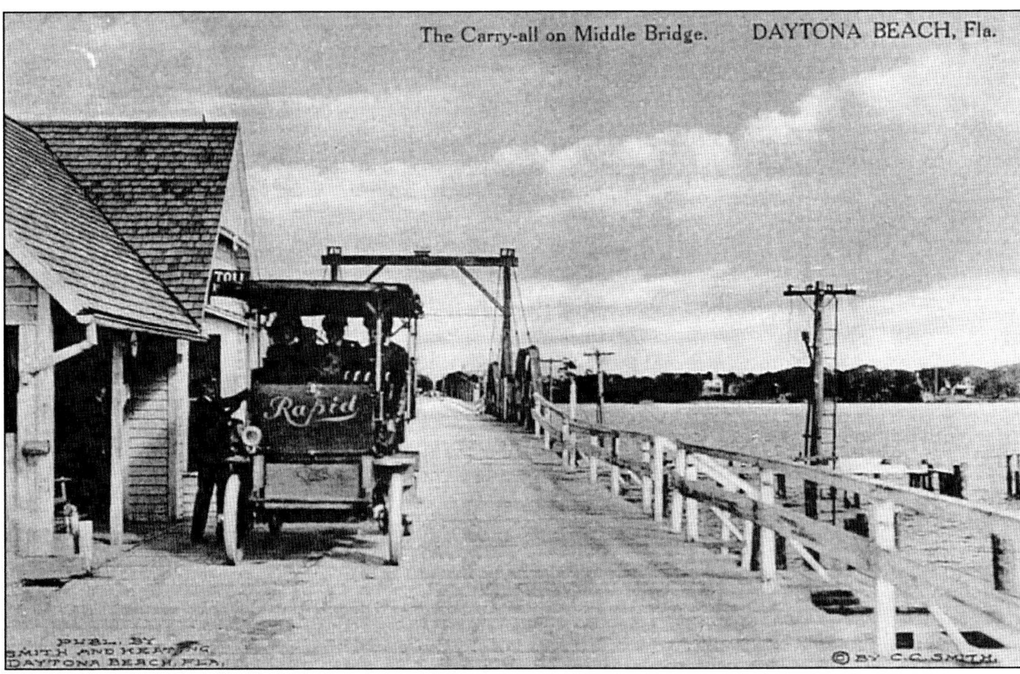

The Carry-all on Middle Bridge. Automobile transportation across the river linked hotels with railroads and boosted the development of peninsula communities. Tolls were charged on Daytona bridges until around 1927. (Postcard courtesy David Findlay.)

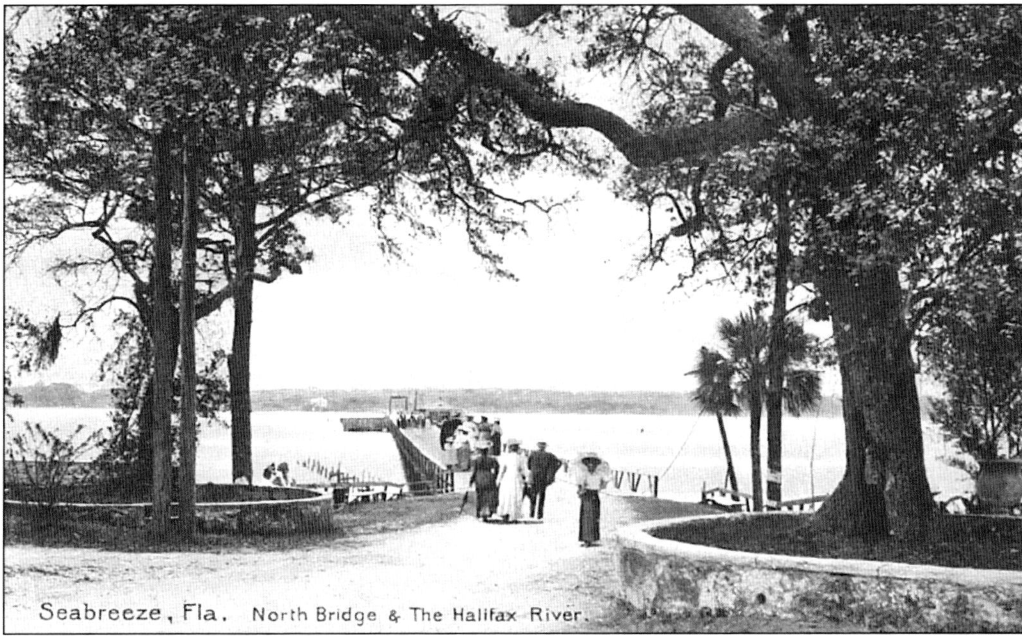

NORTH BRIDGE, SEABREEZE. Seabreeze was reached from the mainland by the North Bridge, also called the Peninsula Bridge, built about 1901. The landing was well-manicured and made an inviting approach to lovely Ocean Boulevard, which extended to the Atlantic Ocean. The home of Seabreeze developers Charles C. and Helen Wilmans Post was on the boulevard at Valley Street by the river.

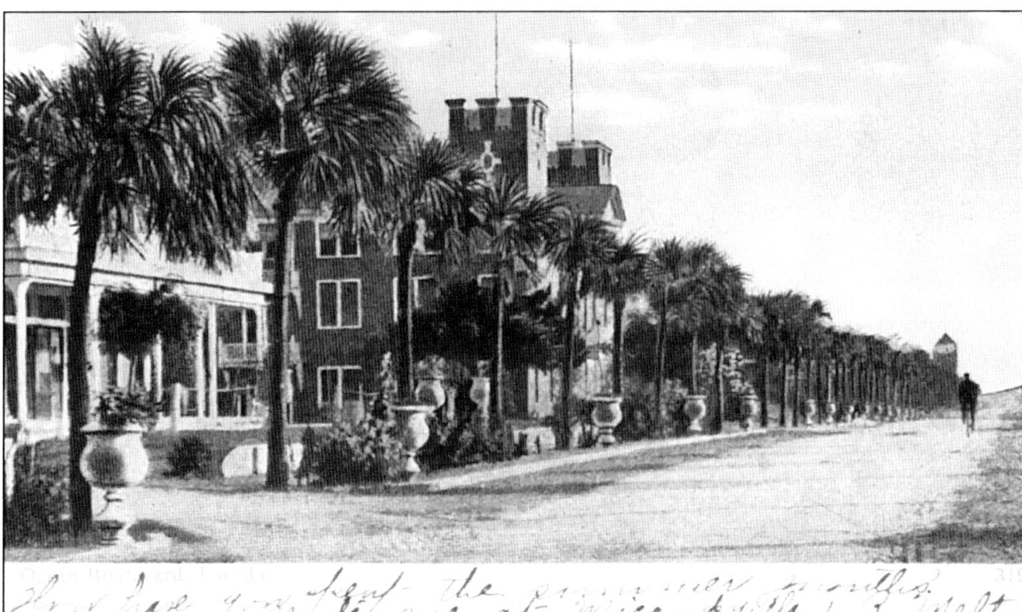

OCEAN BOULEVARD, *c.* 1907. Seabreeze's most prominent street was designed by the Posts. It was landscaped with tall palm trees and lined with ornamental planters. The Posts built the Wilmans Opera House, shown here, as well as a department store and several other buildings on Ocean Boulevard. This is an eastward view.

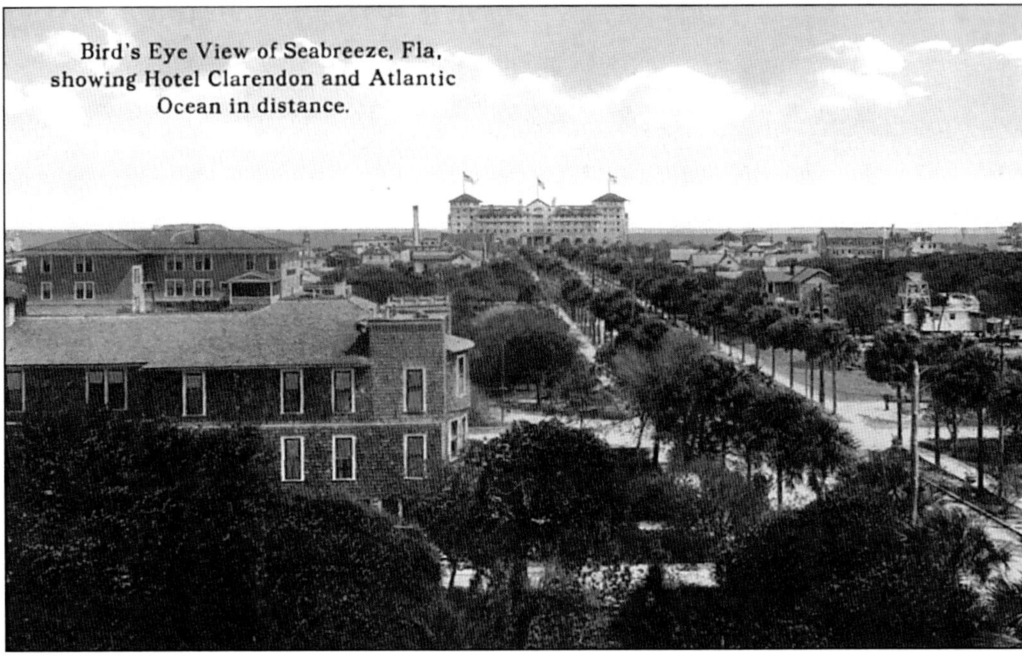

BIRD'S-EYE VIEW OF SEABREEZE AND OCEAN BOULEVARD, *c.* 1915. The Clarendon Hotel was at the east end of Ocean Boulevard.

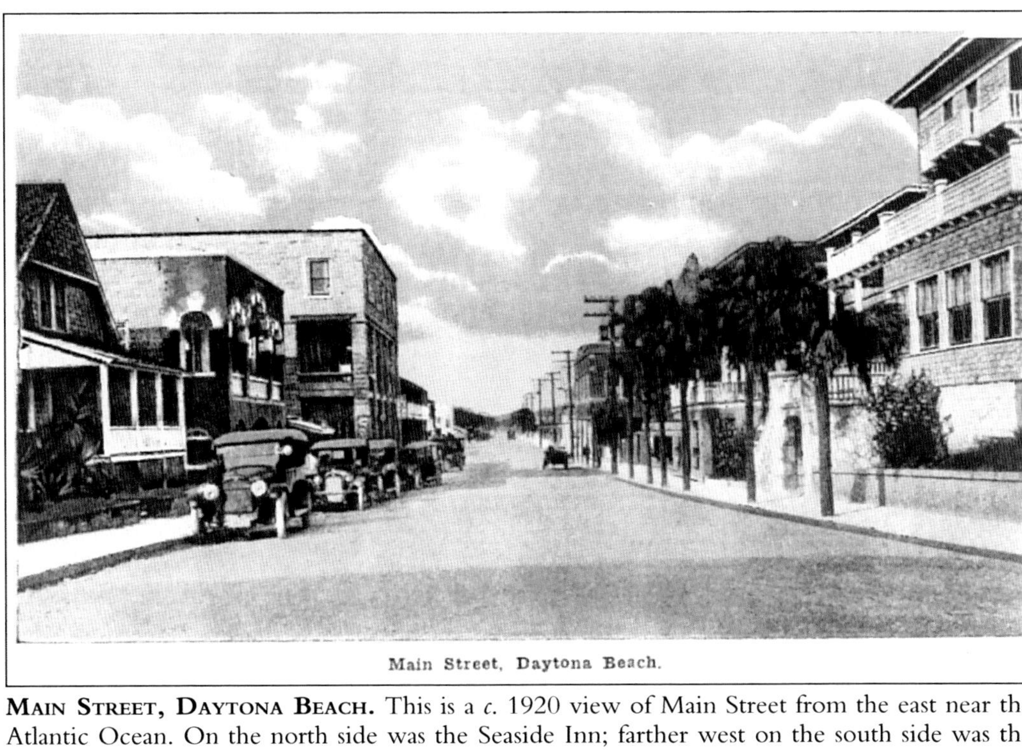

MAIN STREET, DAYTONA BEACH. This is a *c.* 1920 view of Main Street from the east near the Atlantic Ocean. On the north side was the Seaside Inn; farther west on the south side was the three-story Van Valzah Hotel.

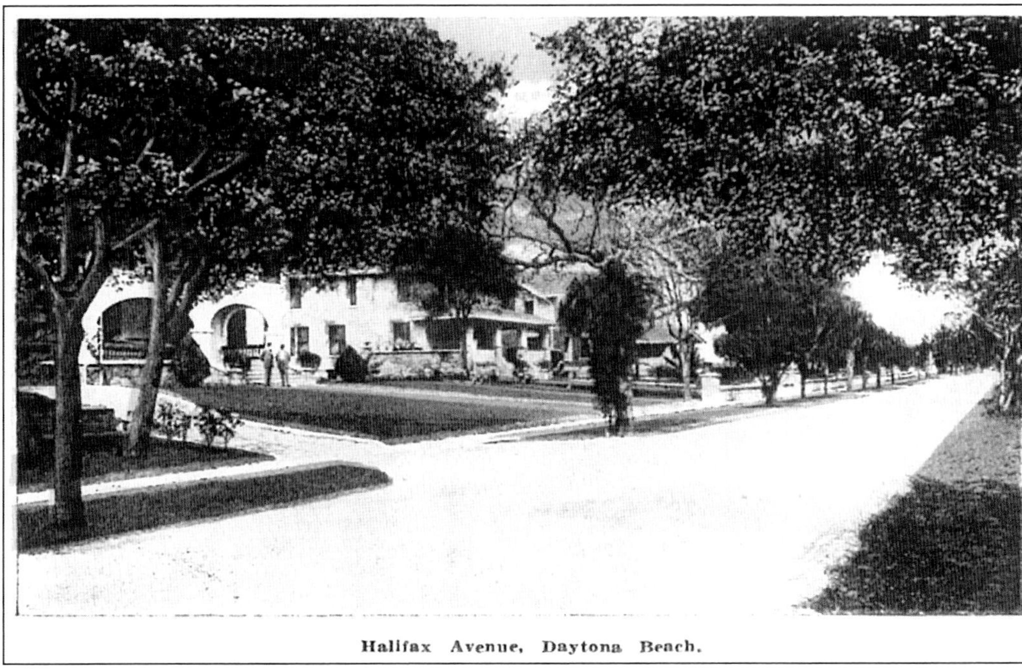

HALIFAX AVENUE, DAYTONA BEACH. Halifax Avenue, primarily a residential district, skirted the east bank of the Halifax River on the peninsula and extended towards Ormond.

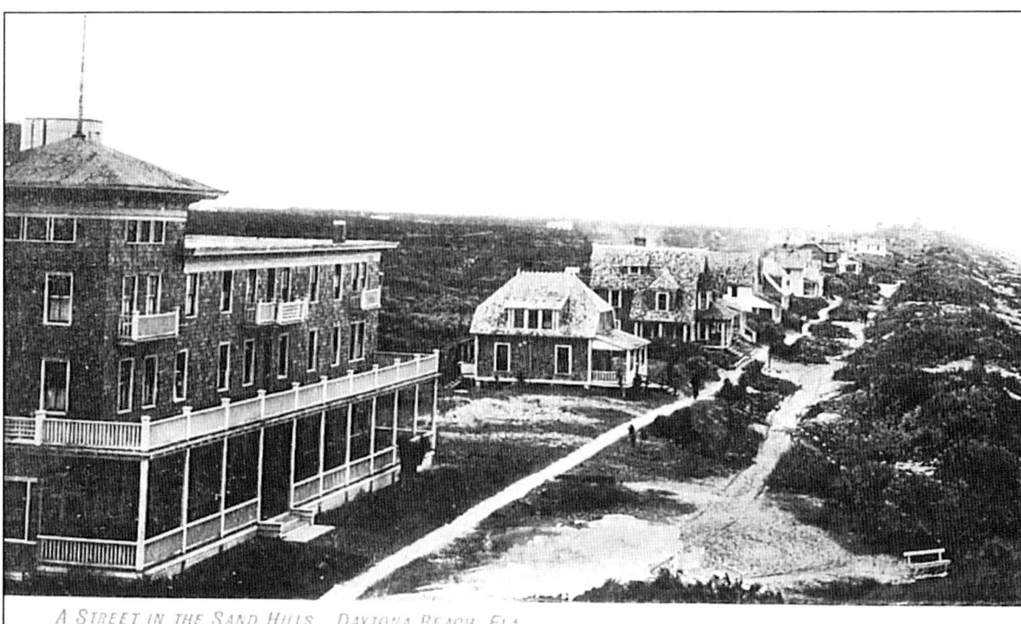

ATLANTIC AVENUE, LOOKING NORTH FROM SEABREEZE AVENUE, DAYTONA BEACH. A sandy path that later became Atlantic Avenue fronted inns, hotels, and cottages in the first decade of the 20th century. The Seaside Inn was at the corner of Seabreeze Avenue, which was later called Main Street. (Postcard courtesy David Findlay.)

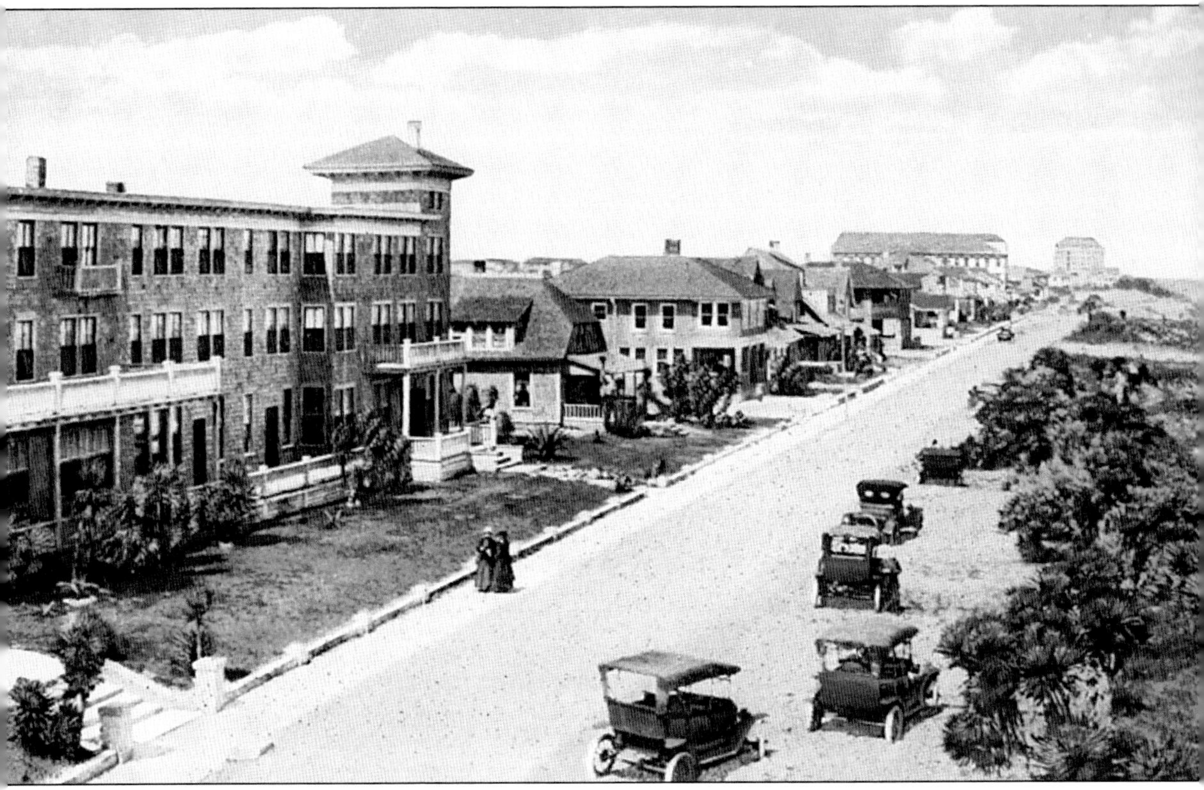

Atlantic Avenue. A later view of Atlantic Avenue shows the enlargement of the Seaside Inn and additional cottages facing the ocean. The silhouette of the new fireproof Clarendon Hotel in the distance dates this card after 1911.

Three

HOTELS, INNS, AND GRAND ACCOMMODATIONS

From the turn of the century to the 1920s, visitors could find accommodations ranging from quaint to grand in a variety of picturesque settings on both the mainland and peninsula. In 1926 incorporated Daytona Beach boasted some 60 lodgings and a winter population of nearly 127,000. The following postcards represent just a sampling of the inns and hotels available to seasonal visitors during the Triple Cities' premier years as a tourist resort.

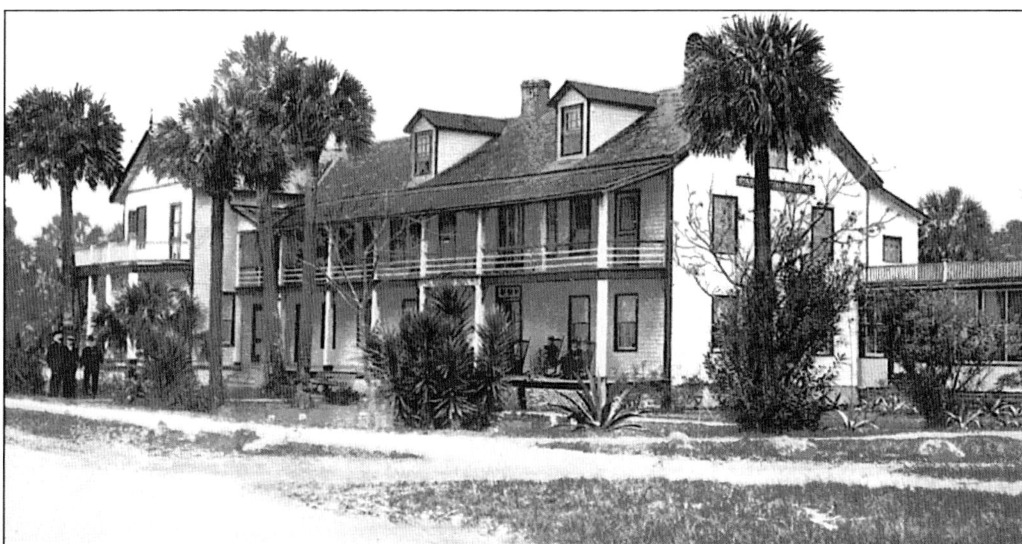

THE PALMETTO HOUSE, DAYTONA. Mathias Day constructed Colony House, Daytona's landmark hotel. The story goes that palmetto fronds were applied temporarily to the roof when a shipment of shingles was delayed. From then on, it was known as Palmetto House. In 1922 the vacant building, destined for demolition, caught fire and burned, prompting the *Daytona Daily News* to comment that the "flames cheated the wrecking crew." A historical marker is located at South Beach Street at Loomis Avenue.

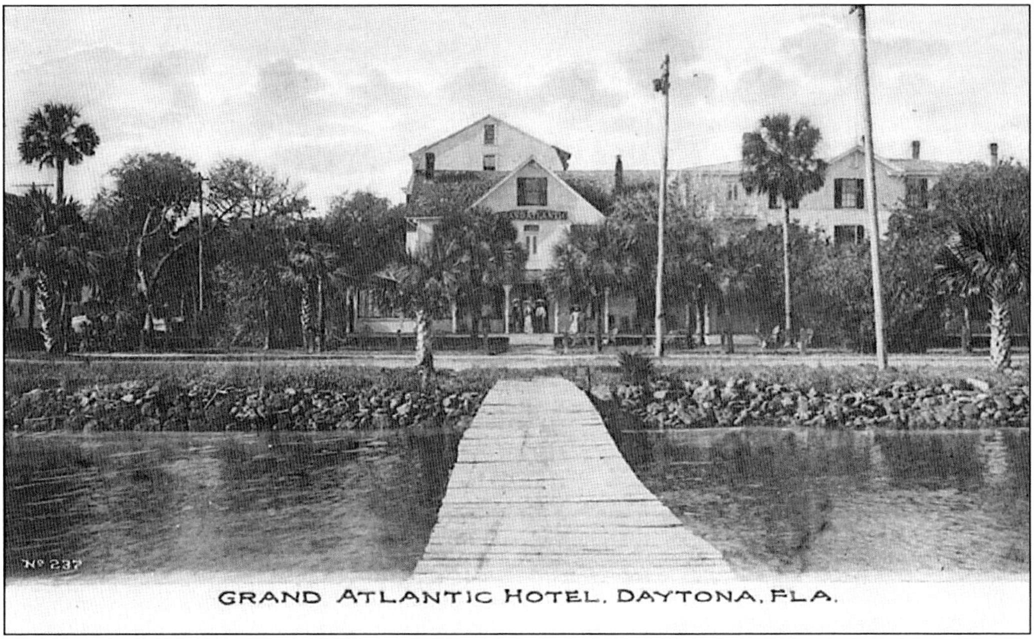

THE GRAND ATLANTIC HOTEL, c. 1906, DAYTONA. Built in the early 1880s on the northwest corner of North Beach Street and Third Avenue, the Grand Atlantic also was known as the Holly Inn prior to 1902, and the Ocean View before that, but may be best remembered as the Prince George. It was one of Daytona's earliest hotels.

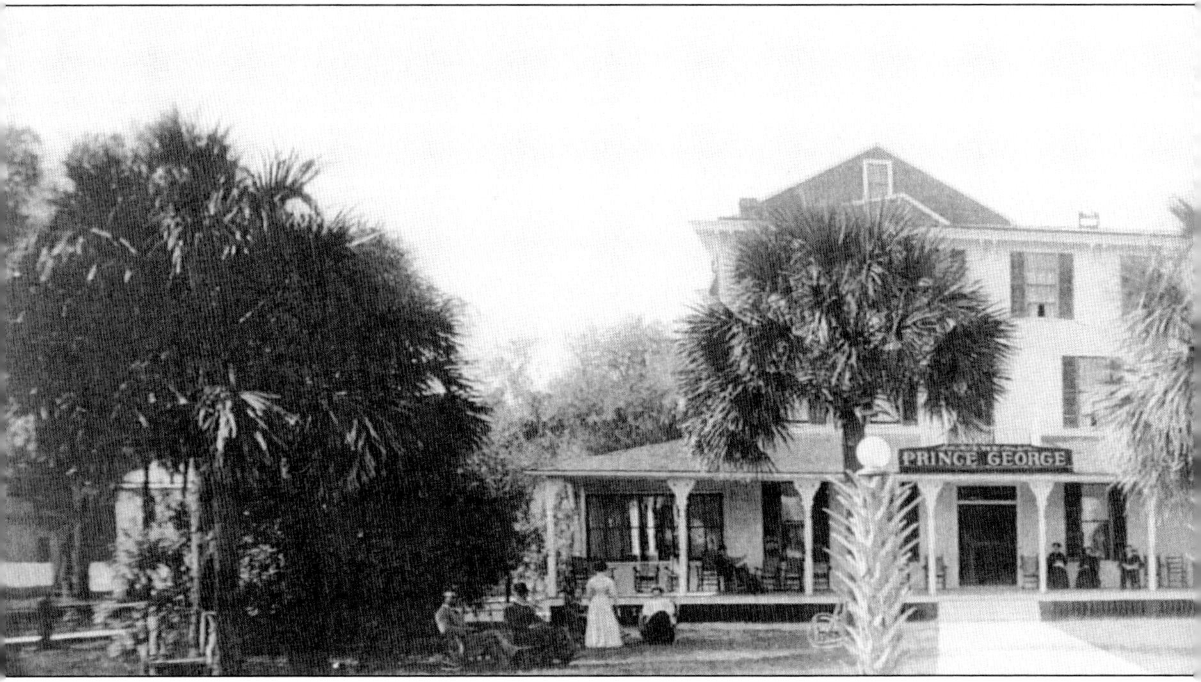

THE PRINCE GEORGE HOTEL. The Grand Atlantic changed hands around 1908 and was renamed the Prince George. Some of the hotel's most inviting features were a wide veranda, a sun parlor, a billiard and smoking room, an orchestra, and a dining room overlooking the river,

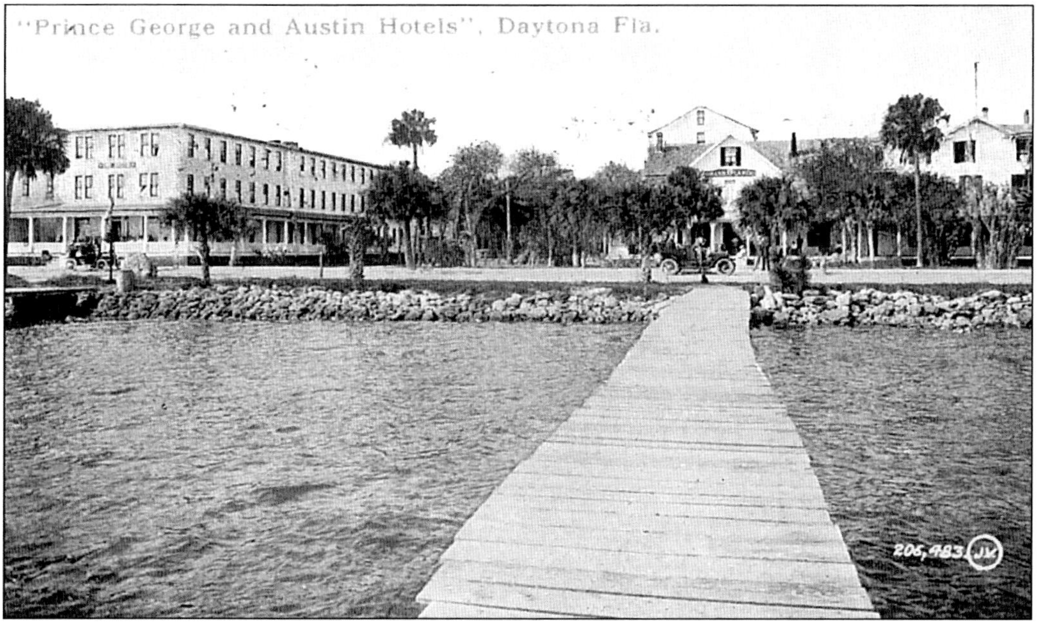

The Prince George Hotel and the Austin Hotel. The Austin also was on N. Beach Street just across Third Street from the Prince George.

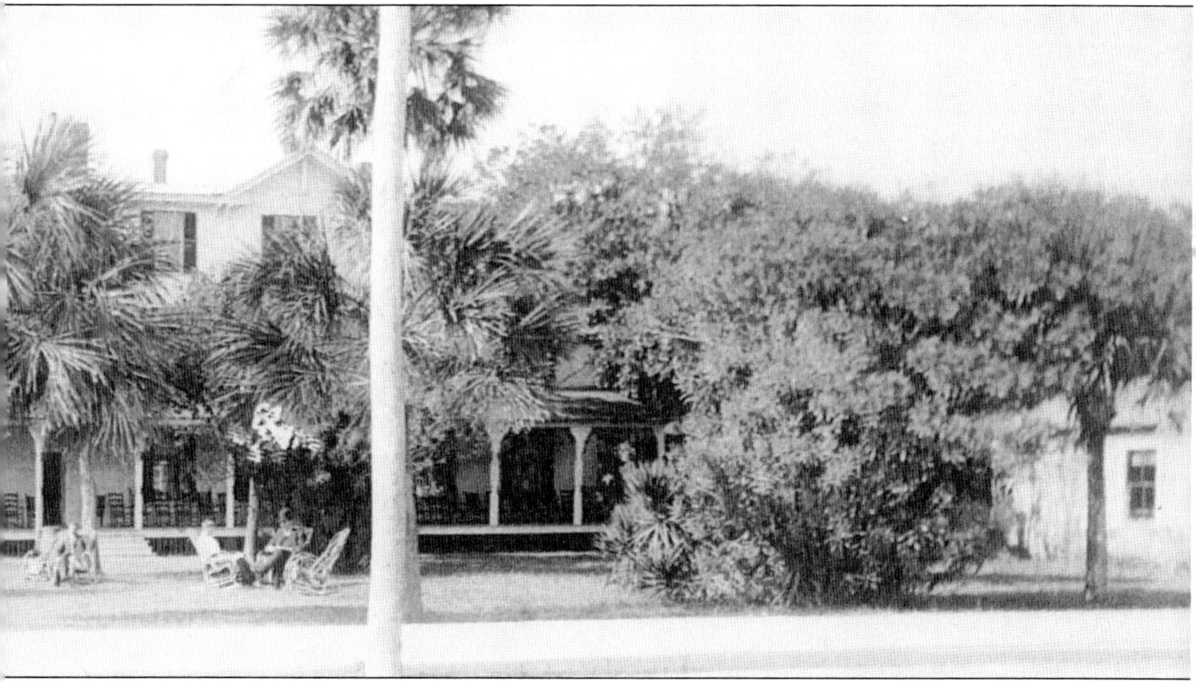

according to 1909 advertisements. This is a rare panoramic view. (Postcard courtesy Shear family.)

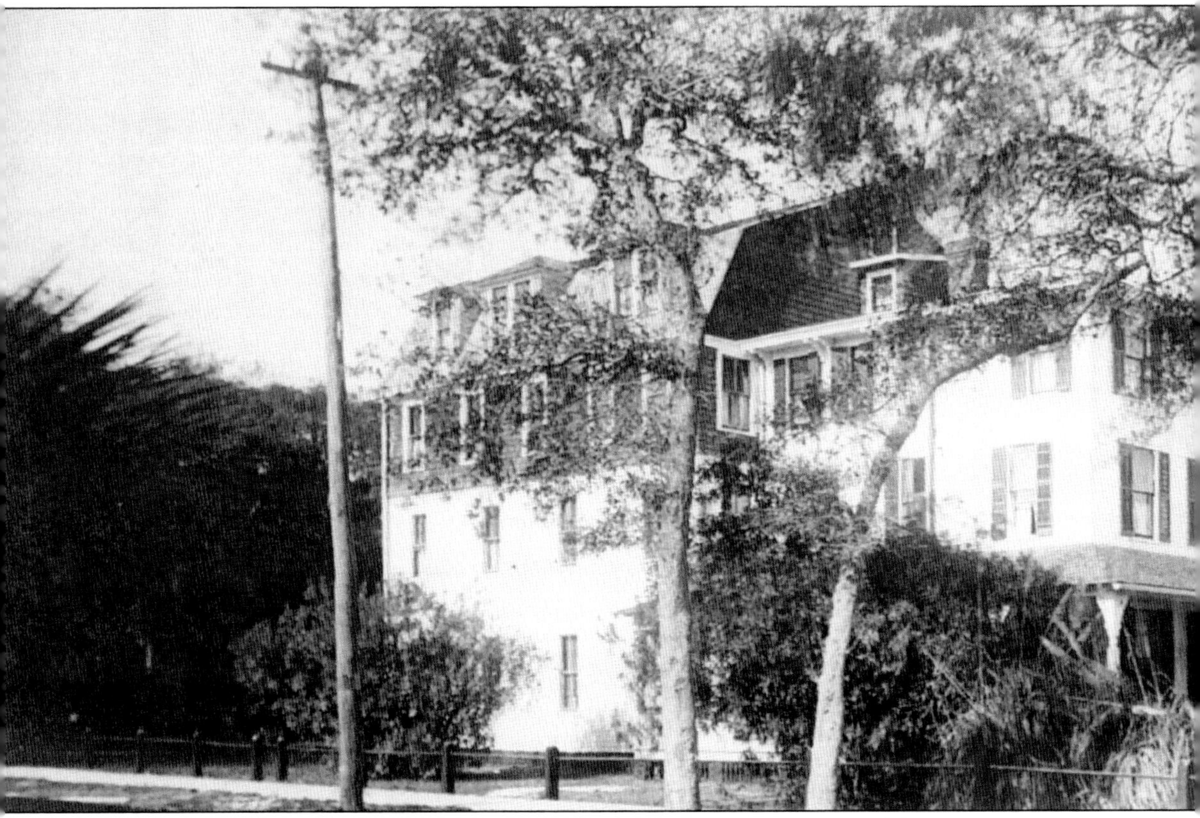

The Prince George Hotel. Another rare panoramic photograph of the Prince George was taken from the Third Street side of the building. Some structural modifications can be observed

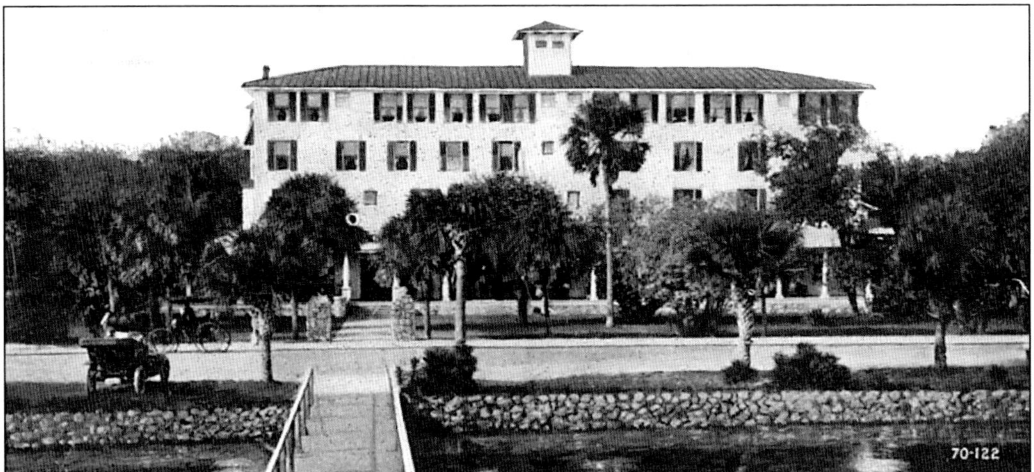

Prince George Hotel After Expansion, c. 1915. Advertisements of the day referred to the Prince George as "Daytona's most select family hotel," touting such improvements as steam heat, hot and cold water in every room, and elevator service. Note the similarities between this card and the one of the Grand Atlantic, both photographed from the hotel's private pier where charter boats were available for fishing or sightseeing excursions. A Sears, Roebuck and Company store was built on the former hotel site in the 1950s.

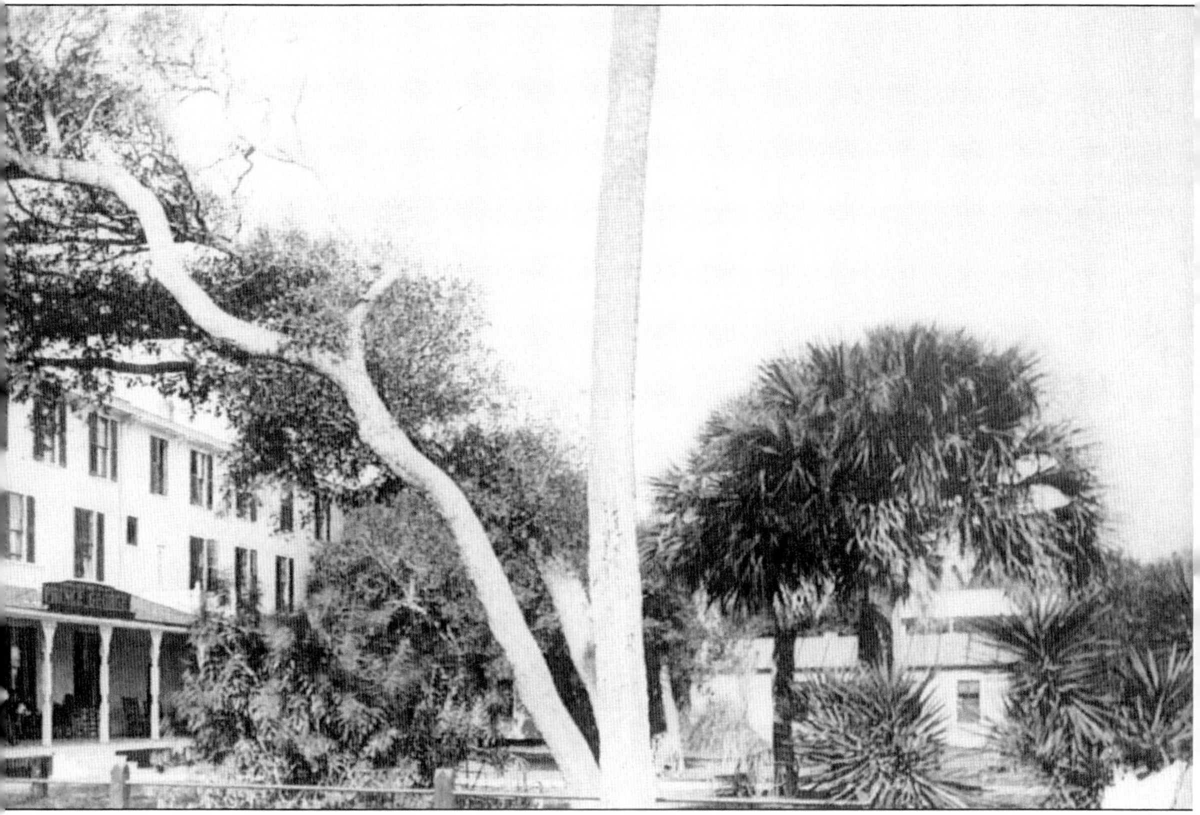

when compared to the previous card of the Grand Atlantic. (Postcard courtesy Shear family.)

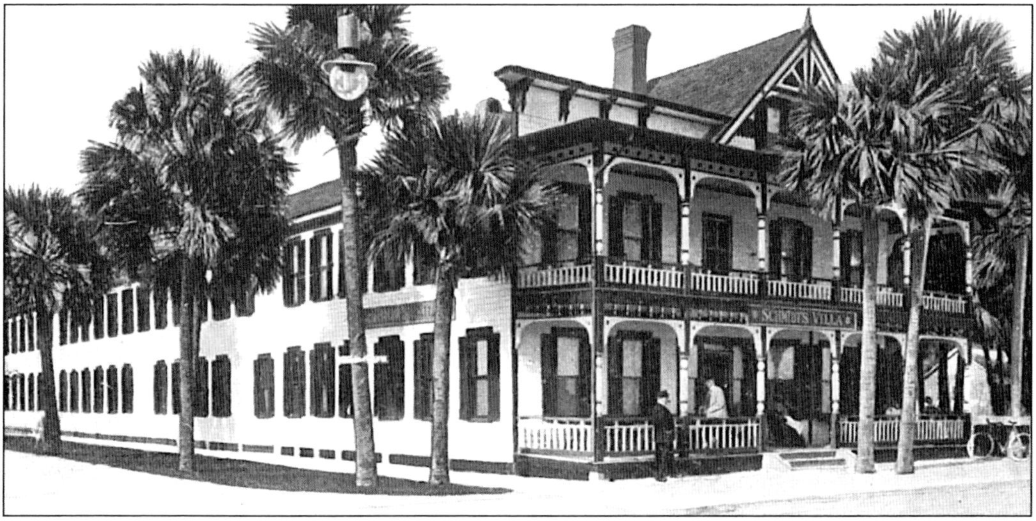

SCHMIDT'S VILLA, *c.* 1905, DAYTONA. Schmidt's Villa, at the corner of North Beach Street and Second Avenue, was another of Daytona's riverfront hostelries. Proprietor Henry Schmidt's hotel advertisements suggested he took great pride in setting a "fine home table" for his guests. Schmidt's Villa was demolished in the 1920s, and an automobile dealership took its place.

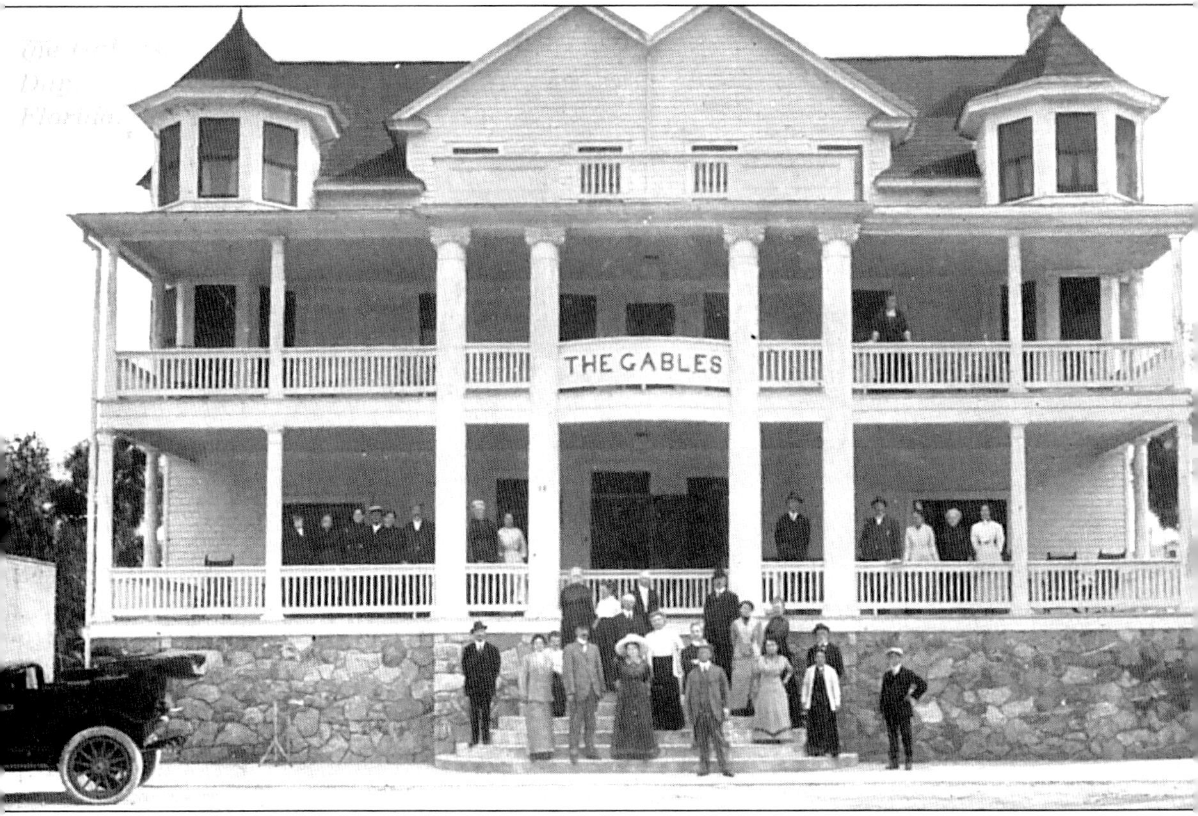

The Gables, Daytona. The Gables was on Volusia Avenue (now International Speedway Boulevard) west of Beach Street near Myrtle Avenue. In 1909 guests could enjoy one of 50 rooms with modern improvements for about $1.50 a day, November to May. By the early 1920s the per diem room rate had soared to $4.50, American plan. The building was condemned about 1960 and torn down to make way for a parking lot.

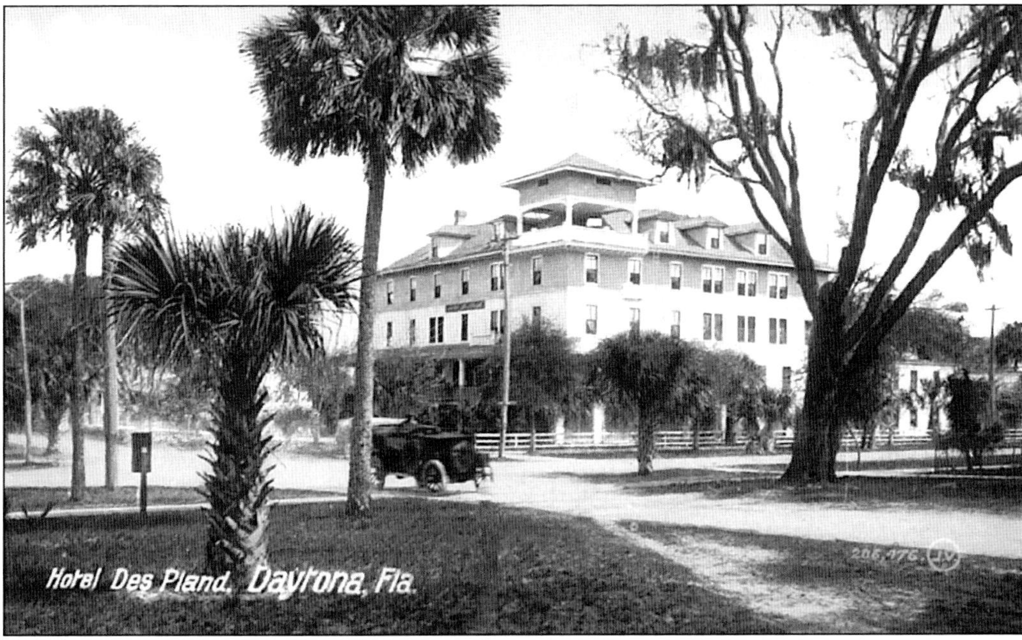

The Despland Hotel, Daytona. Leon Despland built this hotel in 1901 on the corner of Palmetto and Magnolia Avenues, where it stood for 66 years. It was sold in 1917 and renamed the Williams Hotel, after the new owner.

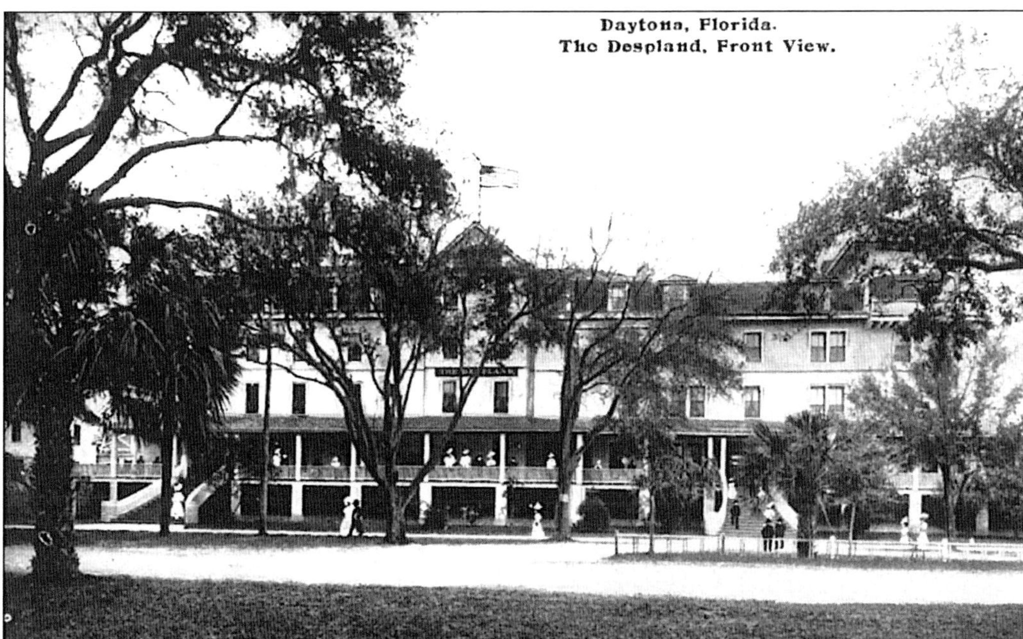

Front View of the Despland Hotel. The hotel fronted Magnolia Avenue. (Postcard courtesy Richard Dragoni.)

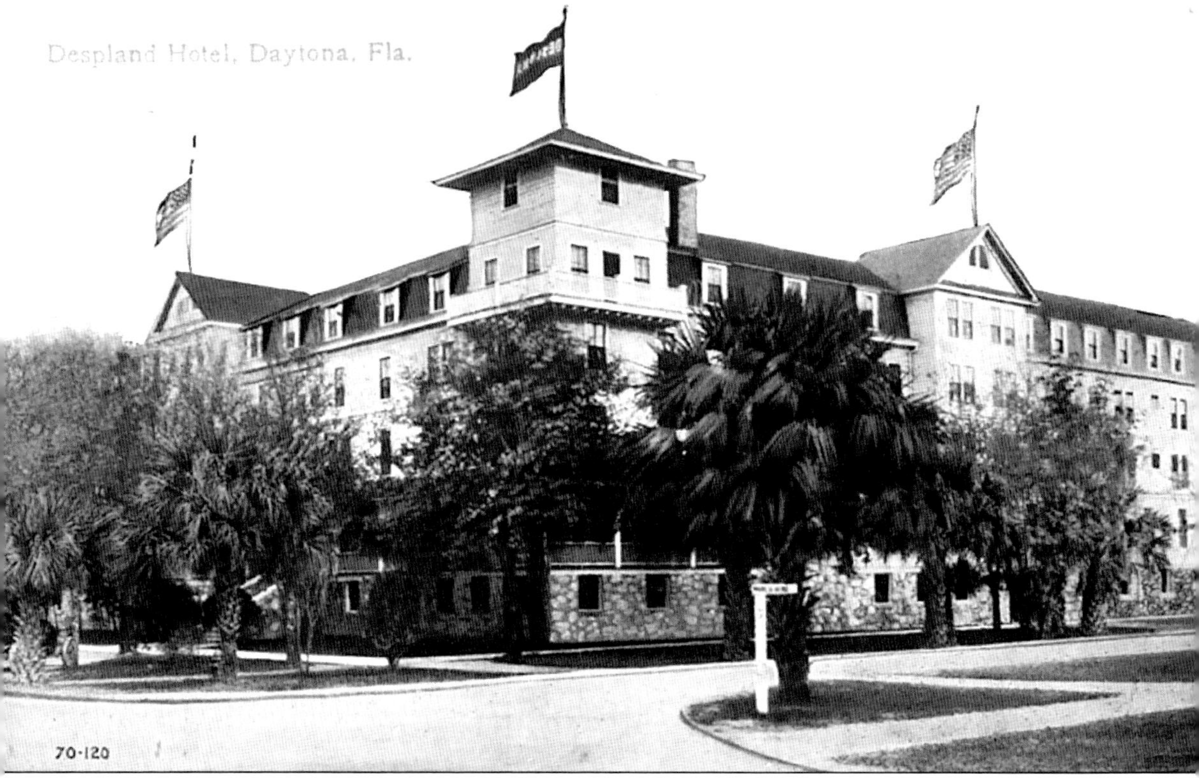

The Despland Hotel, after Expansion. The Despland shown here could accommodate up to 250 guests after it was enlarged to twice its original size. On the premises were a telegraph office, a public stenographer, a manicurist, and a barber. After declining as a resort it operated as a boarding house, then a retirement habitat. When the building was torn down in the late 1960s, the wrecking company claimed that the demolition project was the largest single job of its kind in city history.

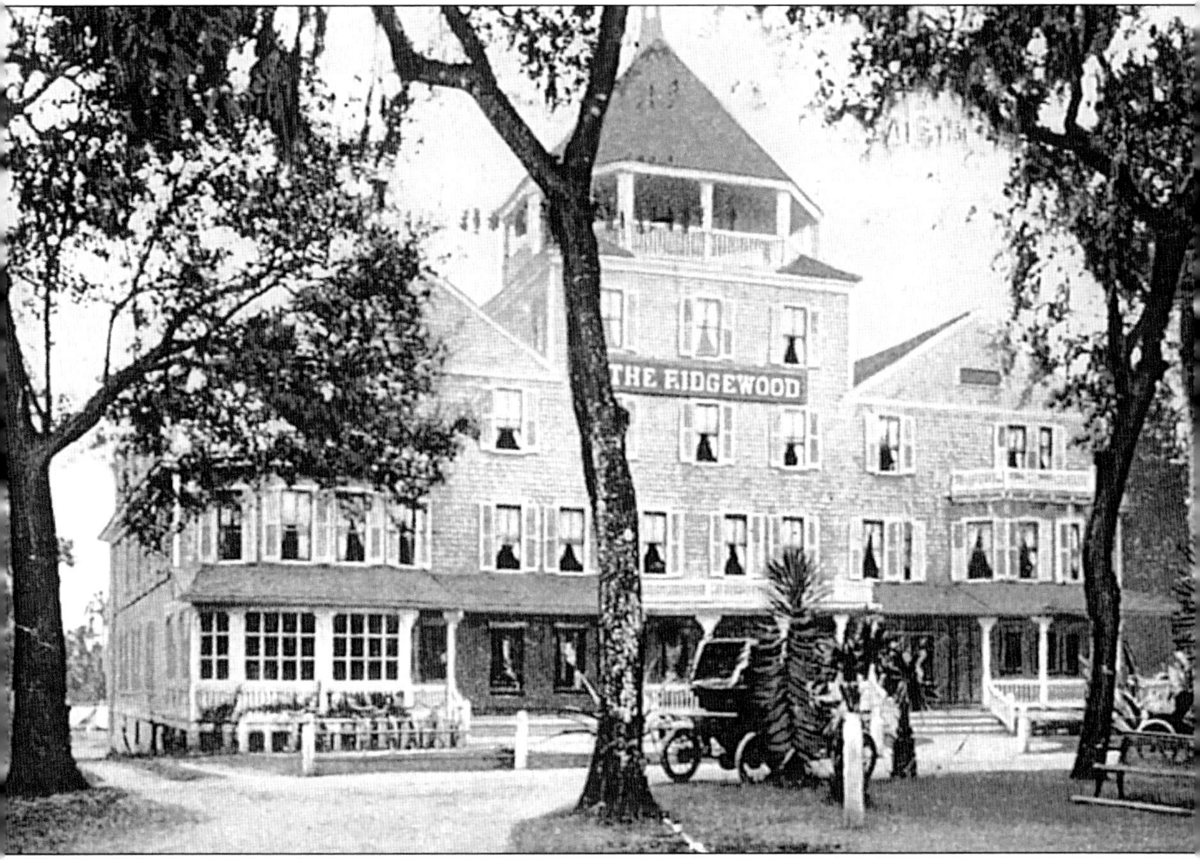

The Ridgewood Hotel, Daytona. This 1904 postcard shows one of the earliest views of the Ridgewood Hotel after it was converted from a private home to one of Daytona's most fashionable places to spend the winter. In its 81-year history, the Ridgewood was damaged by two major fires, yet returned both times from the ashes to reclaim its place on the west side of beautiful Ridgewood Avenue between Magnolia and Orange Avenues. (Postcard courtesy David Findlay.)

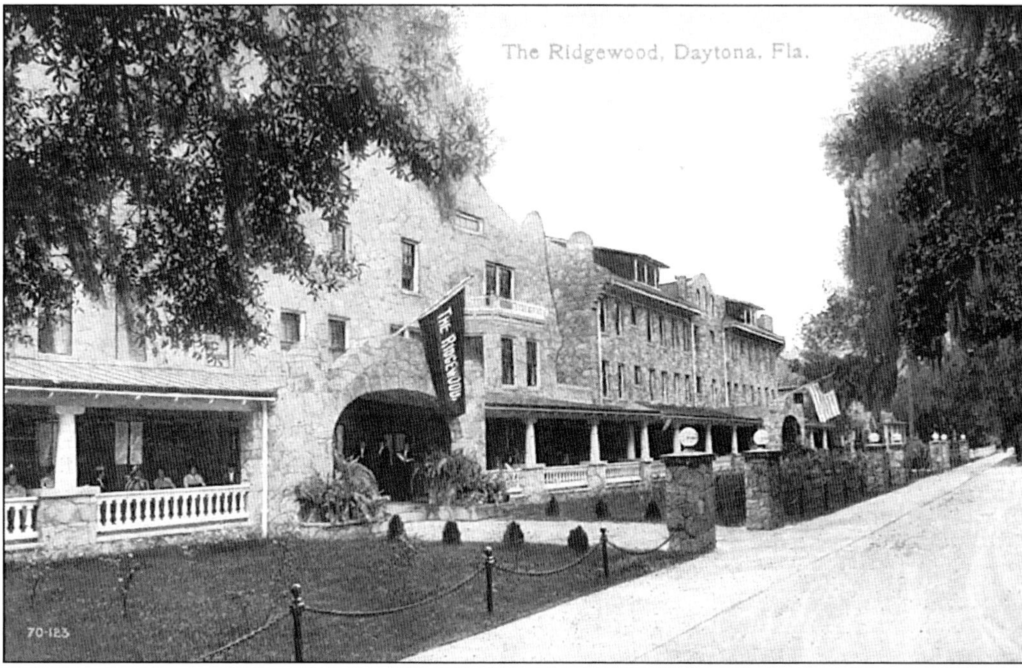

The Ridgewood Hotel, Renovated. The stone facade shown on this 1916 postcard was of local coquina rock, a limestone mixture of clam shells and coral. The hotel had one hundred rooms en suite with baths and single rooms fitted with running water. The long veranda was an ideal place to spend balmy evenings while listening to the faint sounds of the hotel's own orchestra coming from inside.

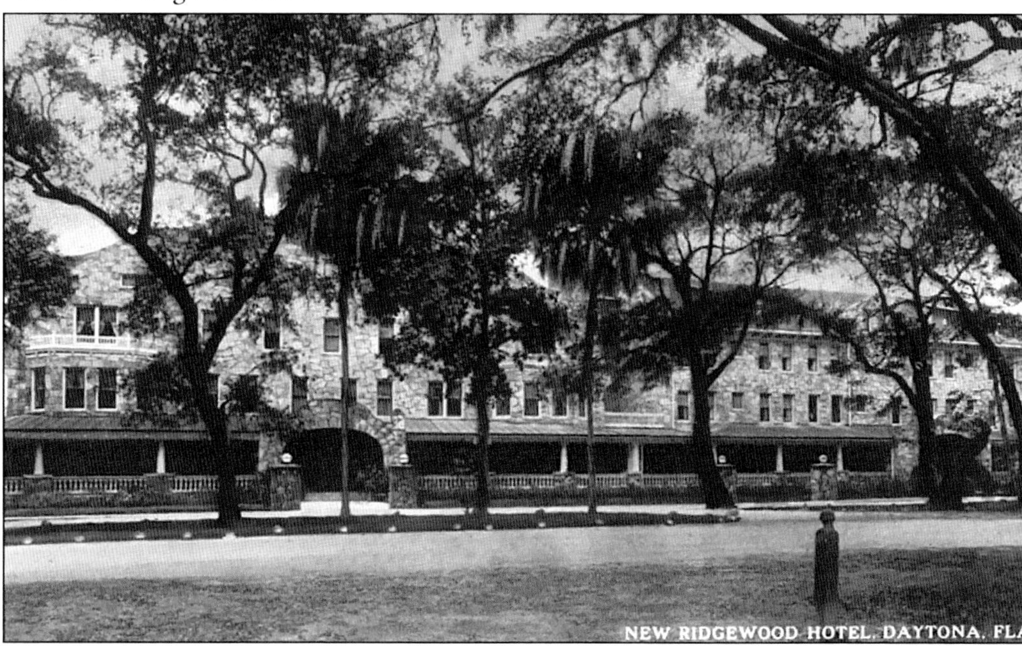

Front View of the Ridgewood Hotel, *c.* 1919. Through a series of owners, the hotel evolved into a sprawling complex. It was refurbished as late as 1971, only to be dismantled about four years later.

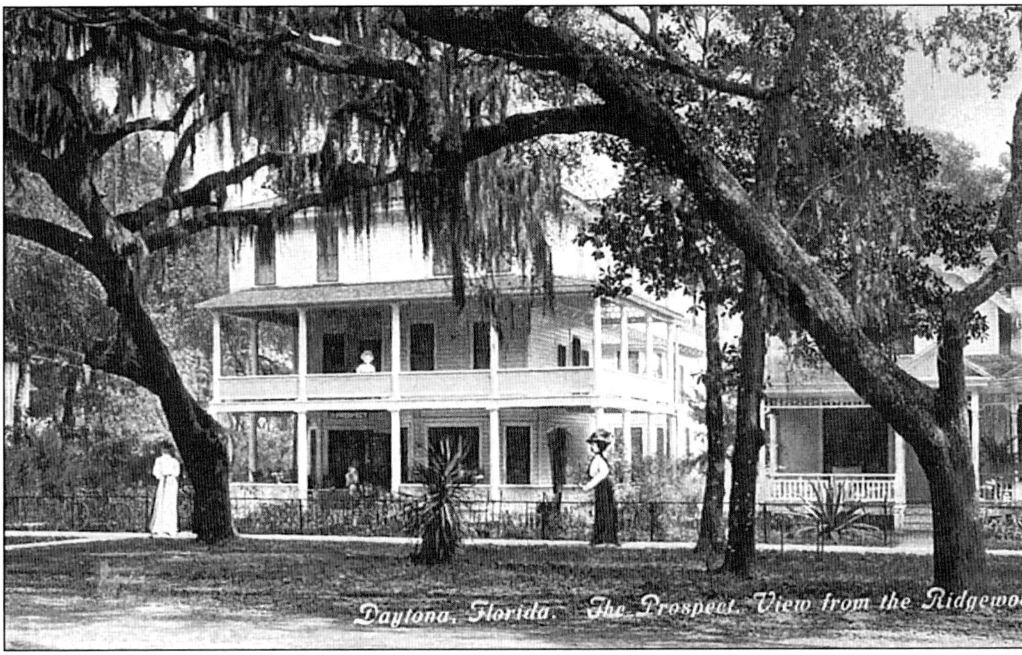

THE PROSPECT, DAYTONA. This 22-room inn was on the east side of Ridgewood Avenue across from the Ridgewood Hotel. The building is still there. (Postcard courtesy David Findlay.)

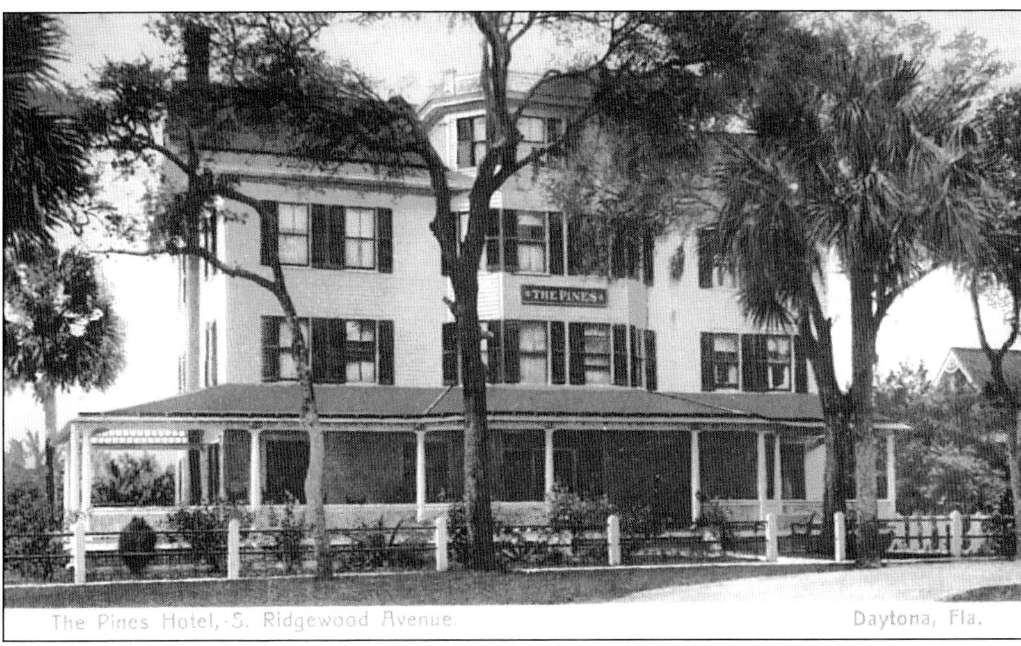

THE PINES HOTEL, DAYTONA. The Pines Hotel debuted on South Ridgewood Avenue between Live Oak and Loomis Streets about 1908. A 1914 advertisement described it as an attractive house with large, airy rooms and modern conveniences including telephone service. Guests were offered sulfur or soft-water baths included in rates that started at $2.50 a day from December to May. The Pines' most unique feature was a rooftop garden with an extended view of the surroundings reaching to the Atlantic Ocean.

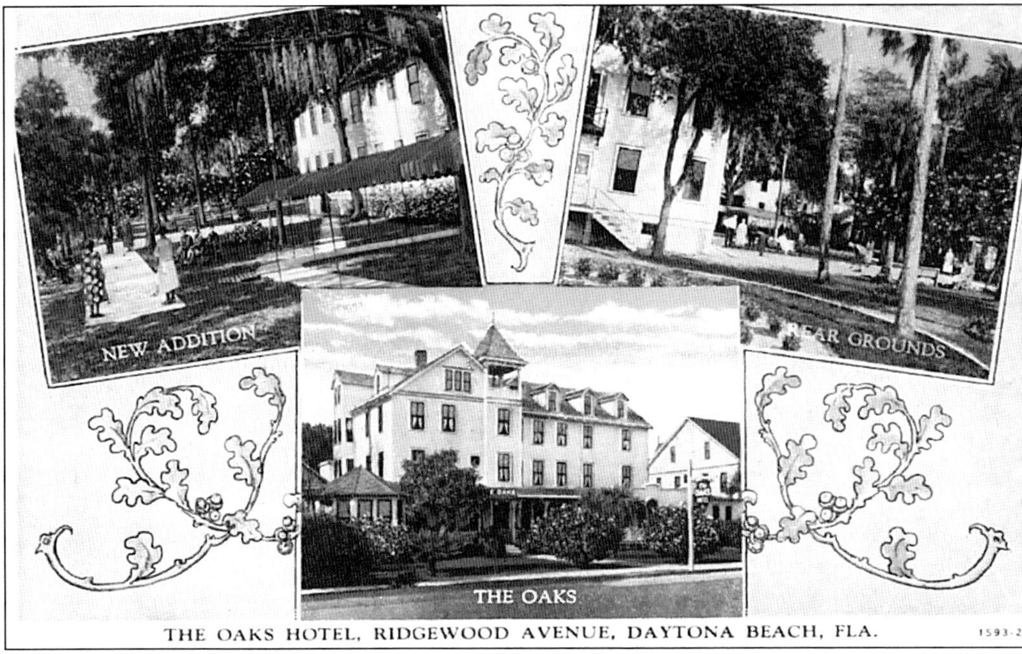

The Oaks Hotel, North Ridgewood Avenue, Daytona. Catering to families was a specialty of this hotel, which offered 40 well-ventilated rooms with electric lights, hot and cold water, and furnace heat. In 1909 a stay at the Oaks cost about $3 a day during the tourist season, November to May. The hotel was between Bay and Third Avenues, not far from the railway station.

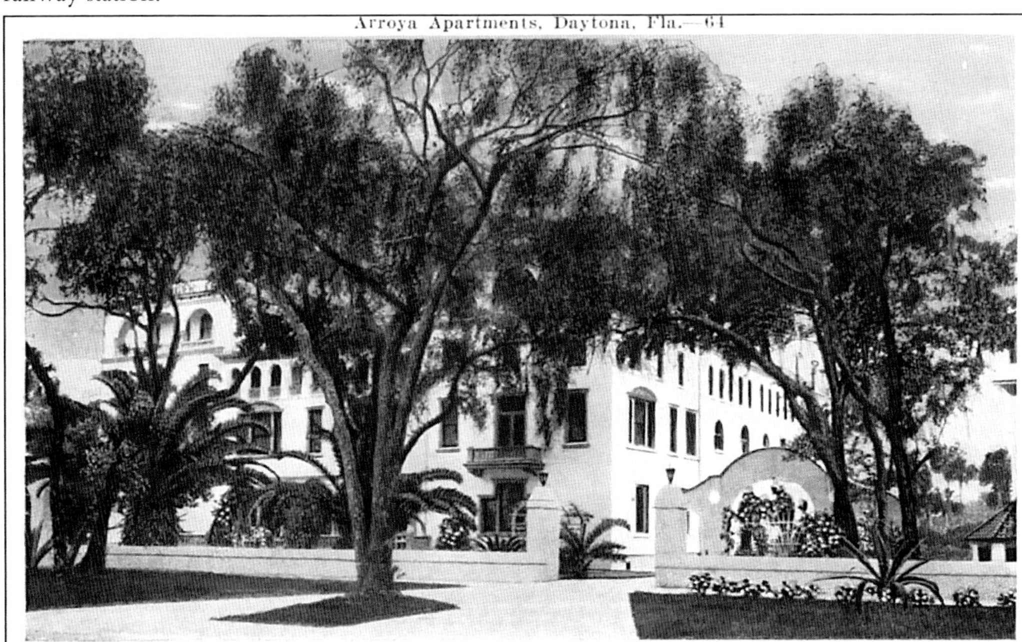

Arroyo Gardens, Daytona. Constructed as an apartment complex in 1923, this 124-room Spanish-Moorish building on a 3-acre estate on Ridgewood Avenue became known as Olds Hall after it was purchased by racing legend Ransom Olds in the 1940s.

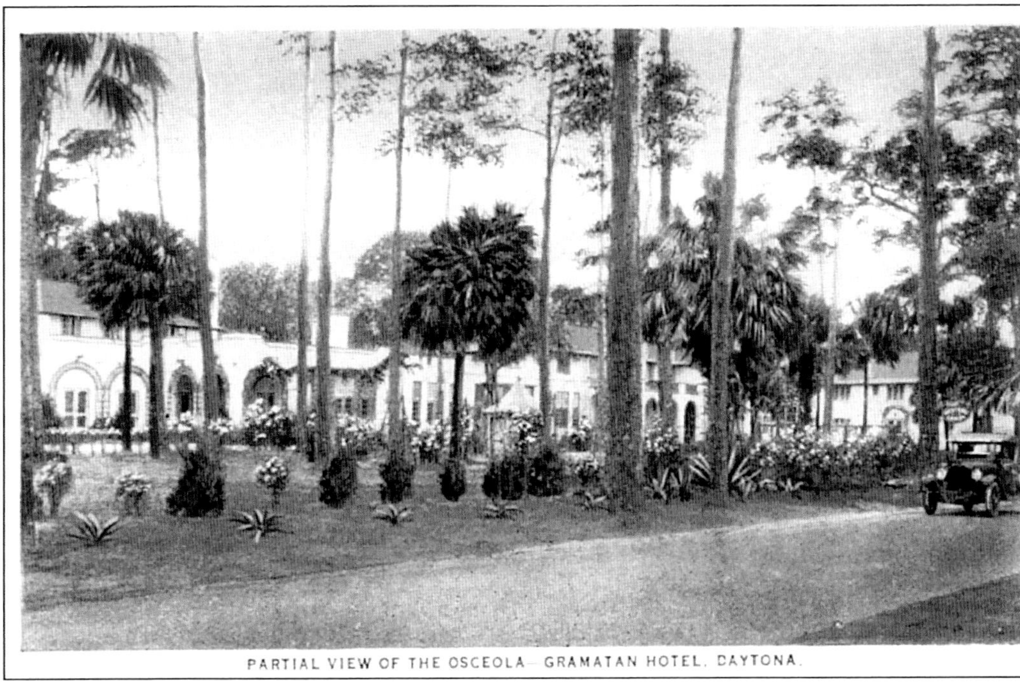

OSCEOLA-GRAMATAN HOTEL, DAYTONA. This seasonal resort hotel also offered 24 cottages situated in an orange grove. Its northern counterpart was the Gramatan in Bronxville, New York. (From Curt Teich souvenir booklet.)

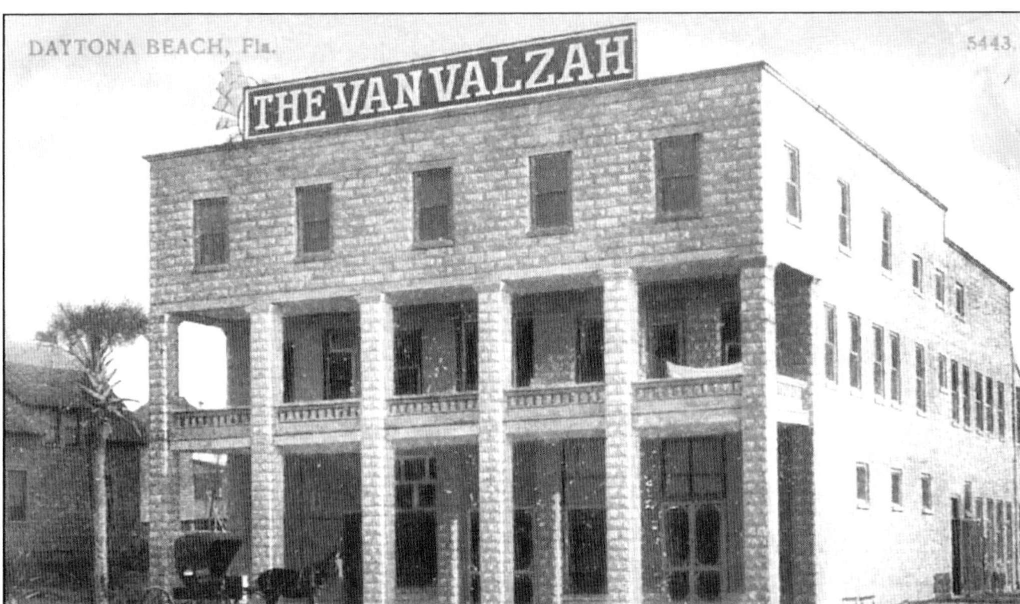

THE VAN VALZAH, DAYTONA BEACH. The cement-stone structure on Seabreeze Avenue (now Main Street) stood apart from the commonplace wooden buildings of the day. It was within walking distance of the beach.

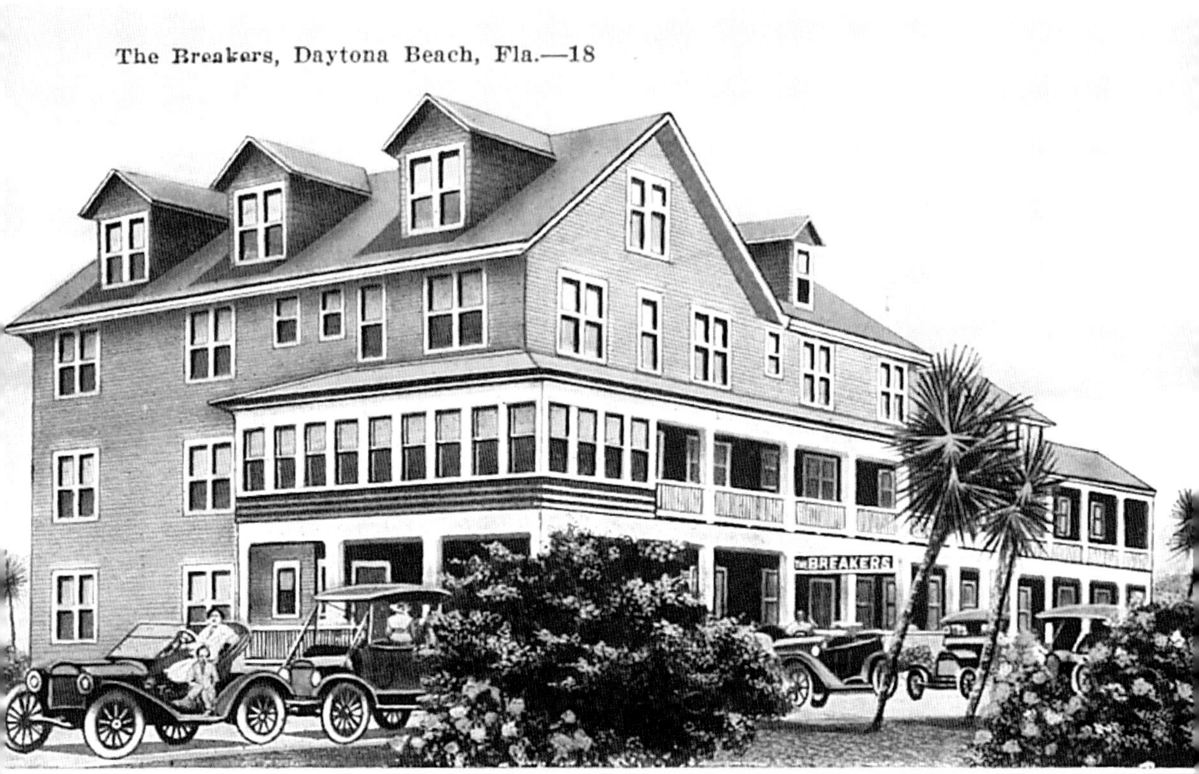

The Breakers, Daytona Beach. According to advertisements, an unrestricted view of the ocean and a spacious veranda where guests could "watch the famous aviatrix, Ruth Law, make daily flights over their heads," were reasons to choose the three-story Breakers Hotel, South Ocean Avenue; another was electric car service from the hotel to the railroad depot. Prospective lodgers were promised pastimes such as bathing, fishing, and motoring on the beach. Built by a DeLand woman in 1914, the Breakers went up in smoke in 1946.

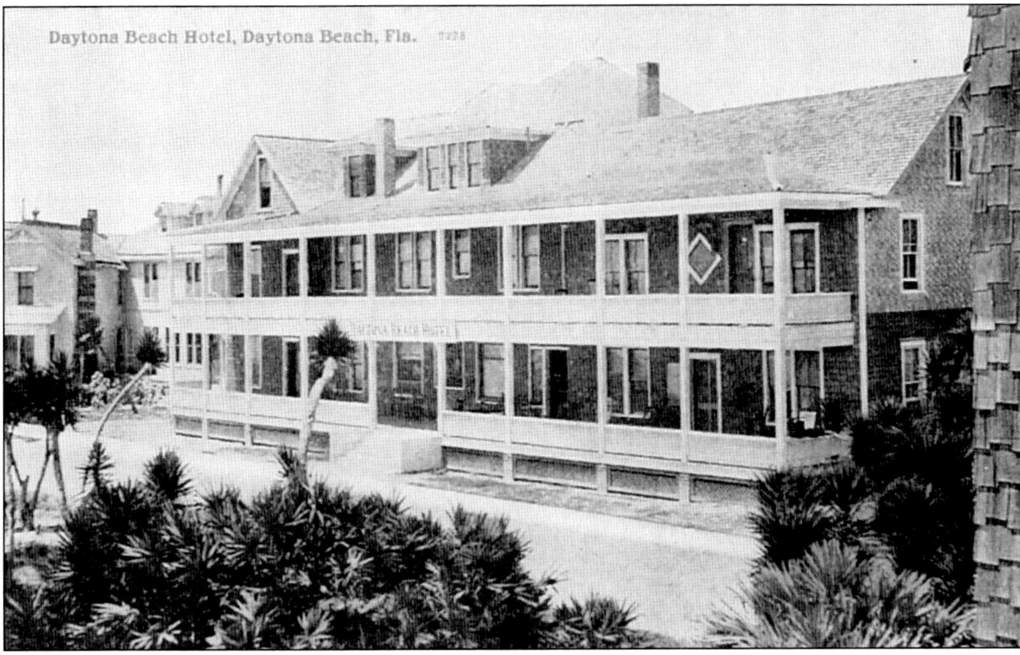

DAYTONA BEACH HOTEL, DAYTONA BEACH. One of Daytona Beach's principal hostelries faced the ocean near Seabreeze Avenue, just 50 feet from the ocean pier built by hotel proprietor Thomas Keating. It opened in 1908. (Postcard courtesy David Findlay.)

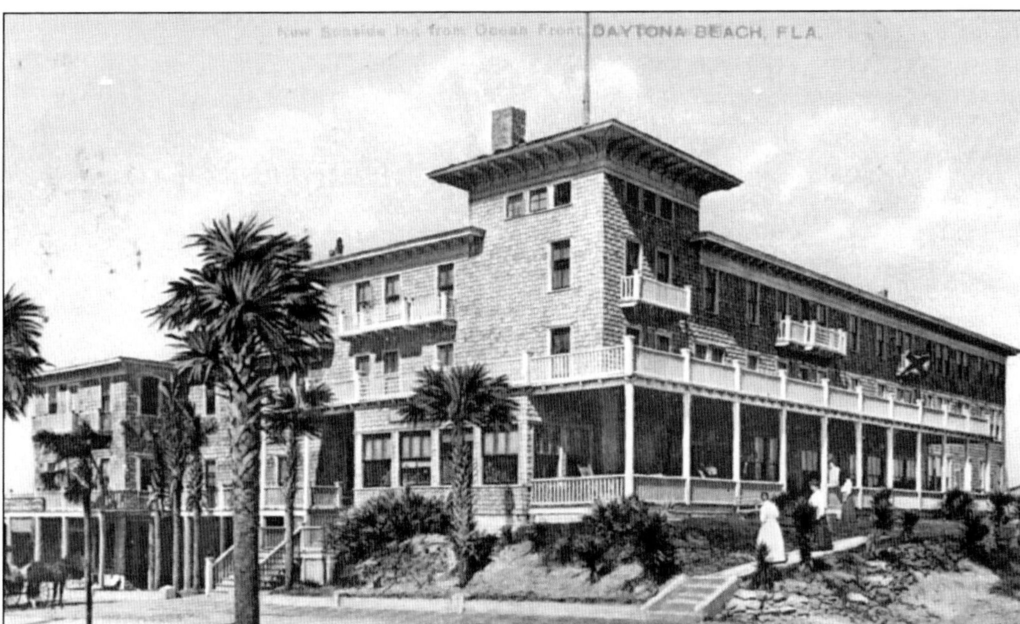

SEASIDE INN, *c.* 1909, DAYTONA BEACH. At Seabreeze and North Ocean Avenues, the inn filled all the requirements of suitable beachfront property when it opened at the dawn of the Gay Nineties. It was outfitted with modern conveniences, overlooked the Atlantic Ocean, and was surrounded by broad verandas fanned by sea breezes. The structure was rebuilt after a fire that occurred about 1898.

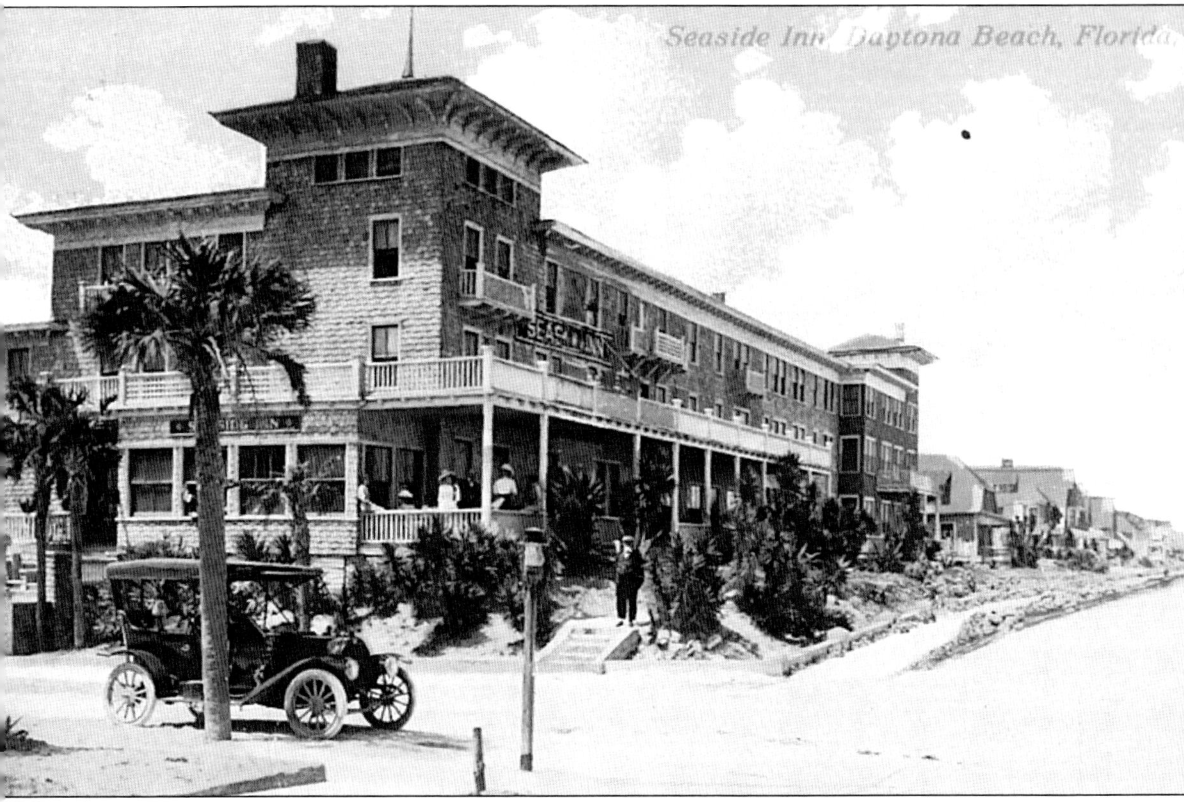

SEASIDE INN ENLARGED, C. 1912–1913. Note the addition on the north end of the hotel. The Clarendon Hotel can be seen in the distance, and Keating's Pier, not shown, jutted into the Atlantic Ocean just south of the inn. The sender of this postcard wrote of catching seven whiting from the pier, while other fishermen pulled in about 150 catfish the same day.

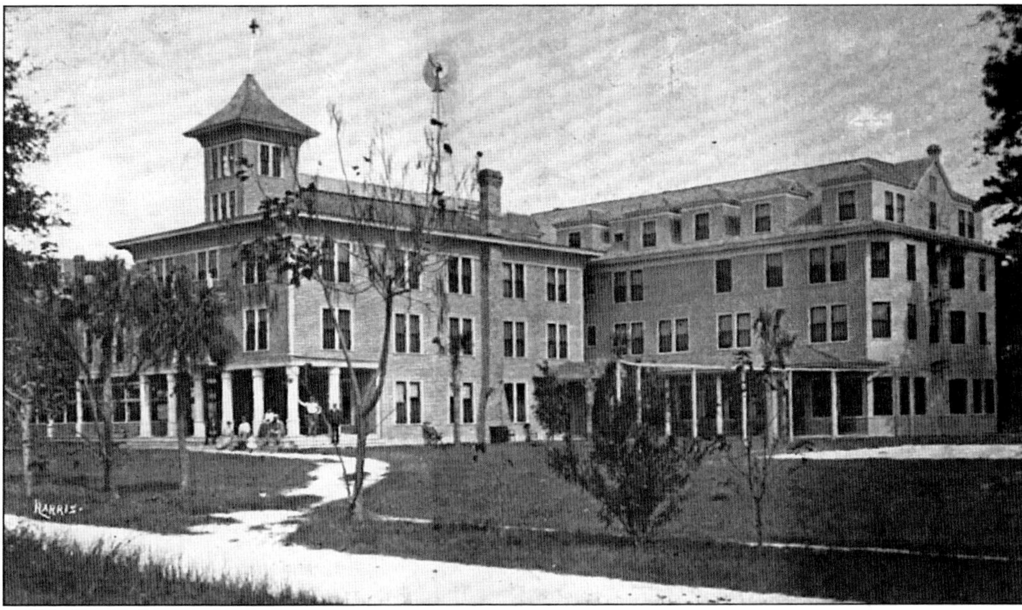

THE COLONNADES HOTEL, SEABREEZE. With the help of pioneer resident C.A. Ballough, Charles C. Post built the Colonnades Hotel in the 1890s as he and his wife, Helen Wilmans Post, developed the town of Seabreeze. The 125-room structure burned in late 1909. Ironically, the Colonnades had taken in the evacuees of a nearby hotel fire several months earlier. (Postcard courtesy Richard Dragoni.)

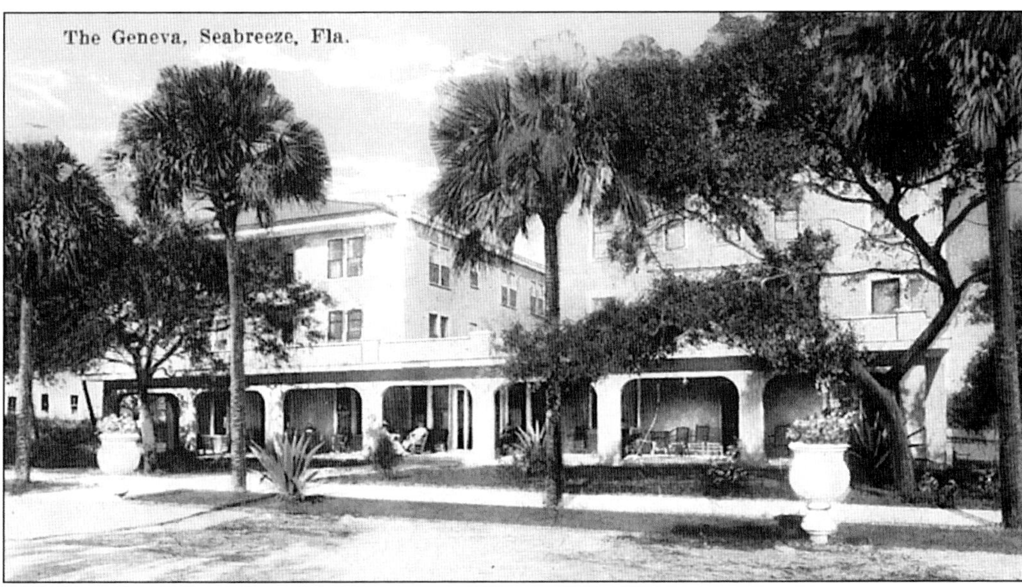

GENEVA HOTEL, SEABREEZE. Northern hotel owners built this Florida counterpart to their New York Geneva Hotel in 1911. After two renovations, the 1924 building offered 75 rooms, each with a telephone. The Geneva was on Ocean Boulevard, midway between the Atlantic Ocean and the Halifax River.

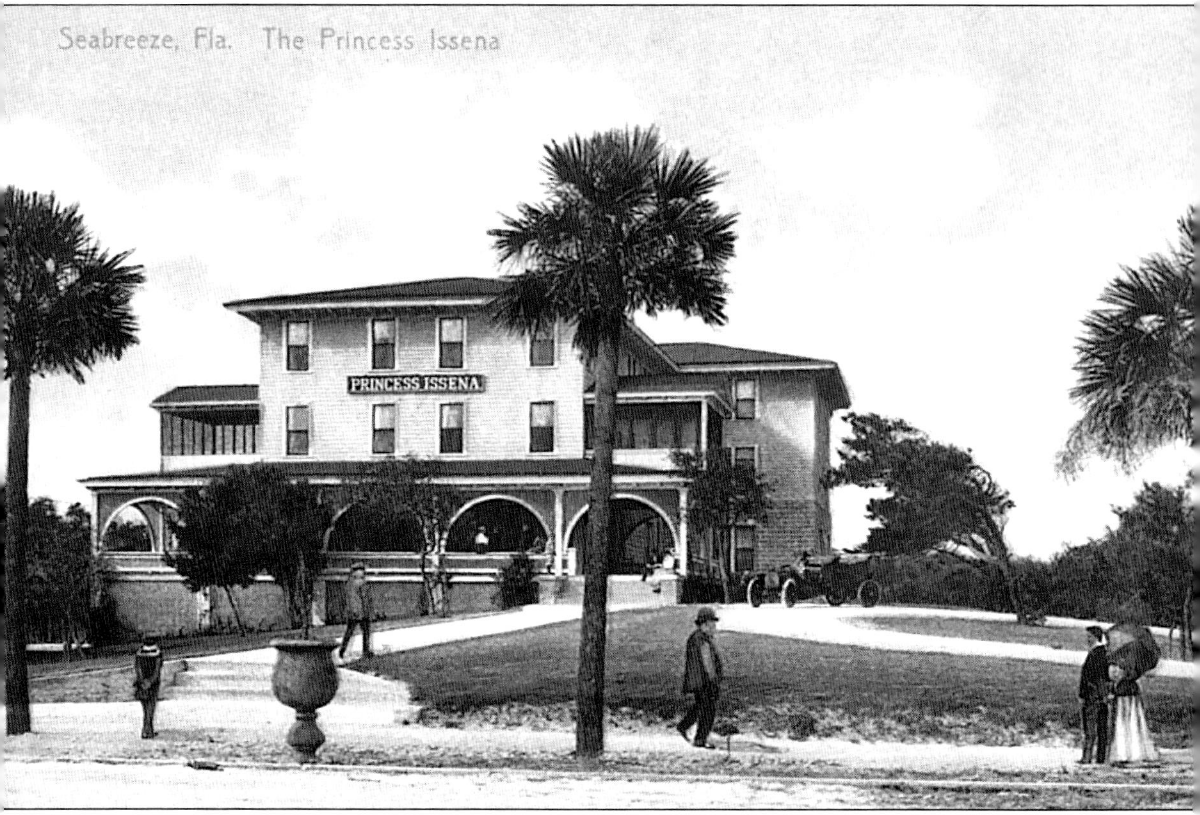

PRINCESS ISSENA HOTEL, SEABREEZE. The legend of a 16th-century Huguenot who married a Timucuan Indian maiden named Issena may have been the inspiration for the name of this hotel, another Post establishment. The elegant, 27-room Princess Issena, situated in the midst of a 5-acre park, opened in 1908 on Ocean Boulevard. Meals were complemented with homemade pastries and canned preserves as well as artesian water and milk from the hotel's own Jersey and Holstein cows, all for about $3 a day.

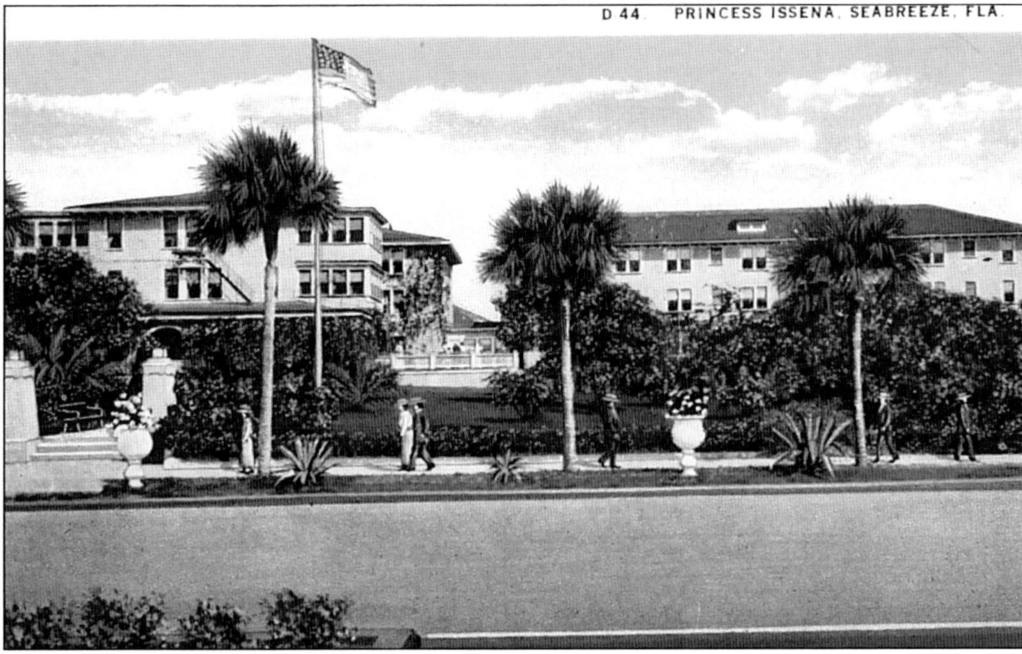

LATER VIEW OF THE PRINCESS ISSENA HOTEL. The Princess Issena blossomed into a resort complex with several cottages, a theater, a 500-seat restaurant, and a swimming pool. It was owned by the Sheraton Corporation in the late 1940s and later operated as a residential community for retired citizens in the 1960s. The cost of maintaining the aging facilities that occupied an entire city block led to the hotel's closing in 1981, at which time a local newspaper gave this final tribute: "The Princess is dead. Long live the Princess."

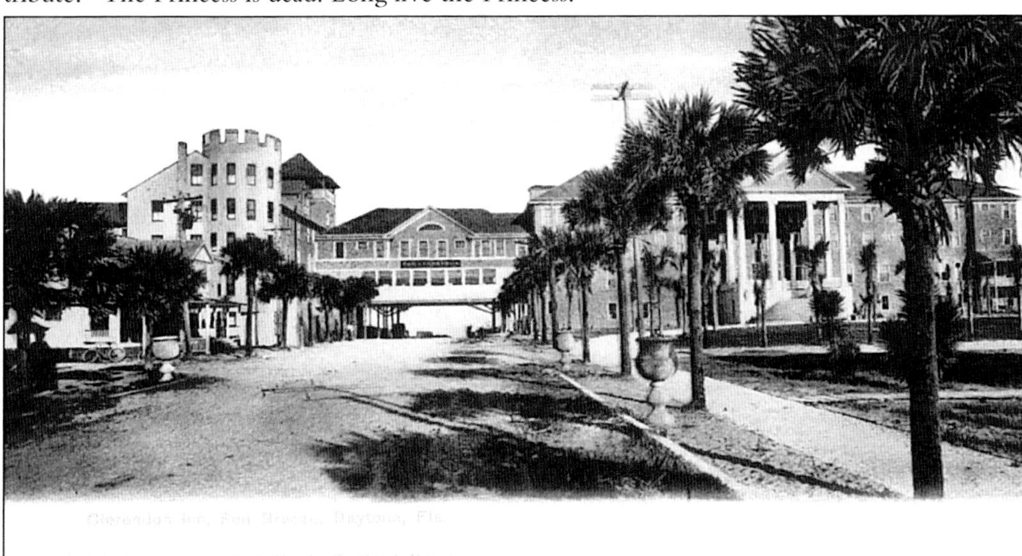

THE CLARENDON INN, FRONTING ATLANTIC AVENUE (NOW SR AIA), SEABREEZE. Two buildings were joined across Ocean Boulevard to form the first Clarendon Inn. The original wood-frame structure shown here was destroyed by fire on St. Valentine's Day, 1909, several months before the Colonnades Hotel burned. The Clarendon was full at the time, as it was the peak of tourist season; fortunately, guests escaped unharmed. It was rebuilt of brick in 1910.

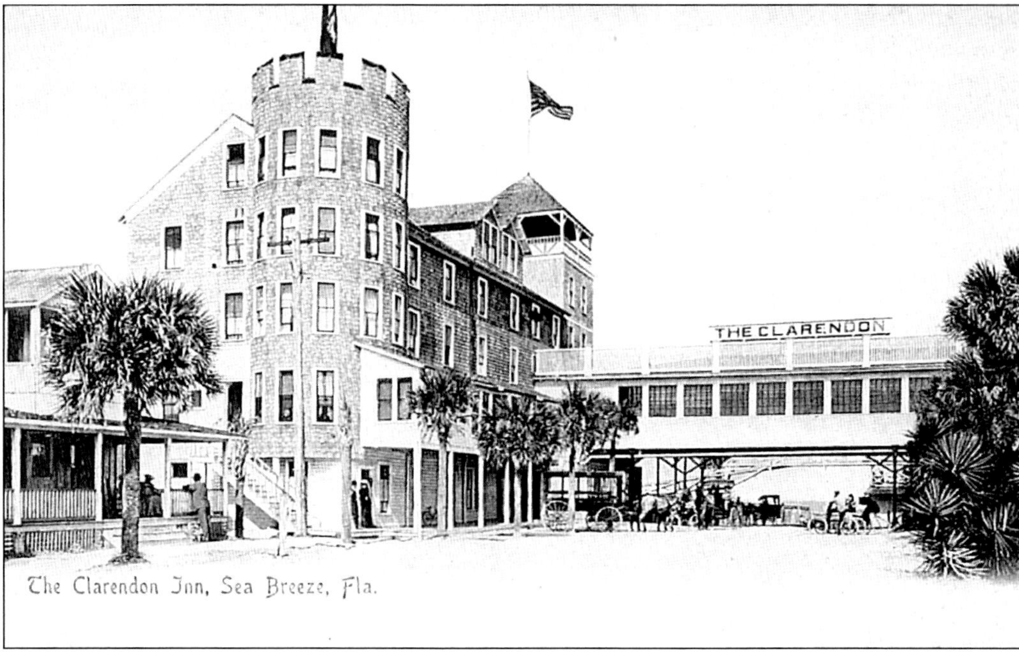

The Clarendon Inn, seen from the West on Ocean Boulevard. A feature unique to the Clarendon was the underpass that led from Ocean Boulevard to the beach. The inn also had its own stable of saddle horses and a livery of carriages. (Postcard courtesy David Findlay.)

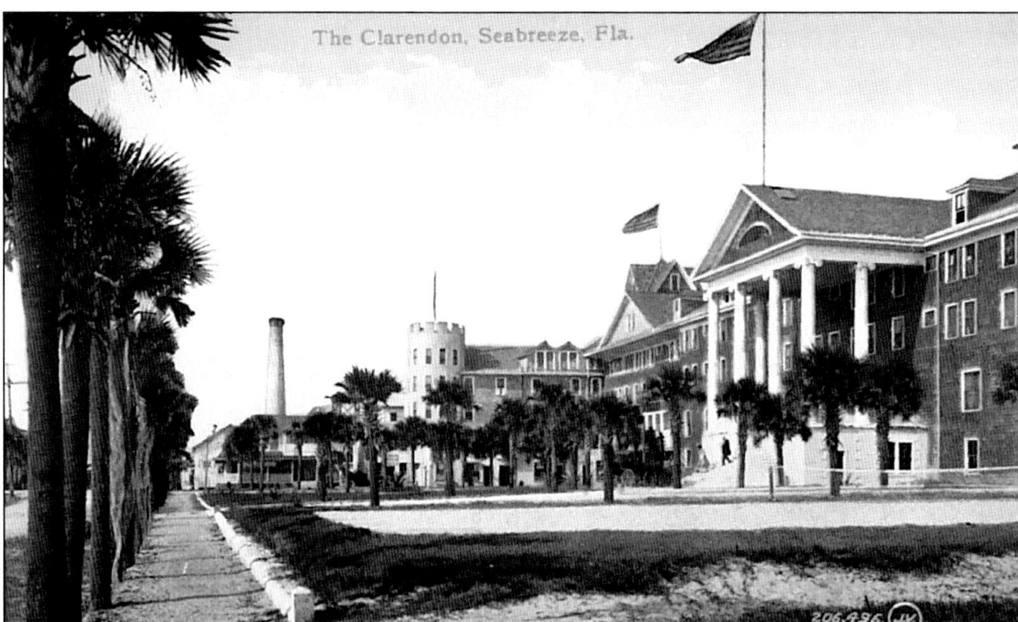

The Clarendon, Looking North on Atlantic Avenue. The hotel had its own electric power plant, as indicated by the smokestack.

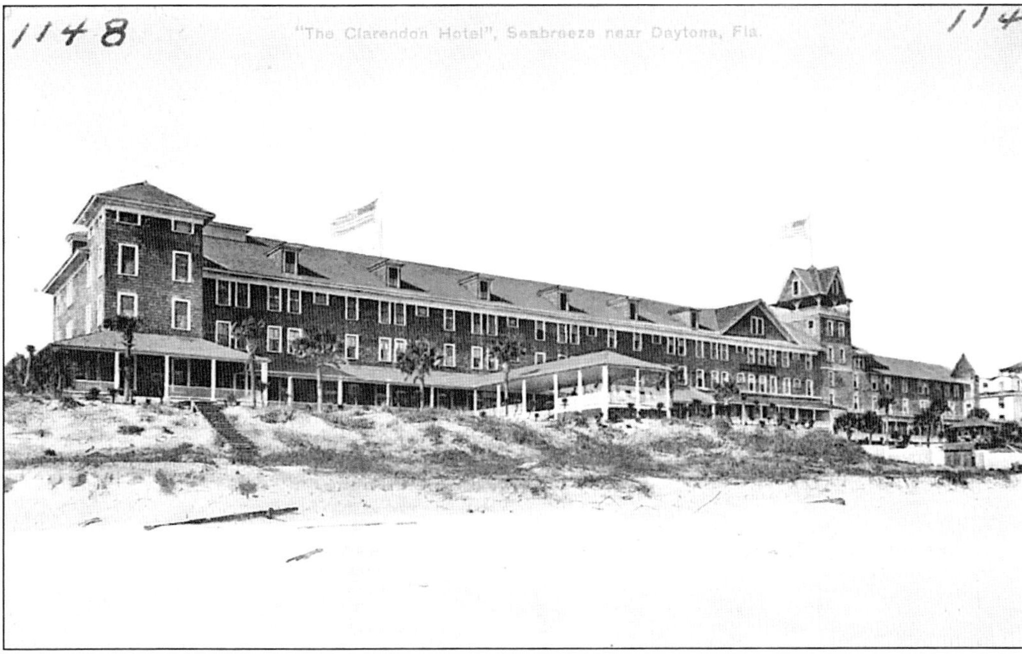

BACK OF THE CLARENDON. The back of the hotel was as impressive as the front. There was a spacious dining room overlooking the ocean and porches ideal for viewing automobile races; it also had a pier that later deteriorated and was not replaced. A stay at the inn in 1908 started at $3.50 a day.

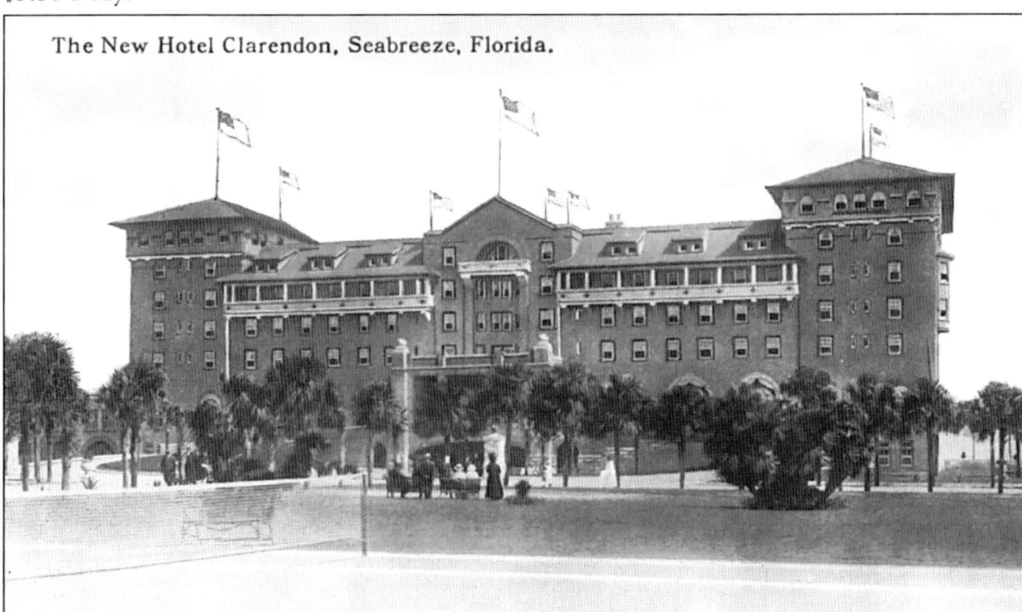

FRONT OF THE 1911 CLARENDON HOTEL SHOWING TENNIS COURTS IN FOREGROUND. The stylish, fireproof hotel opened for business in 1911. It provided guests a full agenda of recreation, entertainment, and social events. In addition to tennis, participatory sports included billiards, bowling, golf, and horseback riding. There was dancing every evening, and for relaxation, one could indulge in a Turkish or Russian bath attended by experts.

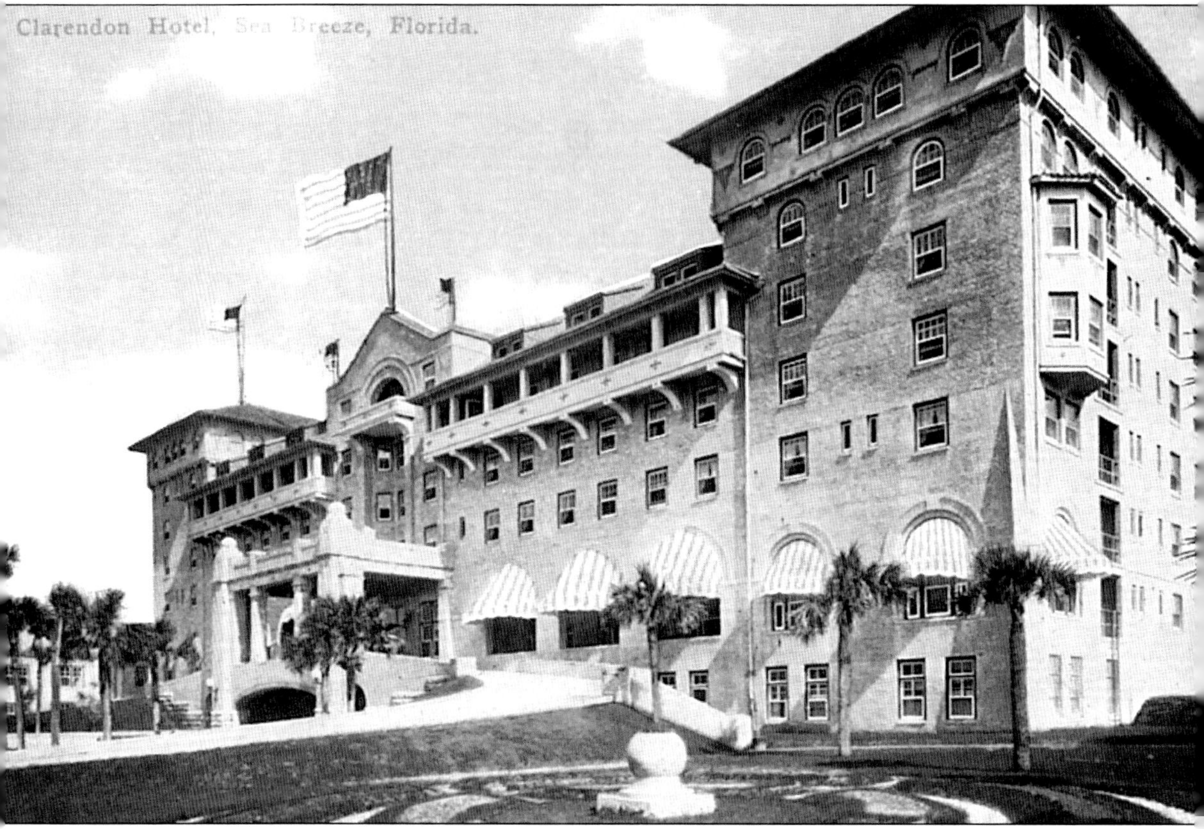

The New Fireproof Clarendon Hotel. While the Clarendon was under construction in 1910, the *Daytona Daily News* gave this preview of what one could expect in the way of appointments: "The guest rooms are being furnished in solid mahogany, making it harmonize with the colonial finish of the white woodwork and mahogany doors. All the baths are being fitted entirely with white enamel; the hardware on the windows and doors is nickel with glass door knobs; and the floor is buff marbleoid."

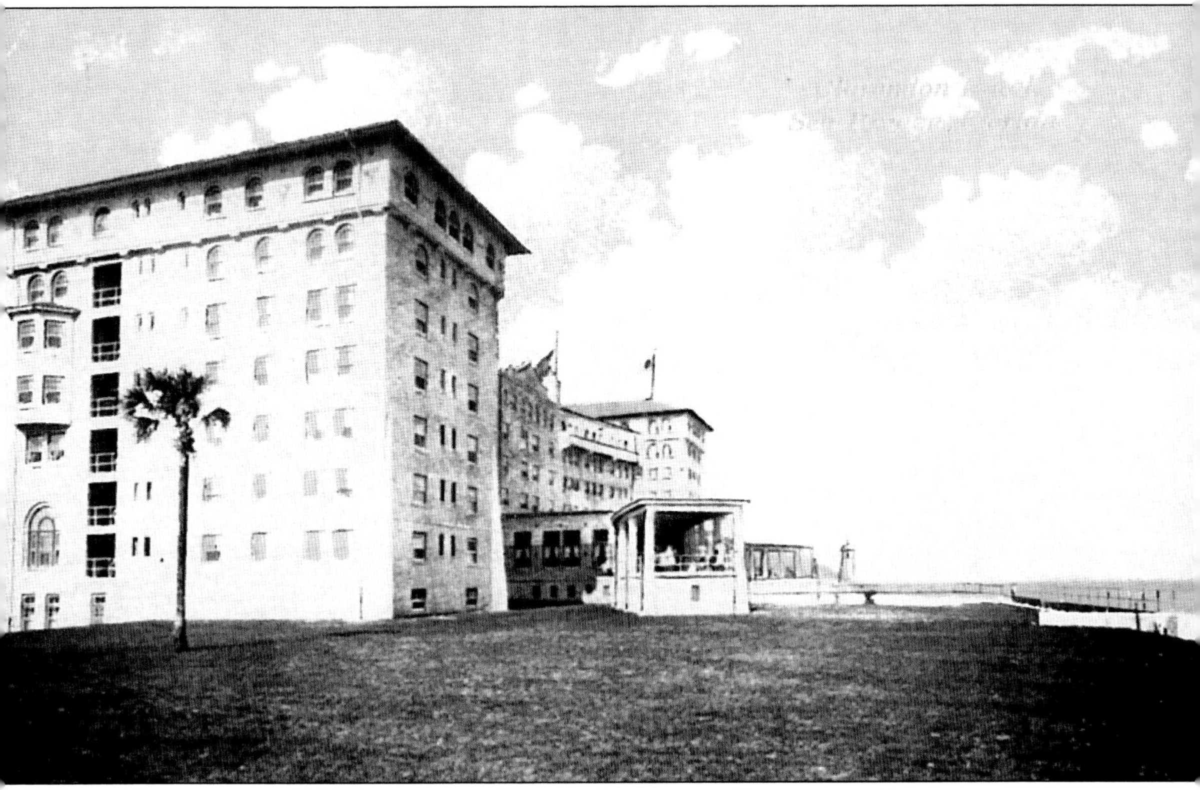

Back View of the 1911 Clarendon Hotel, Showing a Breezeway Overlooking the Ocean. The Clarendon became part of the Sheraton hotel chain in the 1940s, and later was known as the Daytona Plaza. The Clarendon was the only hotel in the area to have its own "aeroplane" livery service, and at one time there were hangars nearby on the beach. (Postcard courtesy Richard Dragoni.)

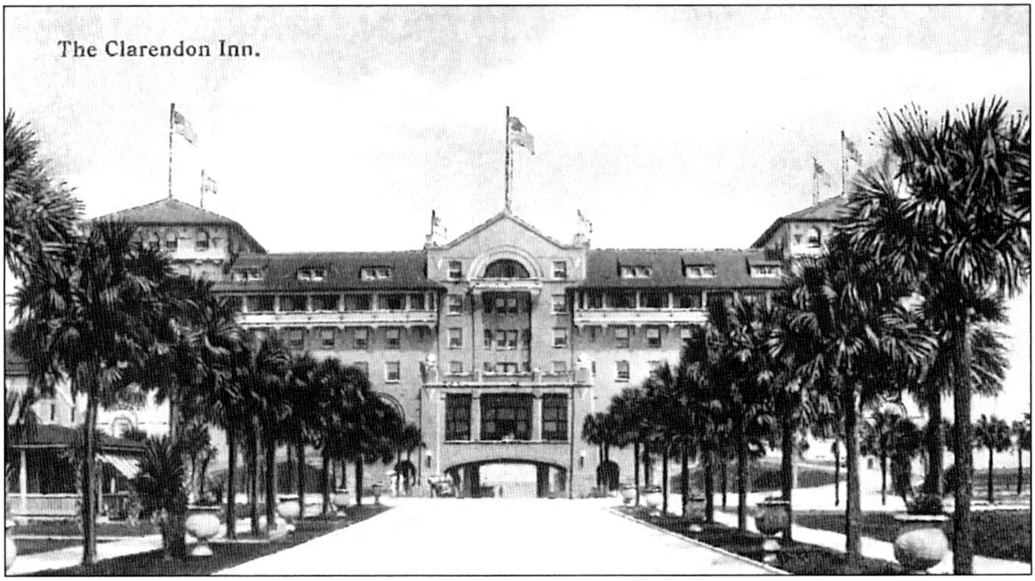

CLARENDON ENTRANCE. The imposing seven-story Clarendon Hotel could be seen for miles along the Ormond-Daytona beach. The entrance to the "new" hotel lined up with Ocean Boulevard. Note the ramps on each side leading up to the hotel lobby and the continuation of the road under the hotel to the beach.

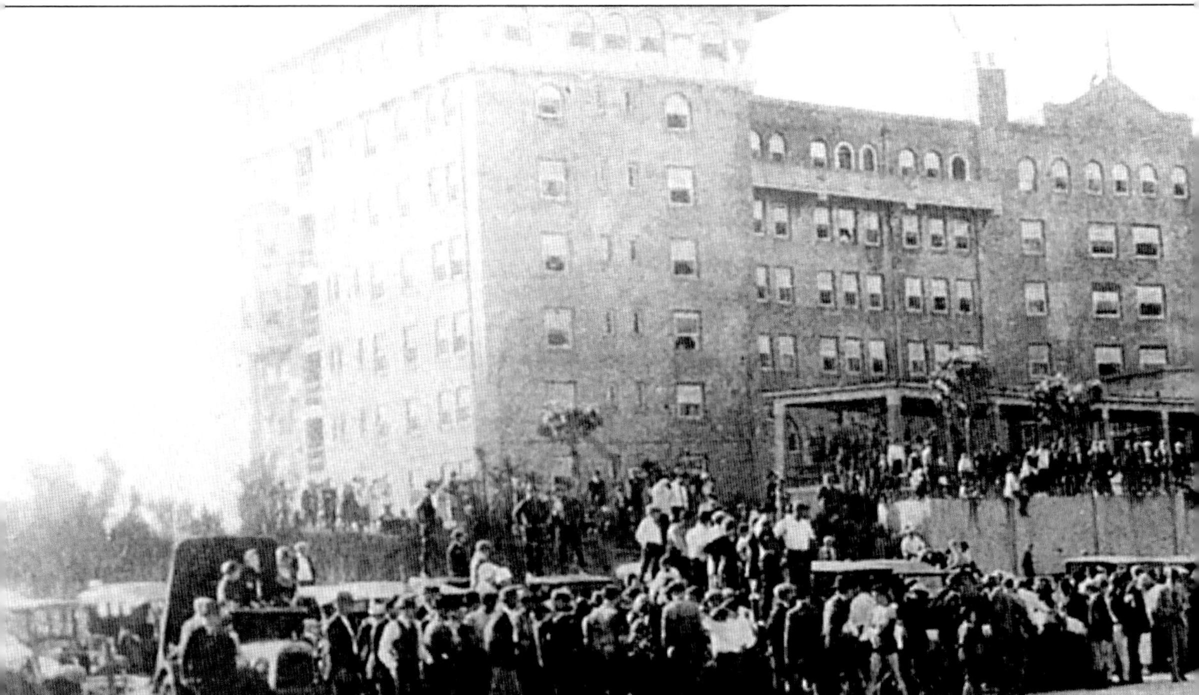

RACE DAY AT THE CLARENDON. This panoramic photograph was snapped on the beach behind the Clarendon Hotel. Two race cars can be seen facing south at the far right. The year and event depicted here cannot be confirmed; however three clues suggest the mid- or late 1920s: This certainly is the 1911 Clarendon Hotel; sanctioned beach racing ended about 1910 and was

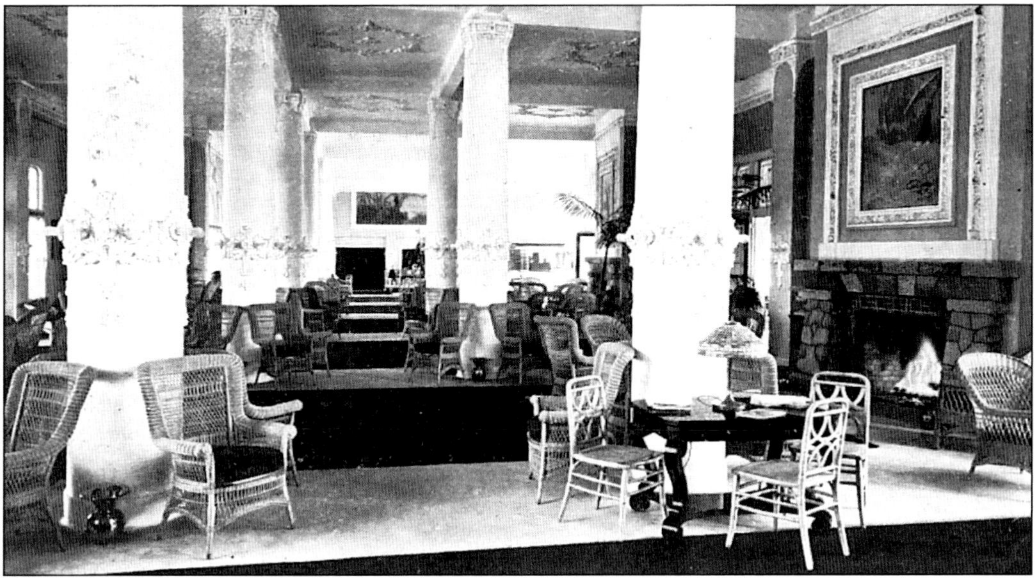

Clarendon Hotel Lobby. The hotel's casual elegance was reflected in both the architecture and furnishings shown on this postcard mailed in 1914. Note how formal features such as massive columns, ornamental friezes, and Tiffany-style lamps were juxtaposed with a rustic stone fireplace, tropical plants, and airy wicker furniture.

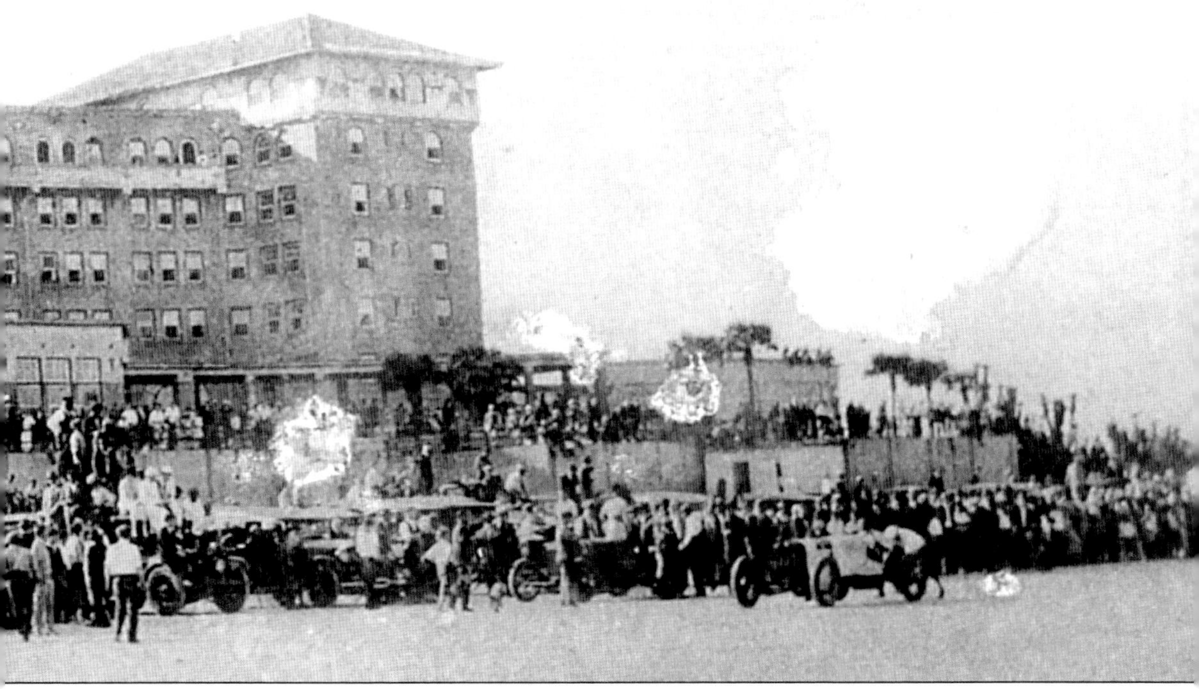

revived about 1919. The year "1928" is scrawled on the back of this picture. A major event occurred in 1927 when Major Henry Segrave set a world speed record here. (Postcard courtesy David Findlay.)

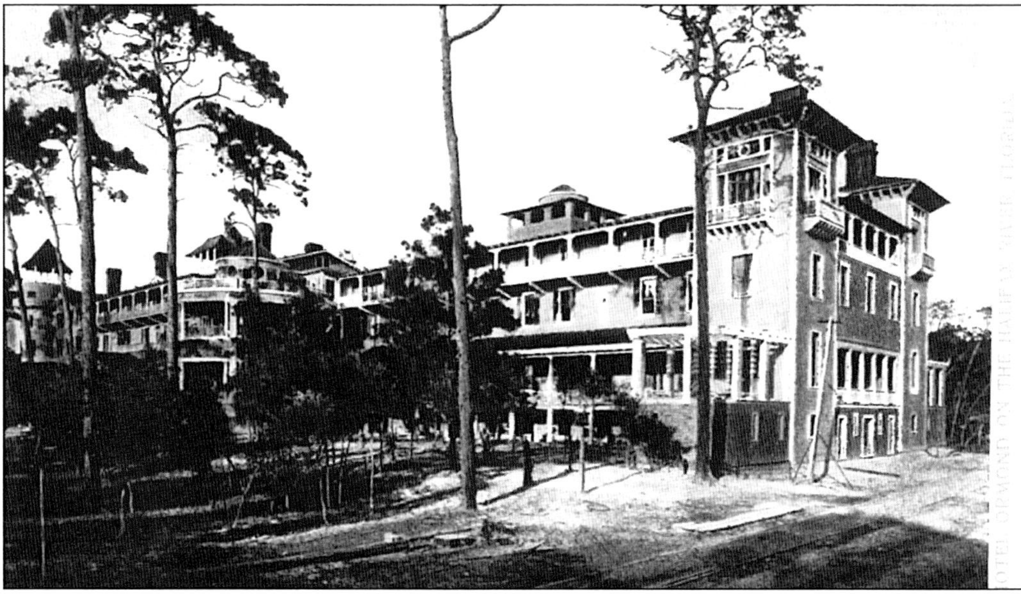

ORMOND HOTEL, ORMOND. John Anderson, one of Ormond's most colorful figures and beloved pioneers, along with partner Joseph Price, opened the 70-room Ormond Hotel on January 1, 1888, with a grand ball attended by some four hundred guests. According to local historians, a 14-year-old boy drew up the plans for the original structure. (Postcard courtesy Richard Dragoni.)

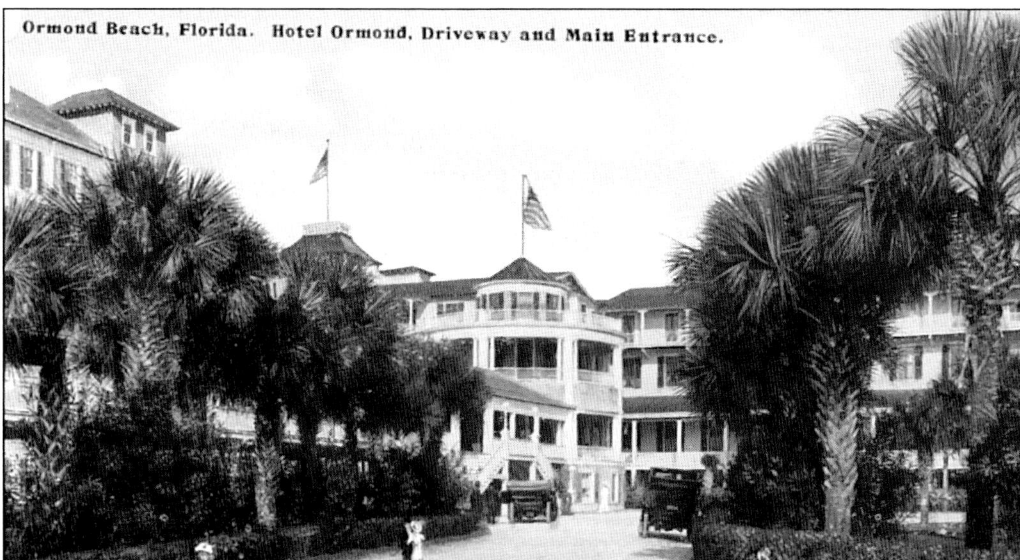

MAIN ENTRANCE TO THE ORMOND HOTEL. Henry Flagler purchased the property in 1891, then brought his railroad across the Halifax River to the doors of the hotel. In typical Flagler style, the Ormond was enlarged, remodeled, and outfitted to suit the clientele that he expected to attract. That clientele—which included Rockefellers, Astors, and other luminaries—soon obliged, making the hotel their winter retreat during the glory days of automobile racing. Hotel guest J.F. Hathaway and former hotel owners Anderson and Price organized the first official meet in 1903.

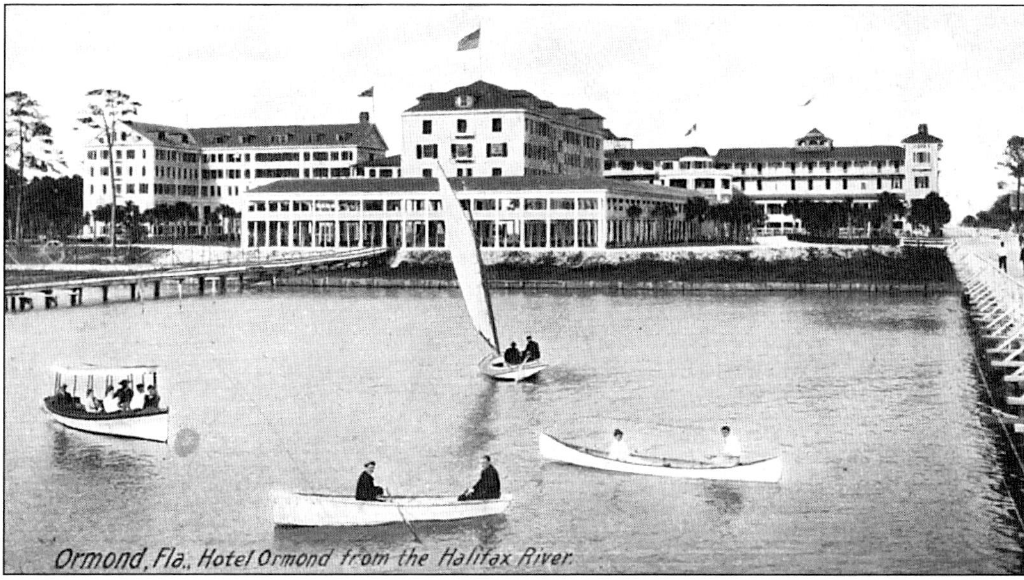

ORMOND HOTEL, AS SEEN FROM THE HALIFAX RIVER. After Henry Flagler took over, the hotel had a capacity for five hundred guests and was said to be the largest wooden structure of its kind in the country. Along with the hotel's extra wings, Flagler installed elevators, a swimming pool, and modern laundry facilities. There also was a private pier with excursion boats that cruised the Halifax and Tomoka Rivers.

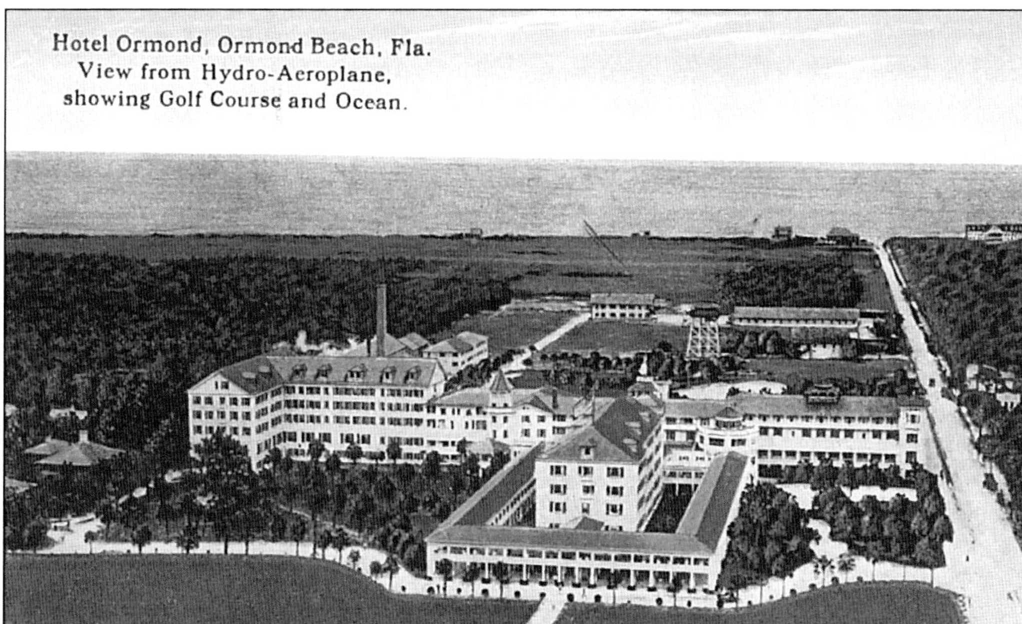

AERIAL VIEW OF THE ORMOND HOTEL TAKEN FROM A "HYDRO-AEROPLANE," OR SEAPLANE. This postcard shows the layout of the hotel around 1916. The rounded portico off Granada Avenue was the hotel entrance, as seen in a previous view. At the end of Granada to the north was the hotel's private 18-hole golf course; the Bretton Inn sat at the southeast corner on a bluff facing the ocean. The Ormond was torn down about 1992. (Postcard courtesy David Findlay.)

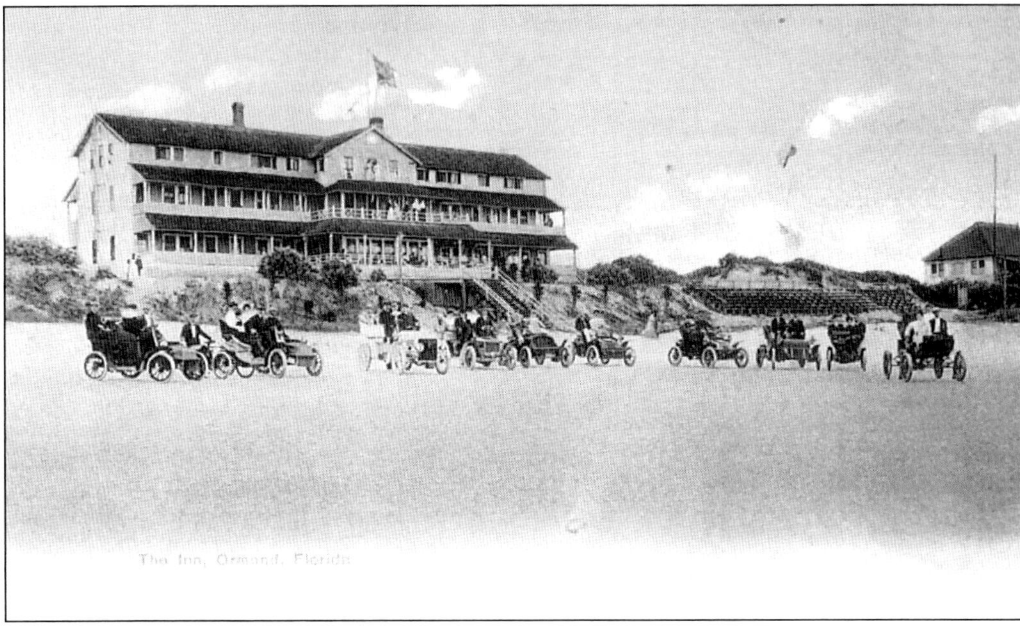

BRETTON INN, ORMOND. The Coquina Hotel, built in 1889, changed hands just after the turn of the century and was renamed the Bretton Inn by new owners John Anderson and Joseph Price. It was demolished about 1923 and a larger Coquina Hotel was built in its place a few years later. The north end of the beach race course was near the Bretton Inn, where guests were ensured exclusive seating for the famous automobile meets. (Postcard courtesy David Findlay.)

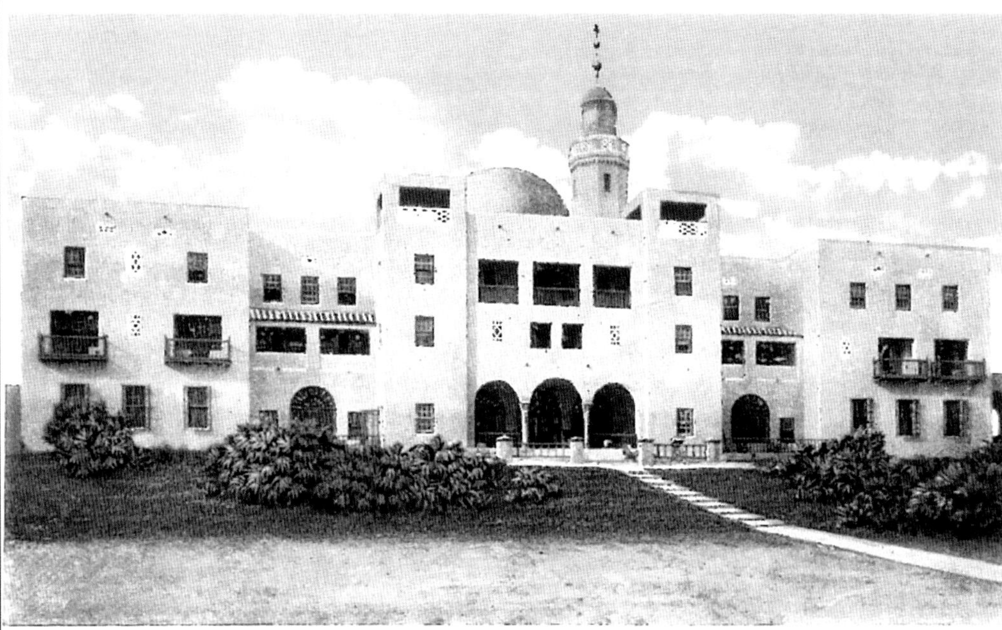

HOTEL COQUINA ON THE ATLANTIC OCEAN, ORMOND BEACH.

THE NEW COQUINA HOTEL ON THE FORMER SITE OF THE BRETTON INN, C. MID-1920S. The Coquina came down in the late 1960s when SR A1A was widened. (From Curt Teich souvenir booklet.)

Four

Pastimes in Paradise
Sports, Recreation, and Entertainment

The cards in this section offer a glimpse of the area's main attractions. This is Florida before theme parks and outlet malls, before spring break and space shuttles, when natural beauty and pleasing climate were the only reasons one needed to travel hundreds of miles and stay several months.

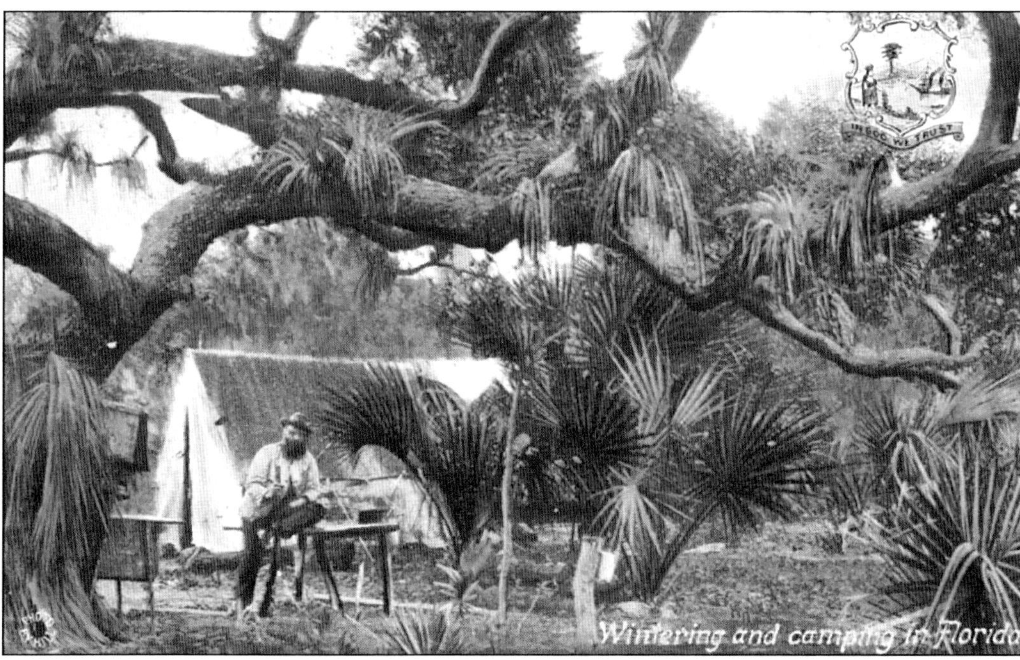

Camping in Florida. Guidebooks were essential reading for Northerners planning a "winter campaign" in the late 19th century. Charles Hallock's *Camp Life in Florida* recommended that sportsmen arrive outfitted with the following: a lightweight tent; a gun and a rifle; woolen clothing, to be worn at all times; a mosquito bar, preferably of lawn; a Dunklee camp stove and kit; whiskey and quinine for medicinal purposes; and for bedding, a hammock to keep the camper away from Florida's "fiercest animal," the flea.

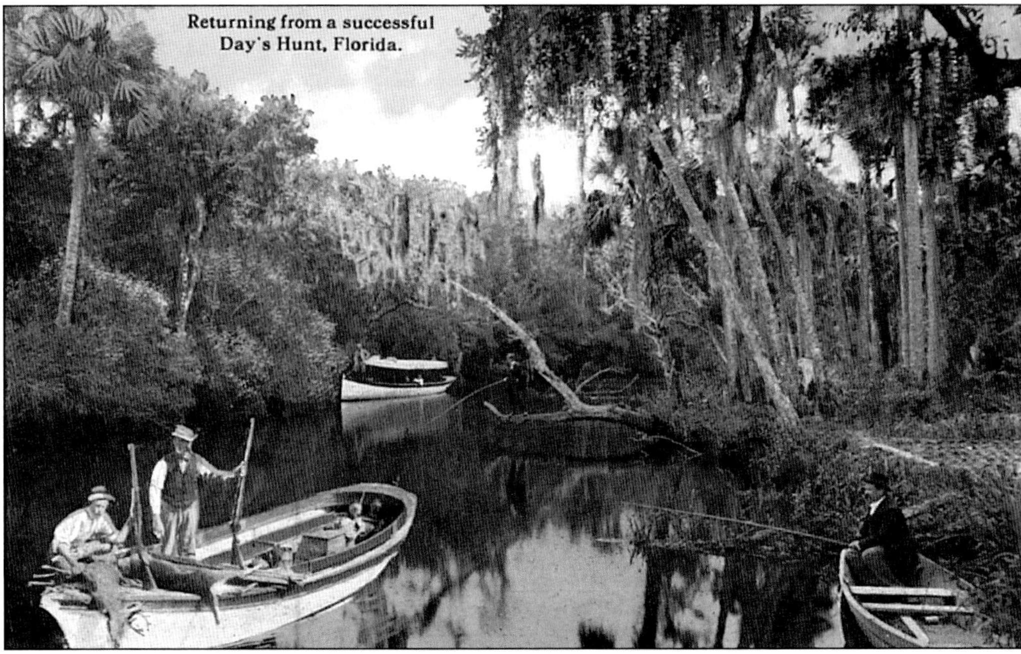

Hunting and Fishing. Florida's rivers and woods were reportedly alive with fish and wildlife, although game laws were in effect as early as the 1880s. One hunting article advised that a patient hunter floating with the current in a flat-bottom boat could easily shoot a deer, just as the two hunters in this picture did.

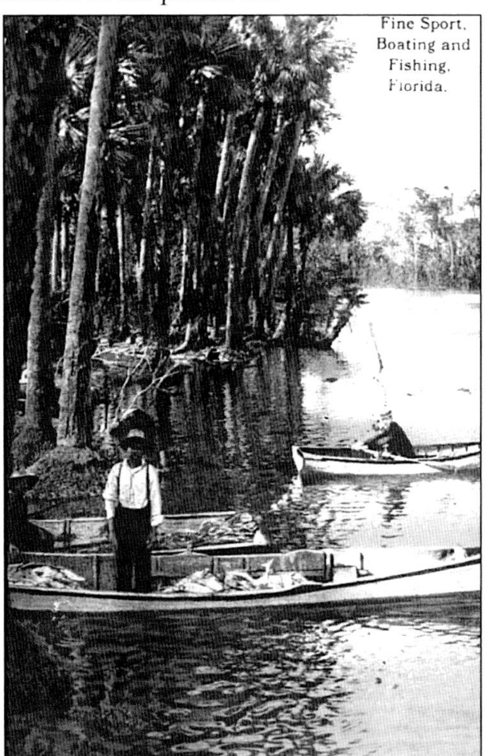

Boating, Hunting and Fishing on a Florida River. In a state that has more than 7,700 lakes, some 2,200 miles of tidal shoreline, and a total water area of approximately 4,300 square miles, a boat was as needful as a horse on the plains, according to *Camp Life in Florida.* (Postcard courtesy Richard Dragoni.)

Fishing in Rivers. Stories about the exceptional size of Florida's black bass prompted experienced angler S.C. Clarke to travel to the Halifax region in 1875. "Having caught these black bass in . . . the St. Johns, the Tomoka, and Spruce Creek," Clarke said, "I find them to be of about the average size of the same species in the western waters, . . . yet I am inclined to think that those weighing from 15 to 20 pounds, said to have been taken here, were estimated rather than weighed." Clarke wrote articles for *Forest and Stream* magazine. (Postcard courtesy Richard Dragoni.)

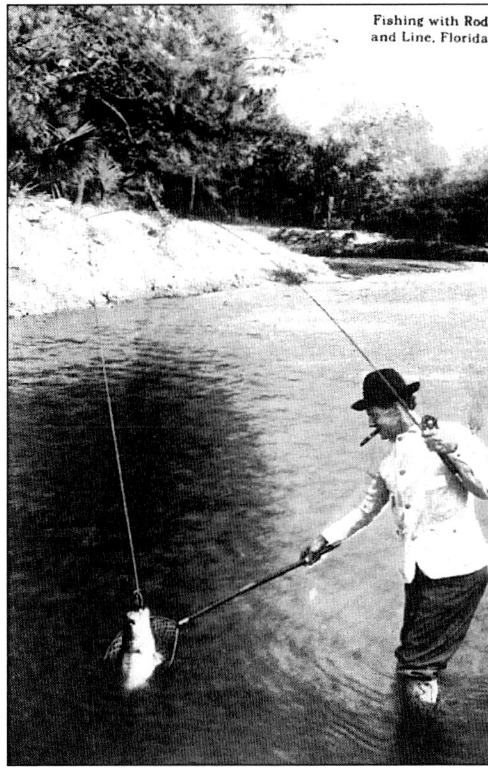

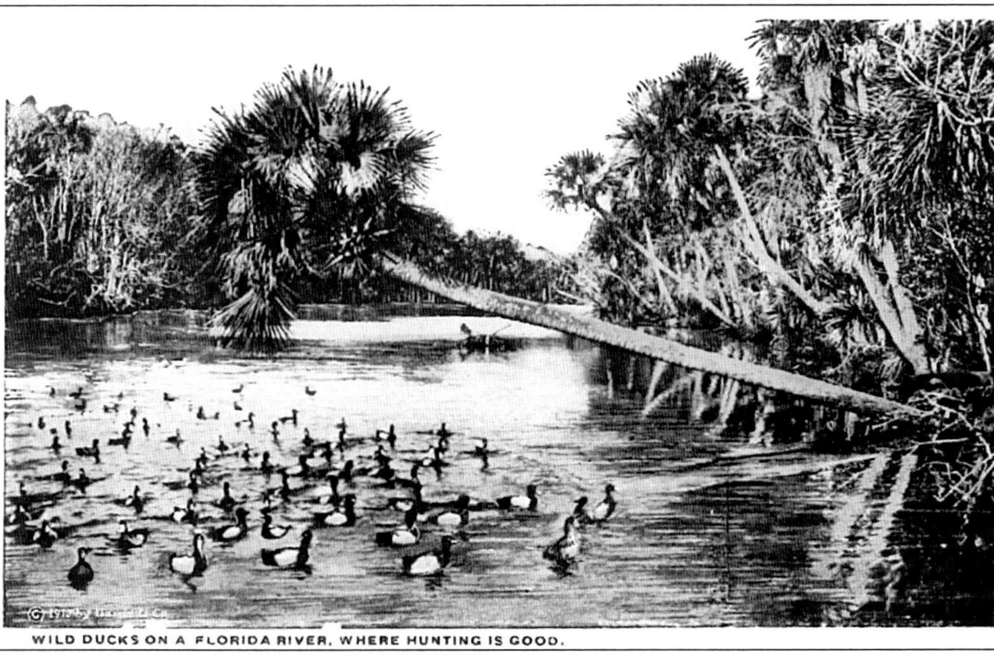

WILD DUCKS ON A FLORIDA RIVER, WHERE HUNTING IS GOOD.

Wild Ducks on a Florida River. Mallards, wingtails, pintails, canvas-backs, and wood ducks were just some of the duck species that could be found in regional waters in winter.

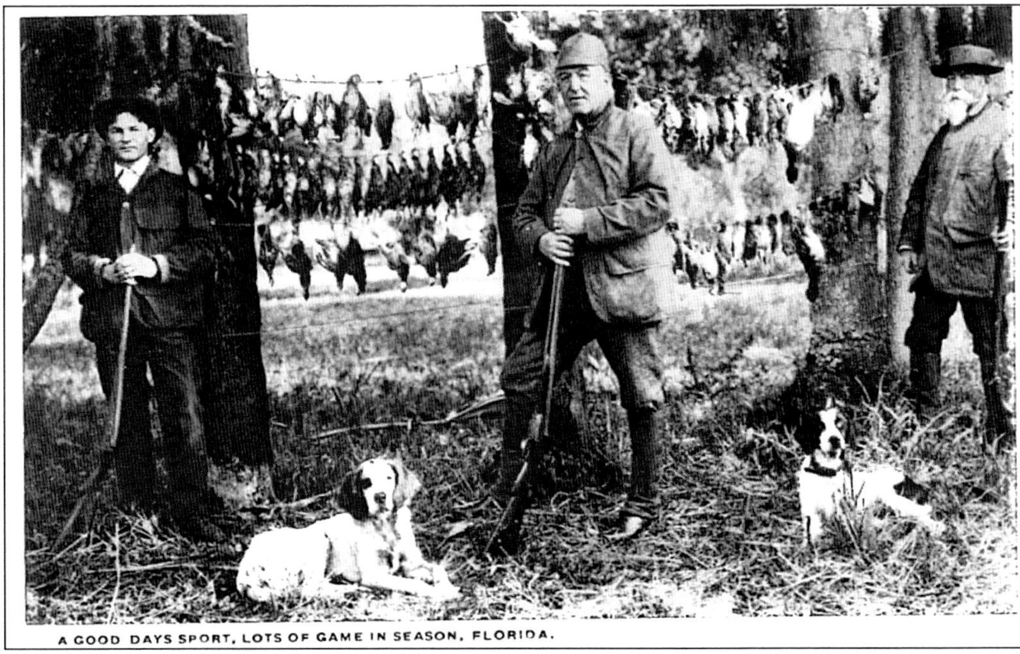

HUNTING GAME BIRDS. Snipe and quail were plentiful in the woods and fields between the Halifax and St. Johns Rivers.

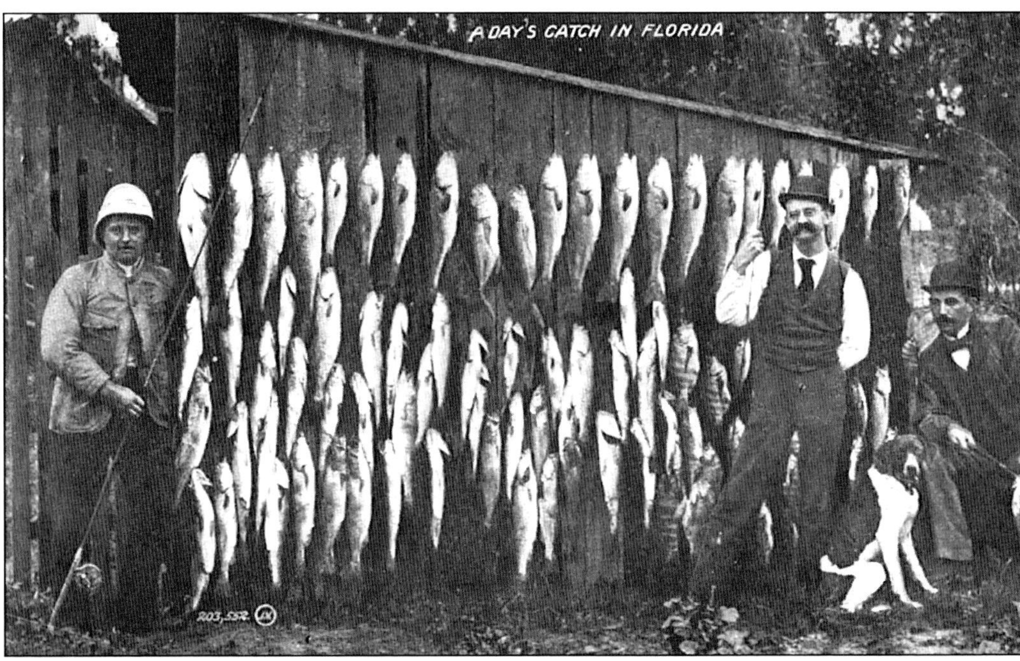

SALTWATER FISHING. A day's catch at Mosquito Inlet (now Ponce Inlet) or on the Indian River in 1912 yielded an assortment of channel bass, grouper, whiting, and even the prized pompano.

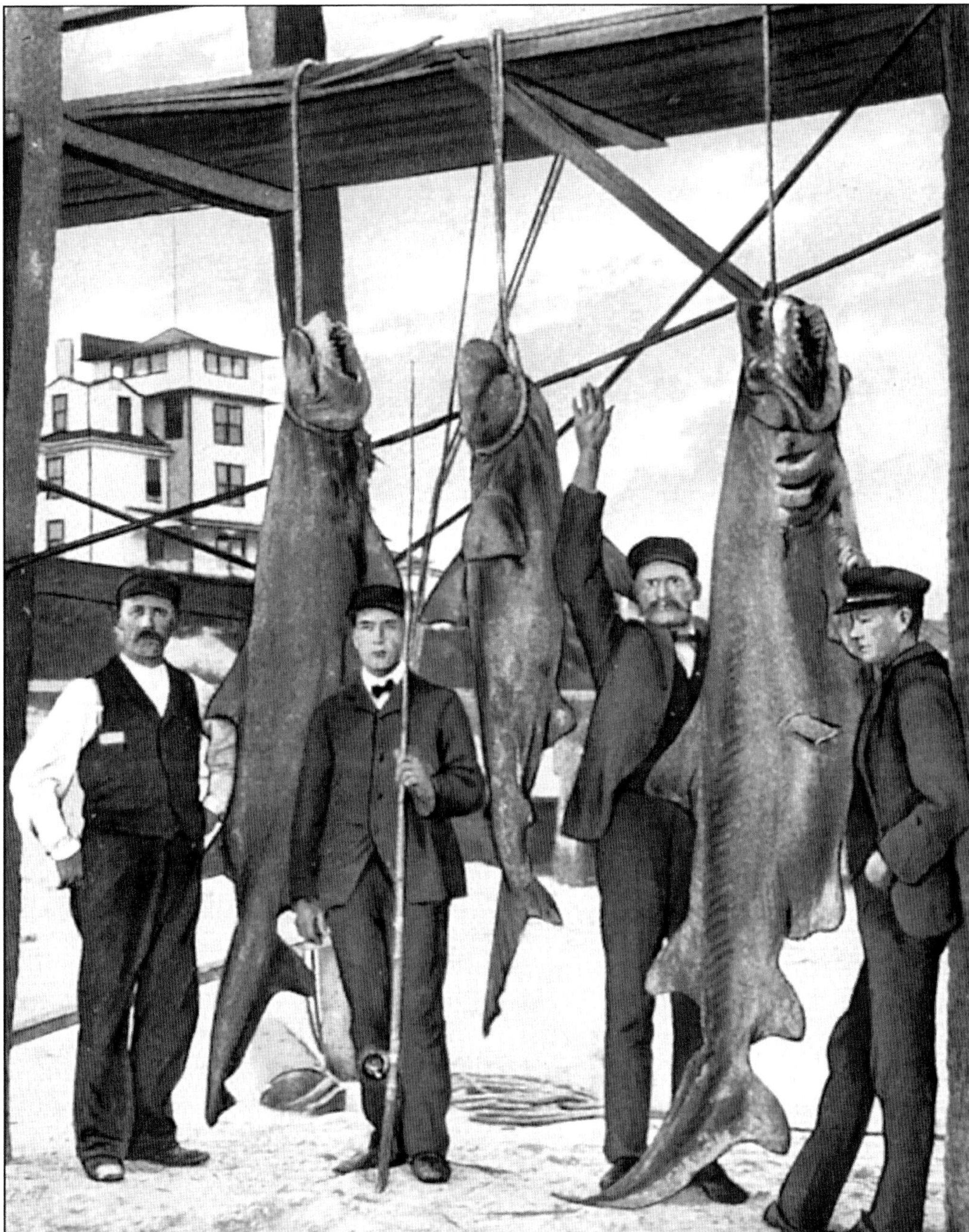

FISHING AT SEABREEZE. Sharks often were caught offshore, and sometimes from ocean piers. If the card's title correctly identifies the location as Seabreeze, chances are this is Post's Pier located behind the Clarendon Inn, just south of the Breakers Hotel (not to be confused with the Breakers in Daytona Beach), shown in the background. Jack, the card's sender, had some fun with his message to the folks back home in Ohio: "I am in the sunny South having a good time. I went fishing the other day—this is what I caught. These are whales." Could Jack be the man waving to the photographer?

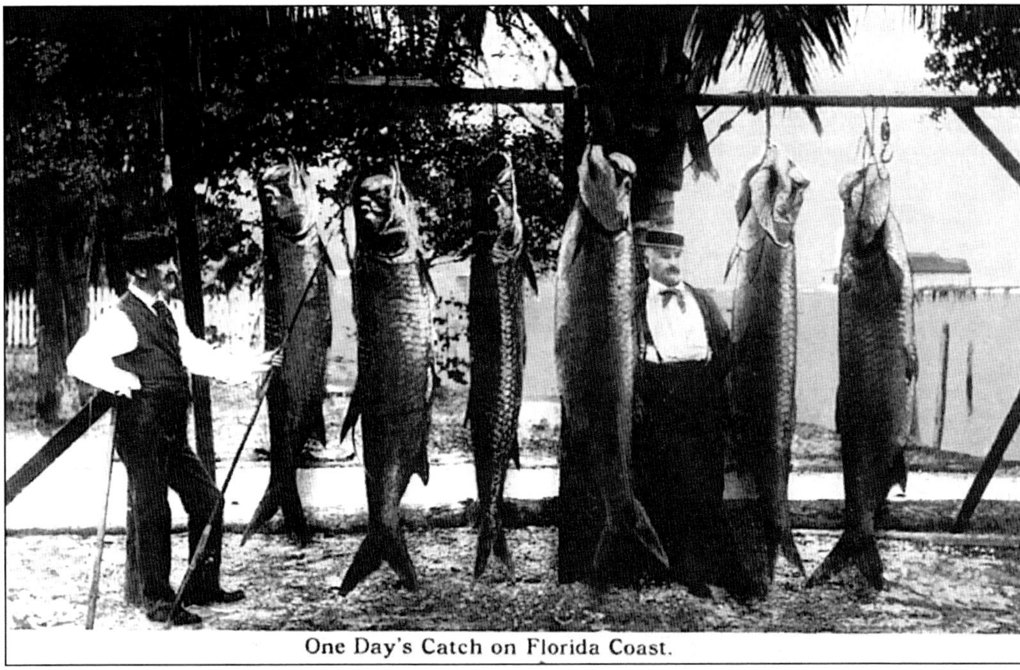

TARPON FISHING. The huge tarpon provided great sport fishing in the Halifax River, according to a 1908 promotional brochure. A contributor to *Camp Life in Florida* advised readers "the only successful way of killing the tarpum is to strike it with a harpoon, to which is attached by a strong line a small empty cask. The fish, by struggling with this buoy, exhausts itself so that it may be approached in a boat and killed with a lance." (Postcard courtesy Richard Dragoni.)

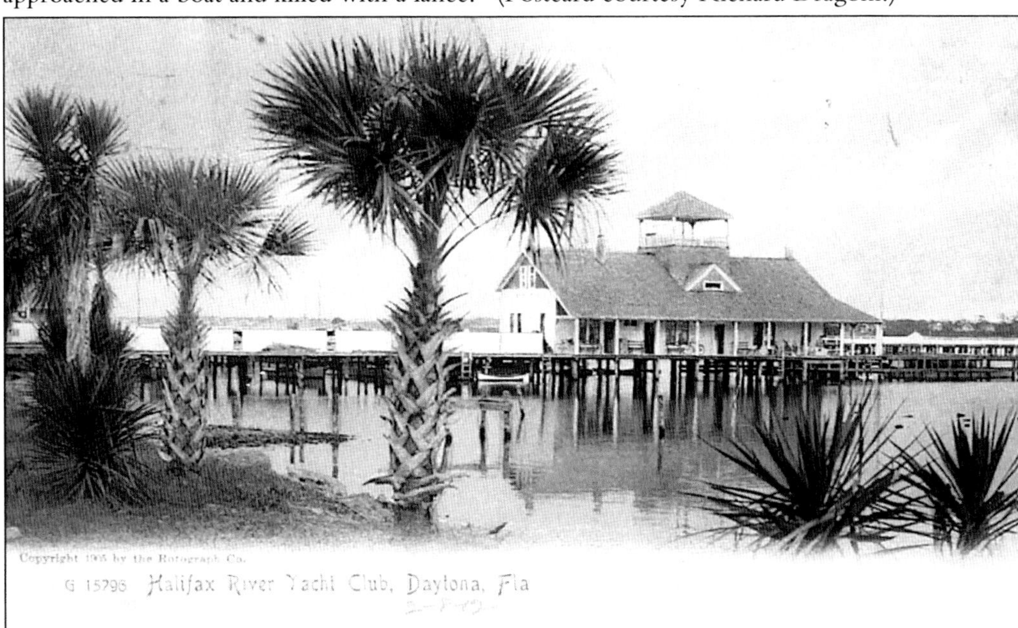

HALIFAX RIVER YACHT CLUB, *C.* 1905, DAYTONA. The Halifax River Yacht Club was organized in 1896 to encourage sailboat racing on the river. It is said to be one of the oldest such clubs on the United States East Coast.

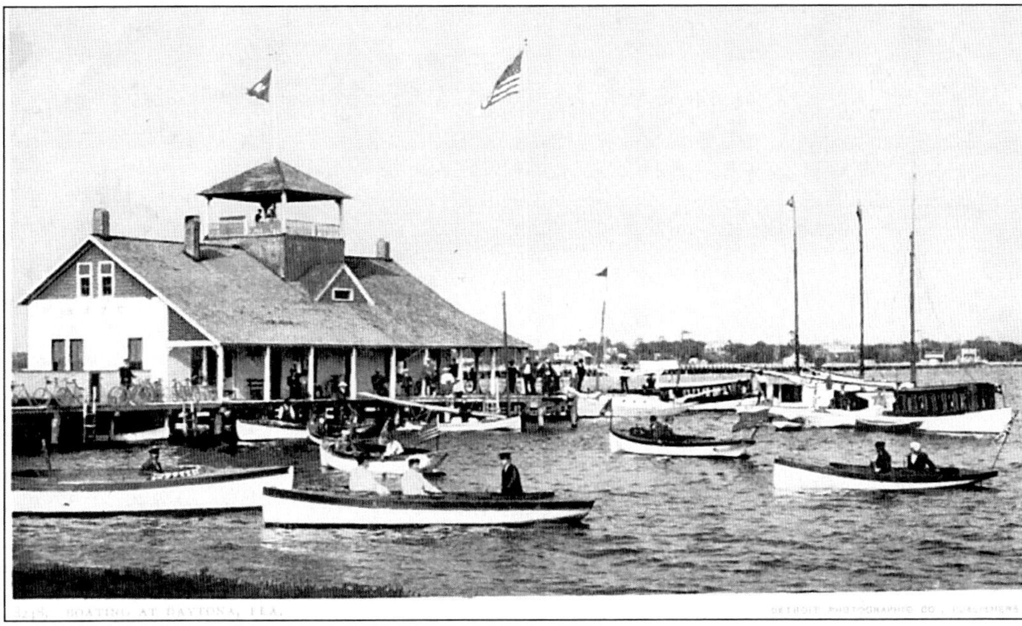

Boating at the Yacht Club, *c.* 1906. Over the years the yacht club has hosted motor launch races and sailing regattas that have attracted participants and visitors from all over the world. In 1899 Charles G. Burgoyne, one of Daytona's leading citizens and an avid promoter of social and leisure activities, became commodore of the yacht club.

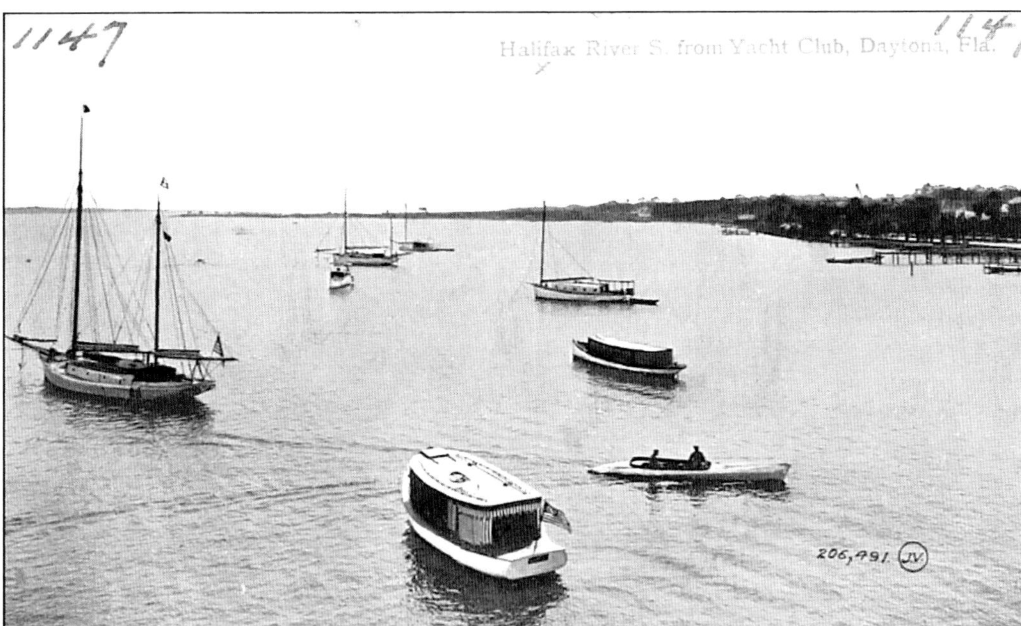

Halifax River Looking South from the Yacht Club, *c.* 1910–1915. Sailboats, yachts, excursion steamers, and motor launches are shown on the river in this card. The sender's message and itinerary hint at his *laissez faire* lifestyle while providing a testimony to the era of leisure travel: " . . . spent June and July at Pablo, near Jacksonville . . . came to Daytona in August . . . going down to St. Petersburg Sept. 20 to settle for the winter season, if not longer."

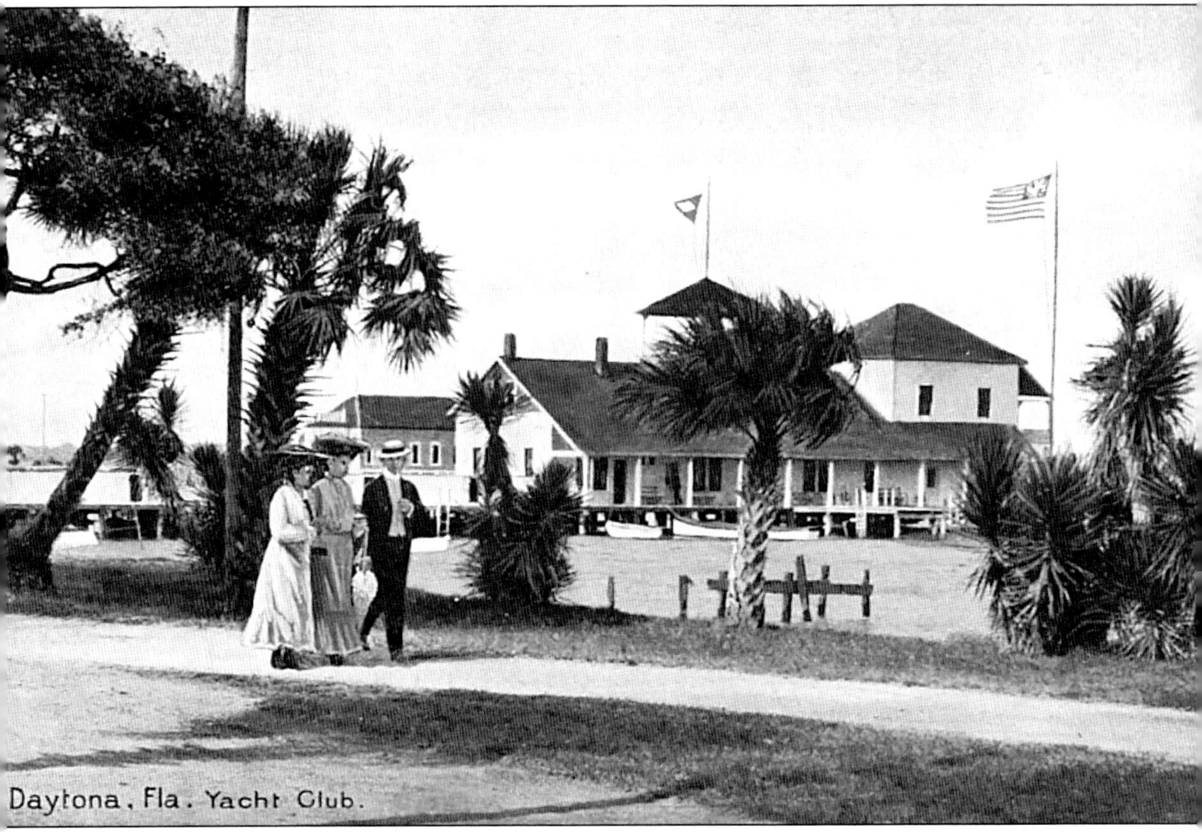

LATER VIEW OF HALIFAX RIVER YACHT CLUB. The marina and yacht club are on the west bank of the river, just south of Orange Avenue. The caption on this card reads: "The Halifax River is a broad tropical lagoon, really an arm of the sea, whose banks are fringed with groves of palm, orange, oak and Southern pine trees. Yachtsmen here find the *Ultima Thule* of their desires."

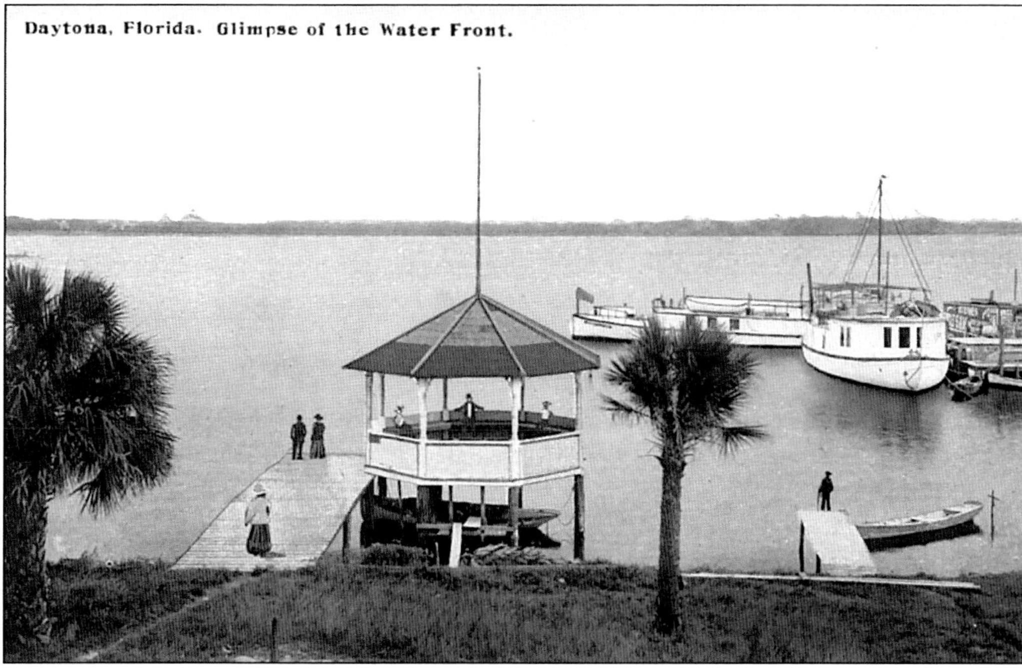

A Public Pier on the Halifax River, Daytona. The pier was off South Beach Street near Volusia Avenue; to the south was the dock for the *Uncle Sam*, a steamer that specialized in Tomoka River excursions.

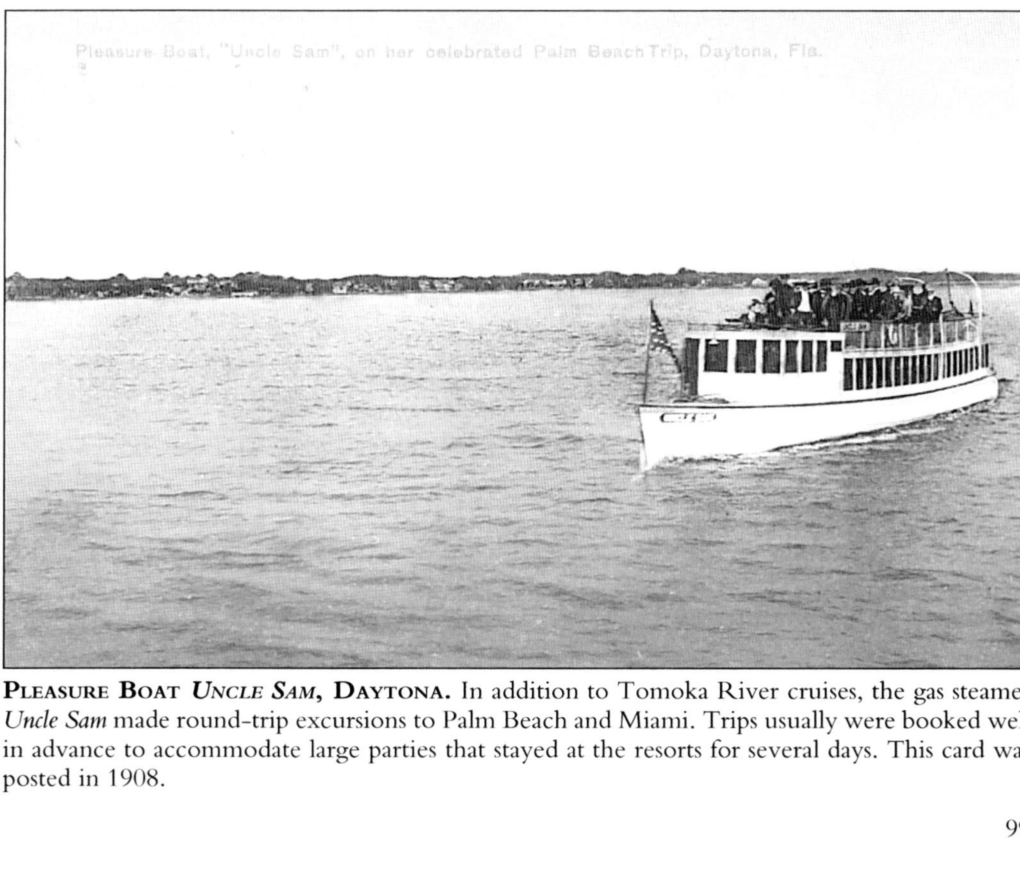

Pleasure Boat *Uncle Sam*, Daytona. In addition to Tomoka River cruises, the gas steamer *Uncle Sam* made round-trip excursions to Palm Beach and Miami. Trips usually were booked well in advance to accommodate large parties that stayed at the resorts for several days. This card was posted in 1908.

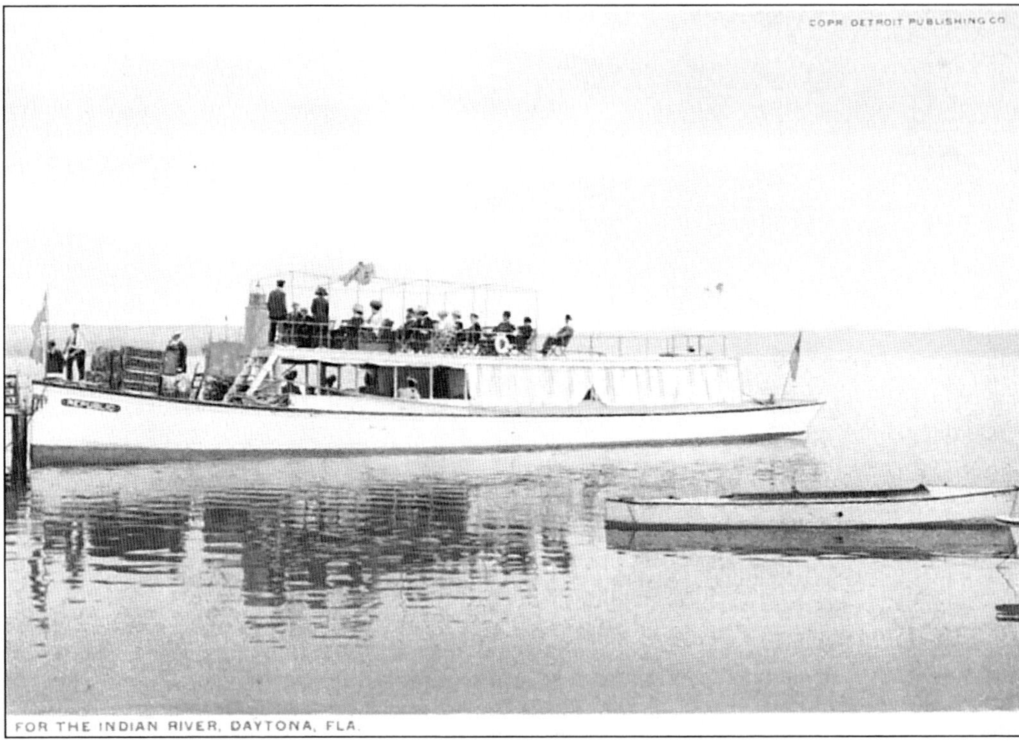

STEAMER LANDING ON HALIFAX RIVER. The sign on the dock indicates this was the landing for the steamers *Republic* and *Constitution*, bound for St. Augustine and Palm Beach. The *Republic* and the *Uncle Sam* (previously shown) were built by a Holly Hill resident who, according to local lore, gained notoriety as a rumrunner in the early 1920s.

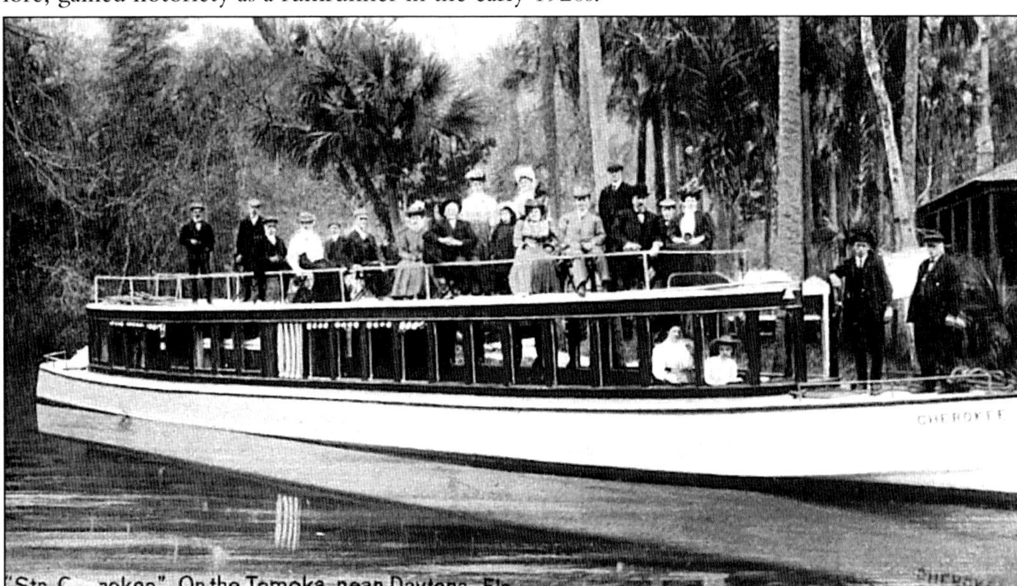

STEAMER *CHEROKEE* ON THE TOMOKA RIVER. The *Cherokee* departed daily from a dock near Volusia Avenue in Daytona, bound for the Tomoka River. Exploring the primitive Tomoka was a favorite pastime of tourists.

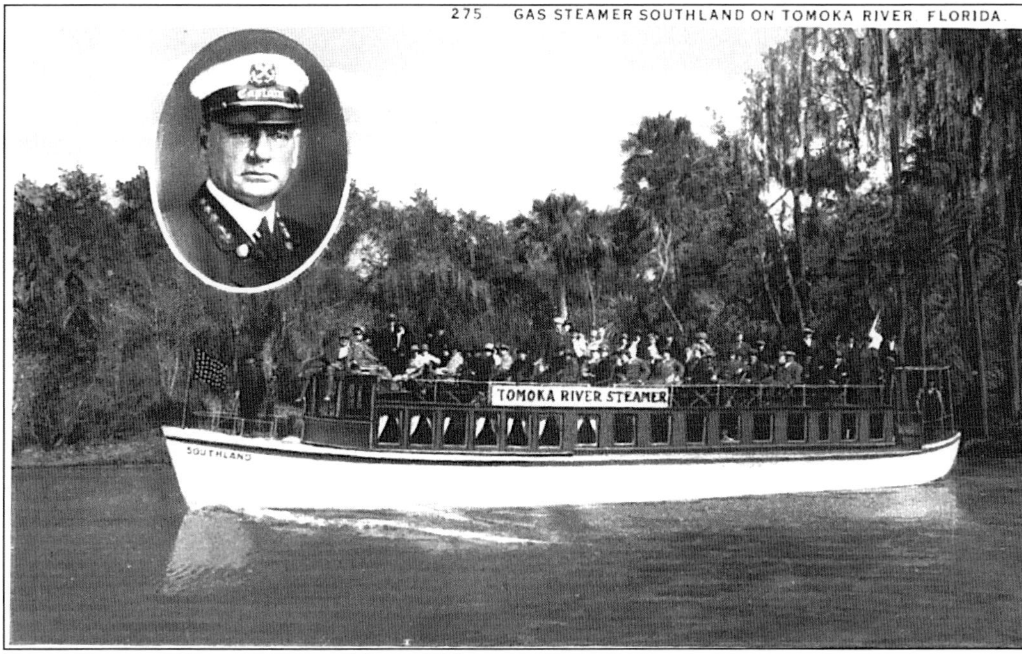

GAS STEAMER *SOUTHLAND* ON THE TOMOKA RIVER. According to this card, the Tomoka River cruise was "one of the best excursions and the finest one-day outing in Florida." Passengers were treated to miles of unspoiled semi-tropical wilderness teeming with alligators, exotic birds, and wildlife. Note the inset picture of the captain, a feature common to early 1900s steamship advertising cards.

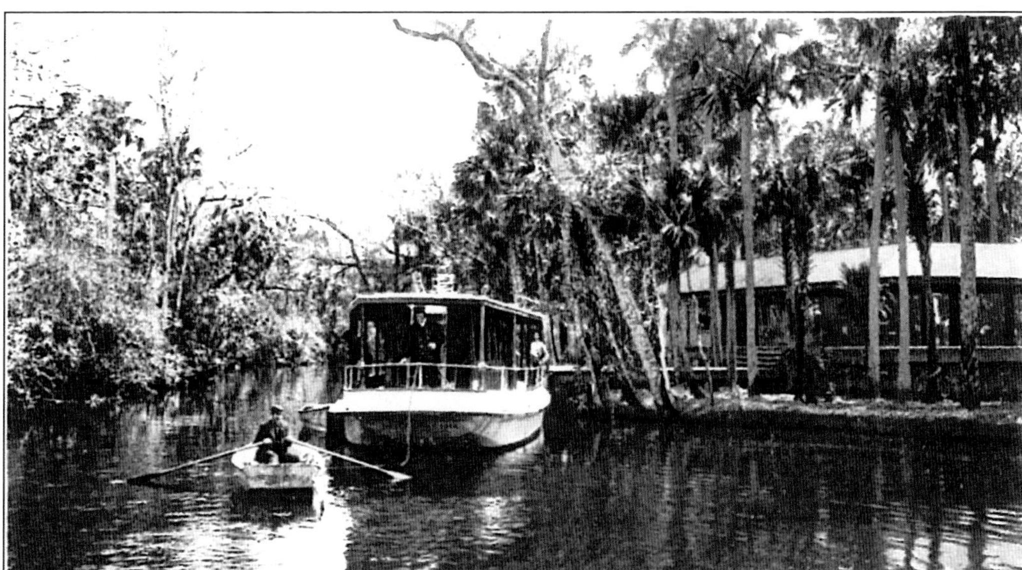

AN EXCURSION LAUNCH ON THE TOMOKA RIVER. A day-long cruise such as the one offered by the Ormond Hotel included a stop for lunch at a Cracker-style cabin. In 1899 trips on the hotel's new 12-knot, 150-passenger Daimler launch departed daily at 3 p.m. and usually lasted about eight hours. (Postcard courtesy Richard Dragoni.)

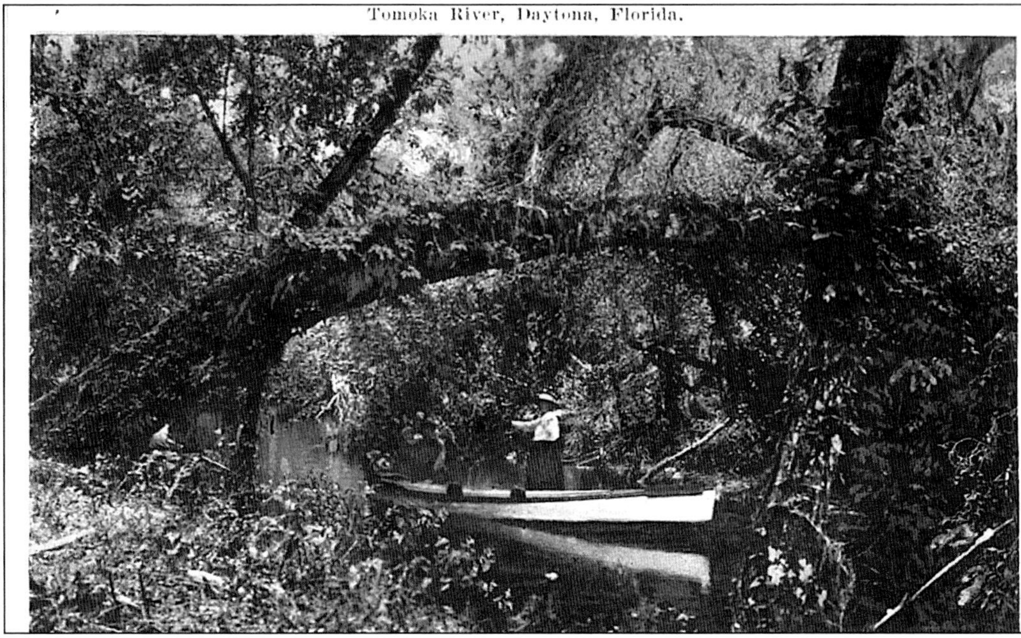

Tomoka River Scenery. The caption on the back of this card offers more words of praise for the unique experience of cruising the Tomoka. "Nowhere in the world is the diversity of scenery to be found that can be observed along the banks of the Tomoka River."

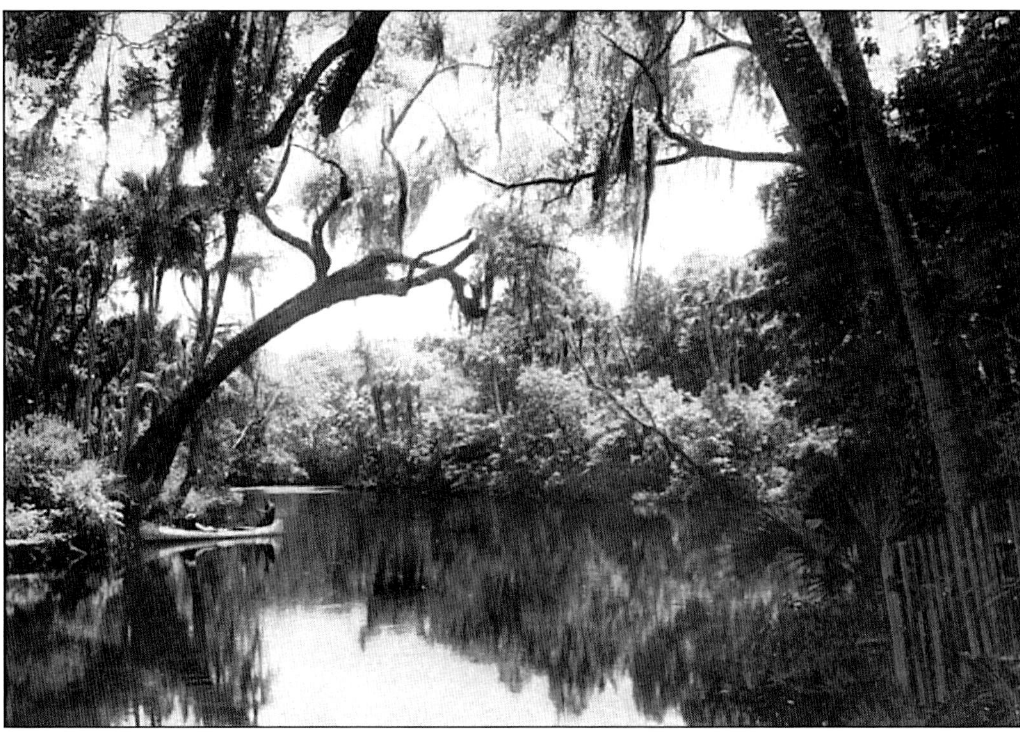

Canoeing on the Upper Tomoka River Near Ormond. The peaceful waters of the Tomoka River, entered at Bulow Bay just north of Ormond, were ideal for canoeing.

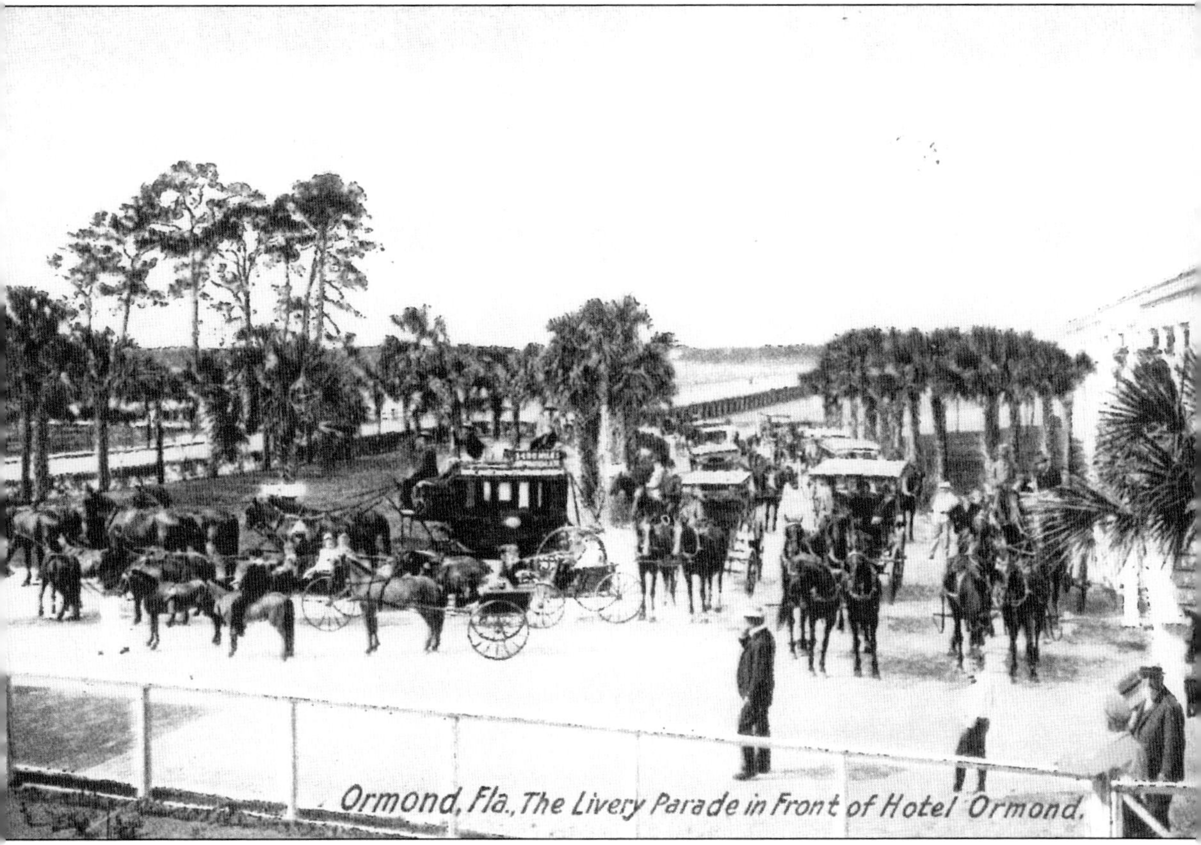

A Livery Parade in front of the Ormond Hotel. The hotel hosted social events and recreational activities, including country drives, beach outings, and trips to nearby orange groves. One of its most popular and unusual equestrian events was the Ring Tournament, a jousting competition using rings suspended from poles as the objects of attack. Among this selection of "turnouts" were a six-team stagecoach, a one-horse buggy, covered carriages, and thoroughbred saddle horses, many from the hotel's stable. (Postcard courtesy Richard Dragoni.)

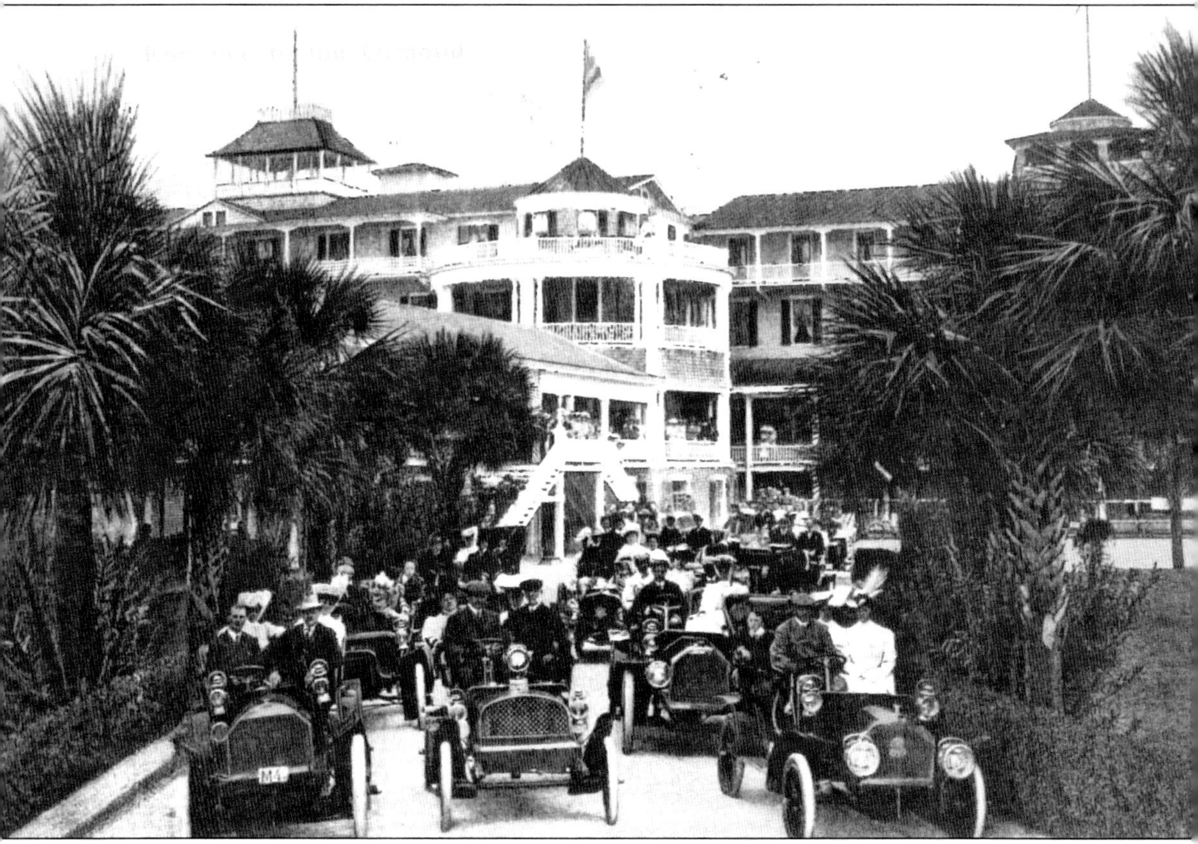

AUTOMOBILES IN FRONT OF THE ORMOND HOTEL, *c.* 1906. Perhaps these motorists were off to the annual automobile meet, held in January. Ormond Hotel owners were instrumental in promoting the first races on the beach in 1903, and the hotel was *the* place to be during racing season. Meets attracted some of the wealthiest men in the country. (Postcard courtesy Richard Dragoni.)

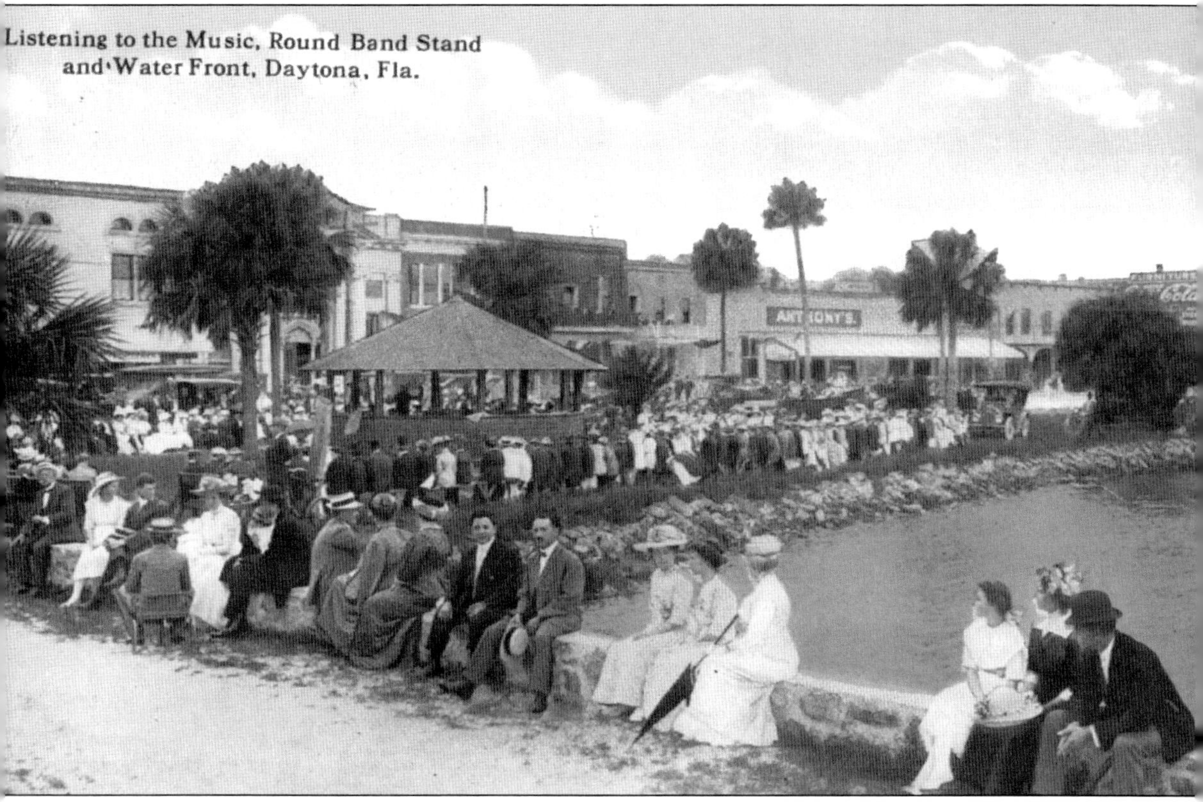

PUBLIC BANDSTAND, DAYTONA. Tourists and residents gathered around the bandstand at the corner of South Beach Street and Orange Avenue for daily concerts sponsored by Charles G. Burgoyne. A lover of music, Burgoyne engaged Saracina's Royal Italian Band for the entire winter tourist season. Concerts were an occasion for turning out in finery, as this 1912 postcard indicates.

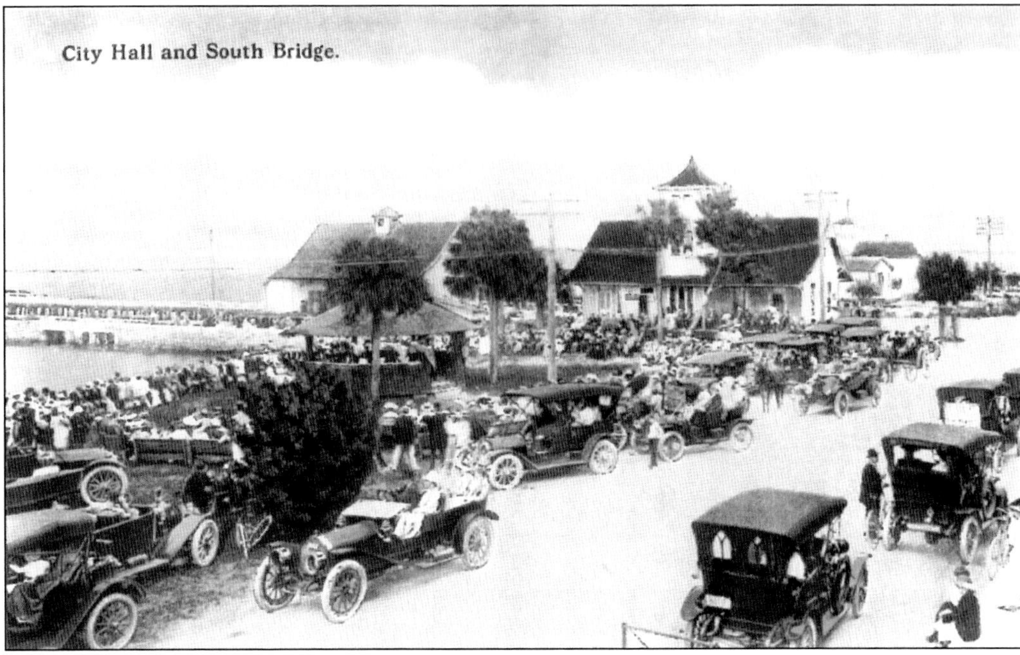

THE BANDSTAND, VIEWED FROM ACROSS SOUTH BEACH STREET. Concerts were so popular that the audience turned to cars, street curbs, and the steps of city hall, formerly the railroad depot, for seating.

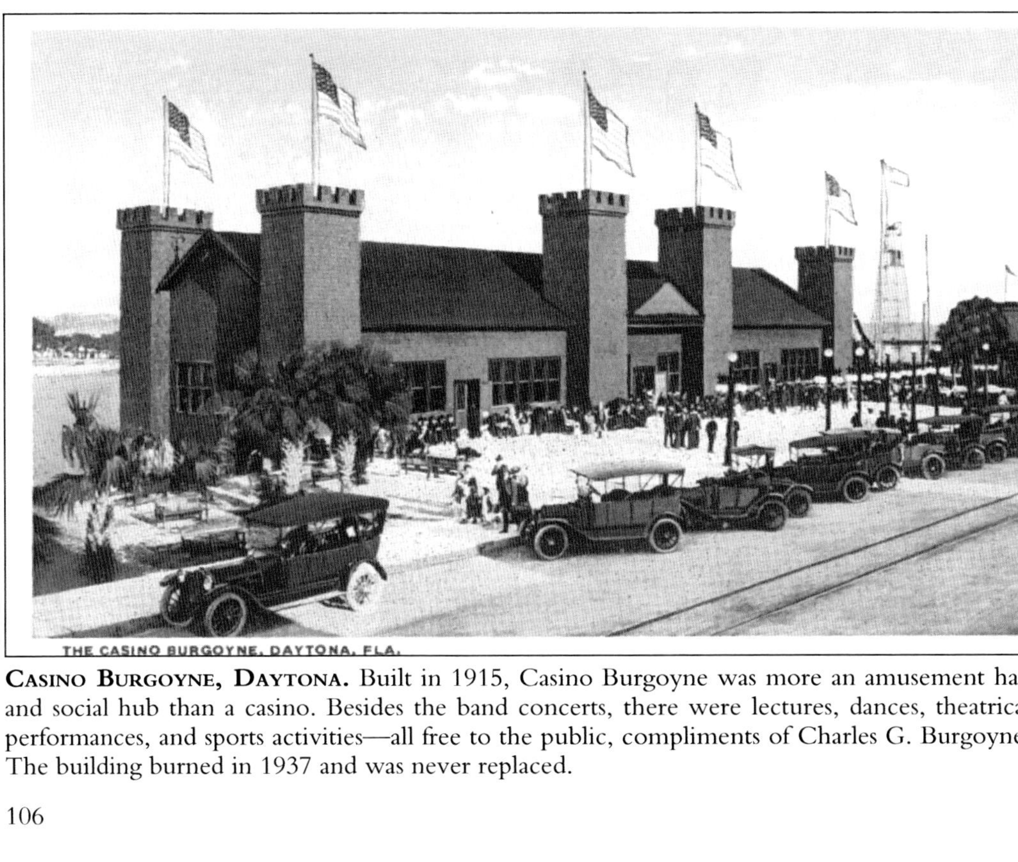

CASINO BURGOYNE, DAYTONA. Built in 1915, Casino Burgoyne was more an amusement hall and social hub than a casino. Besides the band concerts, there were lectures, dances, theatrical performances, and sports activities—all free to the public, compliments of Charles G. Burgoyne. The building burned in 1937 and was never replaced.

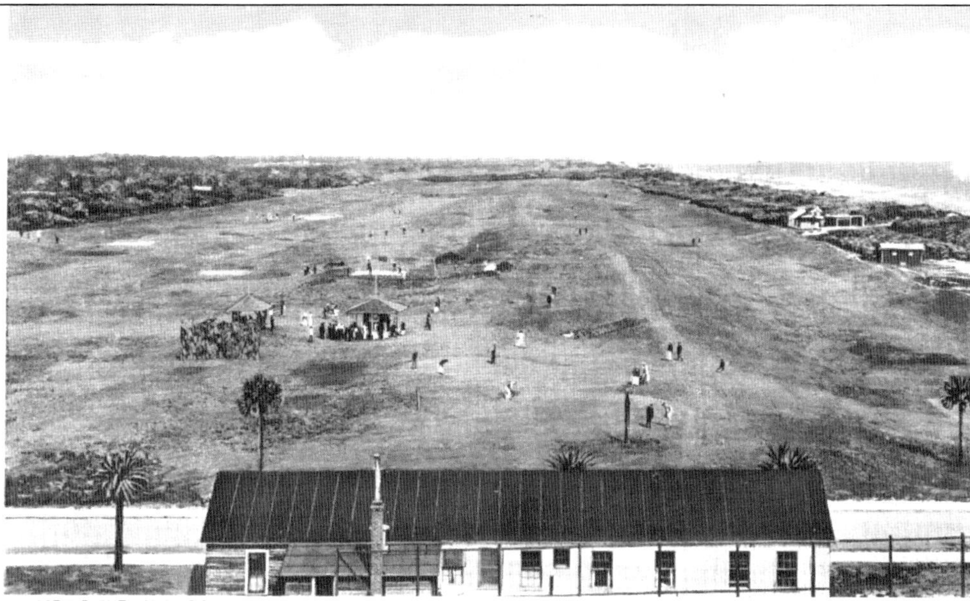

BIRD'S EYE VIEW, GOLF LINKS, ORMOND, FLA.

GOLF LINKS, ORMOND. The Ormond Hotel's golf course was beside the Atlantic Ocean, about one-half mile from the hotel. One of the green's most frequent patrons was John D. Rockefeller, who played nearly every day while in residence at the Casements, his winter home just across from the hotel on Granada Avenue.

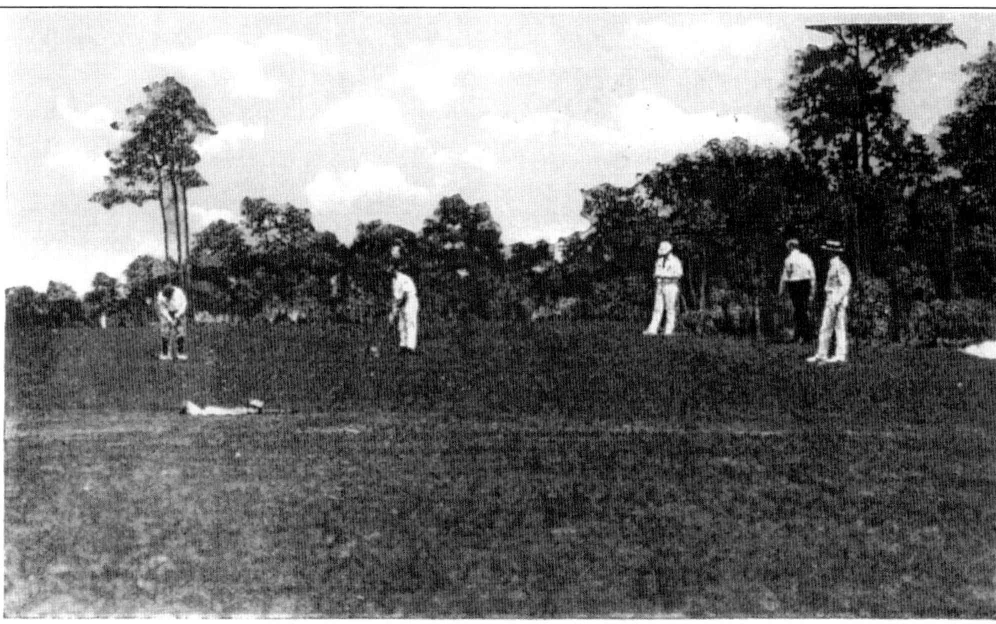

Golf Links at Country Club.

DAYTONA GOLF AND COUNTRY CLUB, DAYTONA. Commentary in a 1920s souvenir postcard folder expressed high expectations for the club: "The Daytona Golf and Country Club, located just south of town and within easy access of all hotels, will, according to Donald Ross, famous golf expert and course designer, be without doubt the prettiest and most unique course in the entire South." The club was organized about 1919.

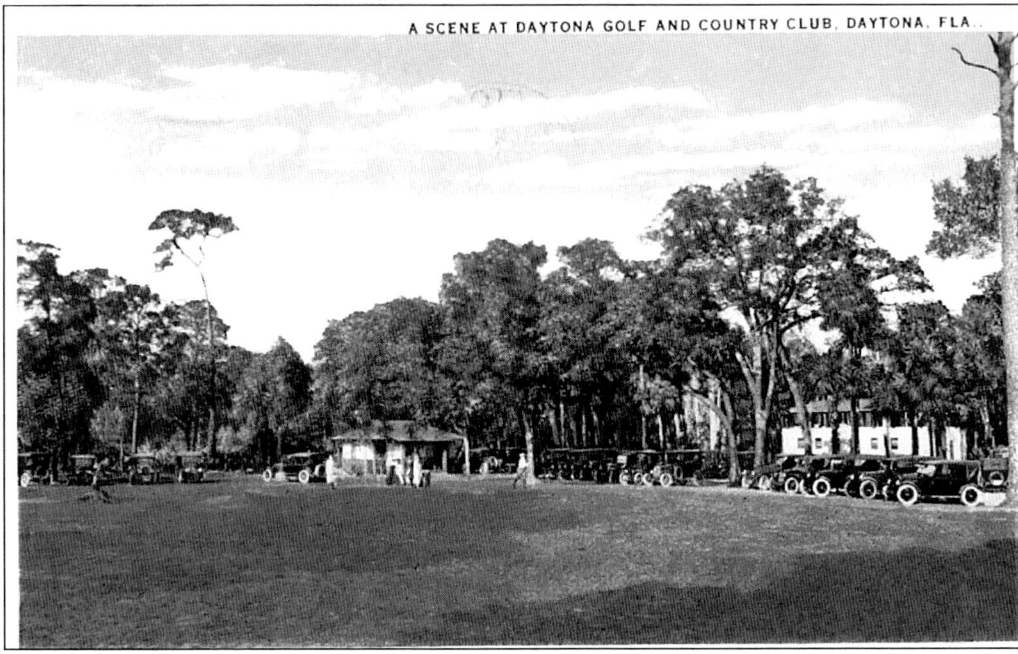

DAYTONA GOLF AND COUNTRY CLUB, *c.* 1925. Many of Daytona's prominent residents and founding citizens belonged to Daytona's first country club. Among these were photographer R.H. LeSesne, civil engineer David D. Rogers, architect John A. Rogers, and merchant Charles Gardiner, as reported in their respective biographies in Pleasant D. Gold's *History of Volusia County*.

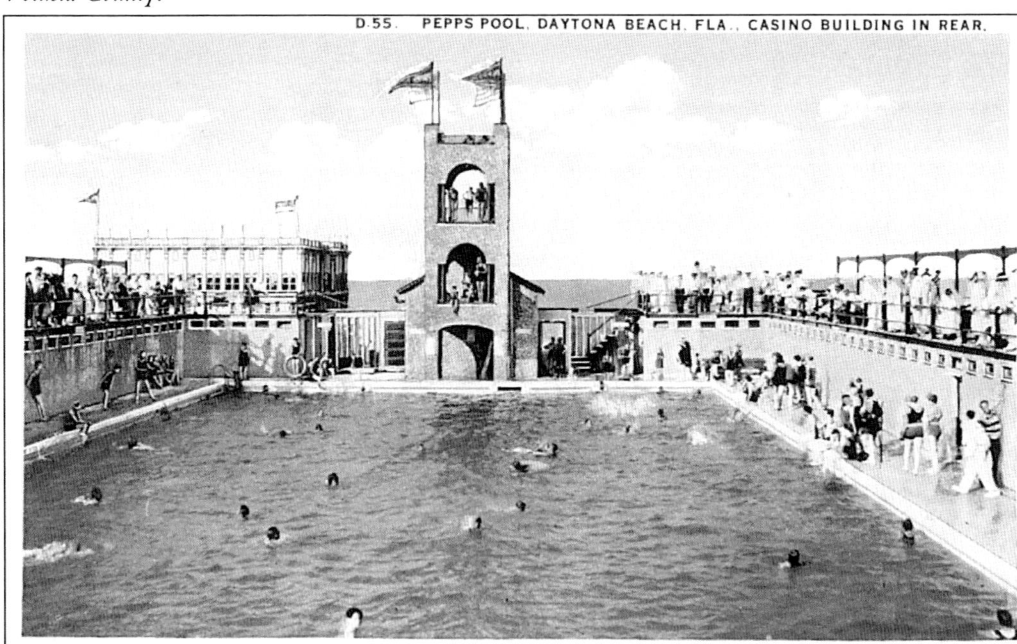

PEPP'S POOL, DAYTONA BEACH. Pepp's Pool and Bath House was a public bathing facility built by Harry Pepper. It opened in 1925, the same year the new Ocean Pier and Casino (left) was completed. The tower topped with flags was a multi-level diving platform.

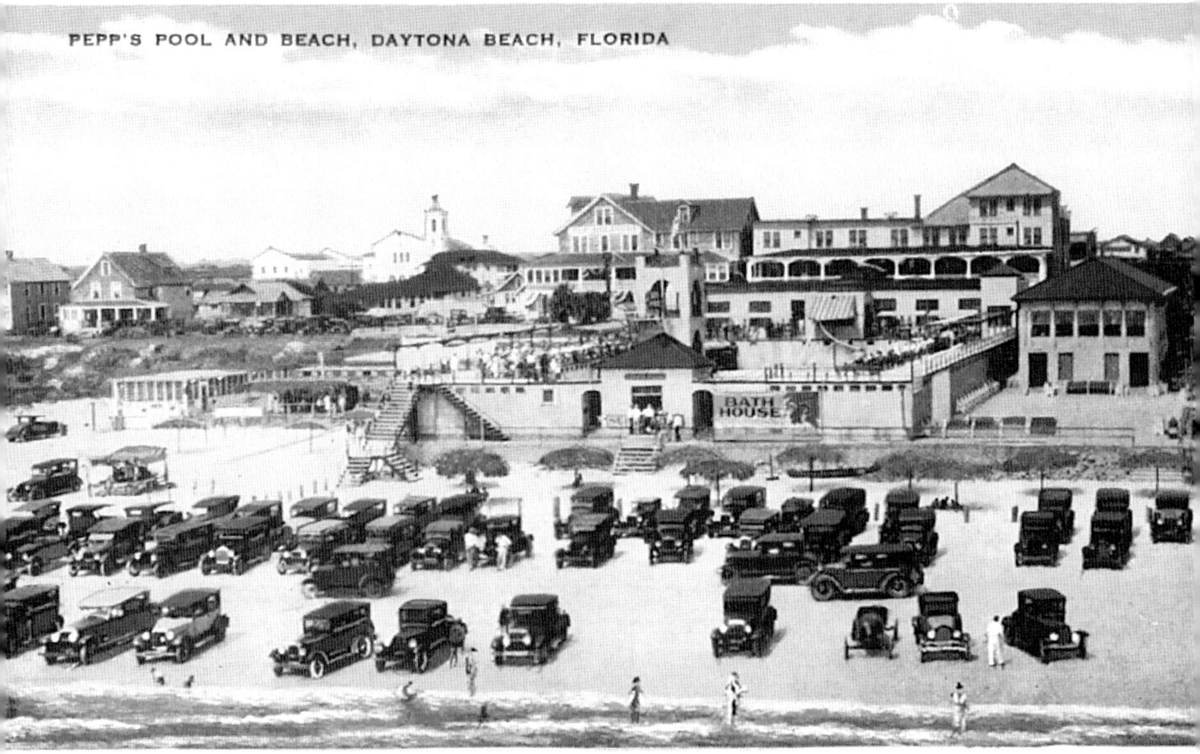

PEPP'S POOL, VIEWED FROM THE OCEAN. The pool was strategically located on the beach so that salt water could be pumped into it from the ocean. But Pepp's was more than a place to take a dip. With dressing rooms, shops, a spectator deck, and eating facilities, this recreational complex hosted diving exhibitions, swim meets, concerts, and supervised activities for children. The pool was flanked by the Breakers Hotel (left) and the Daytona Beach Hotel (right).

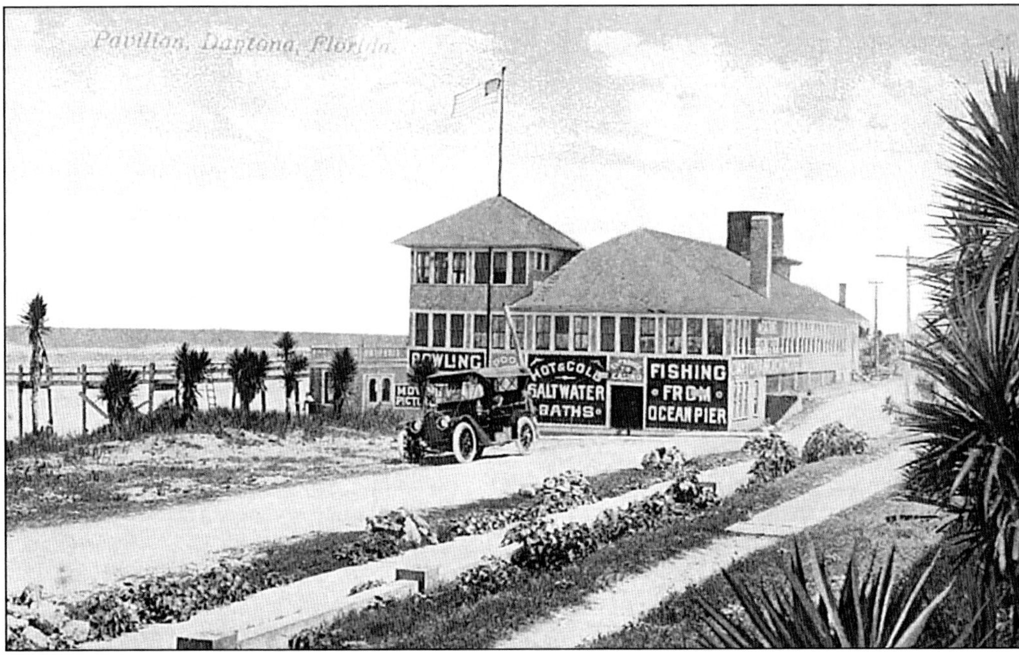

Keating's Pier on the Atlantic Ocean, Daytona Beach. Thomas Keating of Palatka built the 600-foot ocean pier near Main Street in 1900. Its palmetto log pilings extended into the ocean from an onshore amusement complex that housed a casino, a bathhouse, a dance floor, and a bowling alley. The lengthy pier afforded good fishing for sea bass, trout, drum, and the occasional shark. (Postcard courtesy David Findlay.)

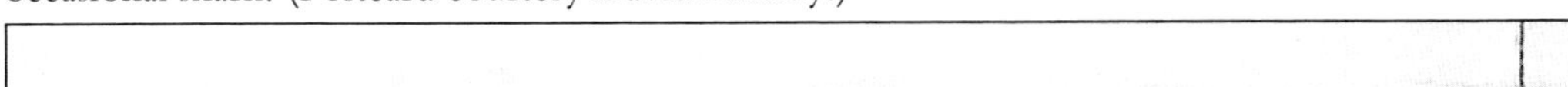

Keating's Pier. This is another view of the pier prior to a 1919 fire that destroyed part of it and all of the adjoining casino. A new 1,000-foot ocean pier was built in 1925. The new owners placed the casino on the pier over the water. It had a ballroom, a rooftop garden, and panoramic view of the ocean through arched windows on all sides. The pier's pilings were spaced to allow automobile traffic to pass underneath. (Postcard courtesy Richard Dragoni.)

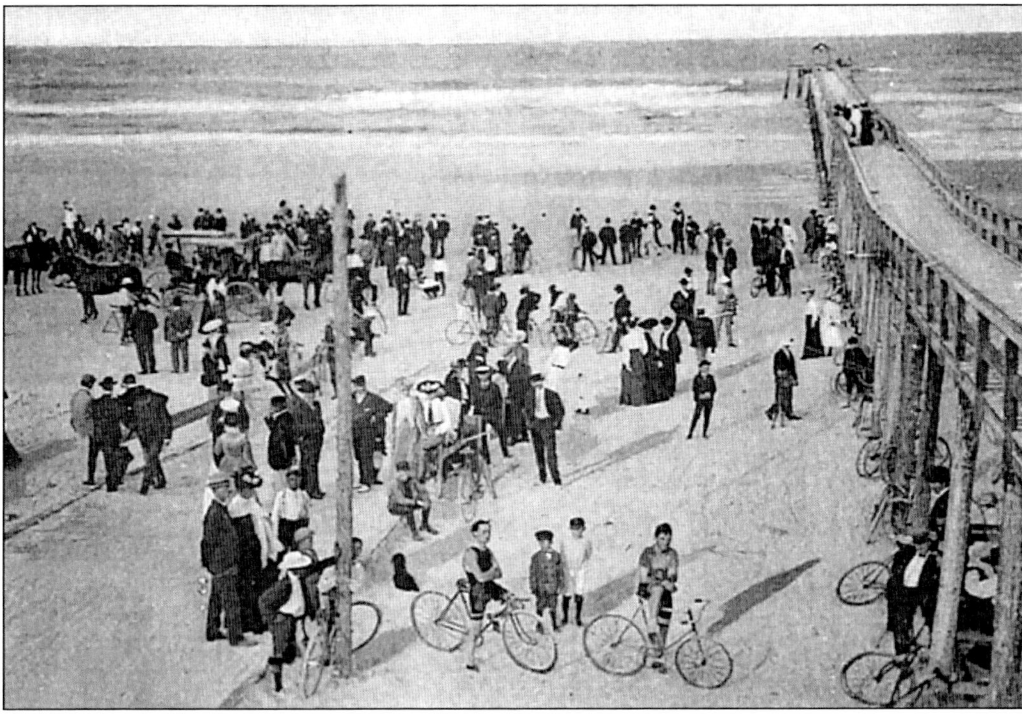

Bicycle Racing on the Beach. Bicycle racing on sand was a popular event in the early 1900s, before automobile meets took center stage. This picture suggests the starting line was near Keating's Pier. (Postcard courtesy David Findlay.)

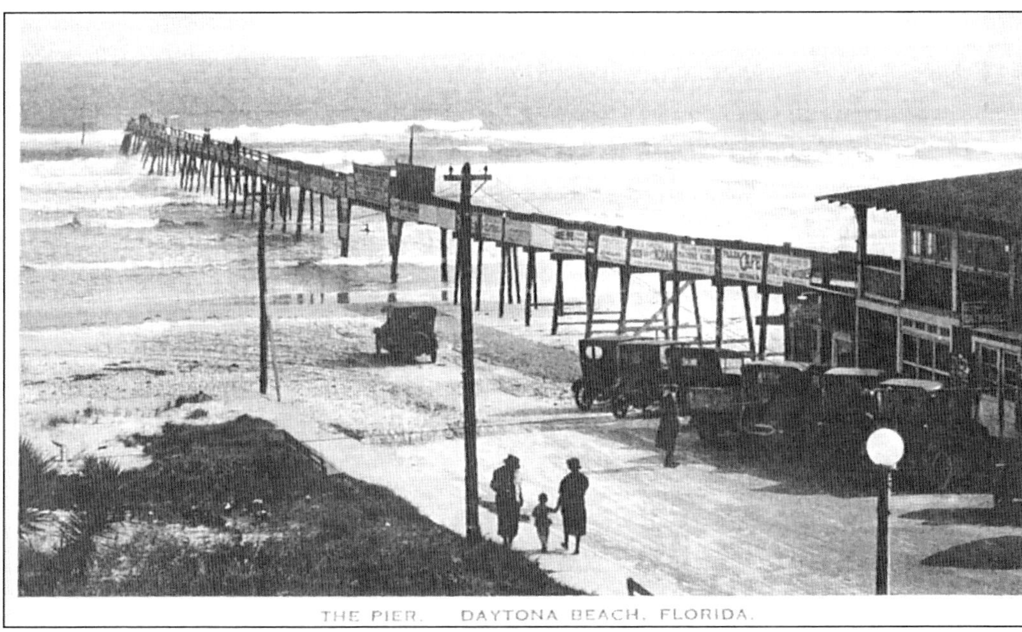

Later View of Keating's Pier. Note the addition of commercial advertisements covering rails on both sides of the pier. (Postcard courtesy David Findlay.)

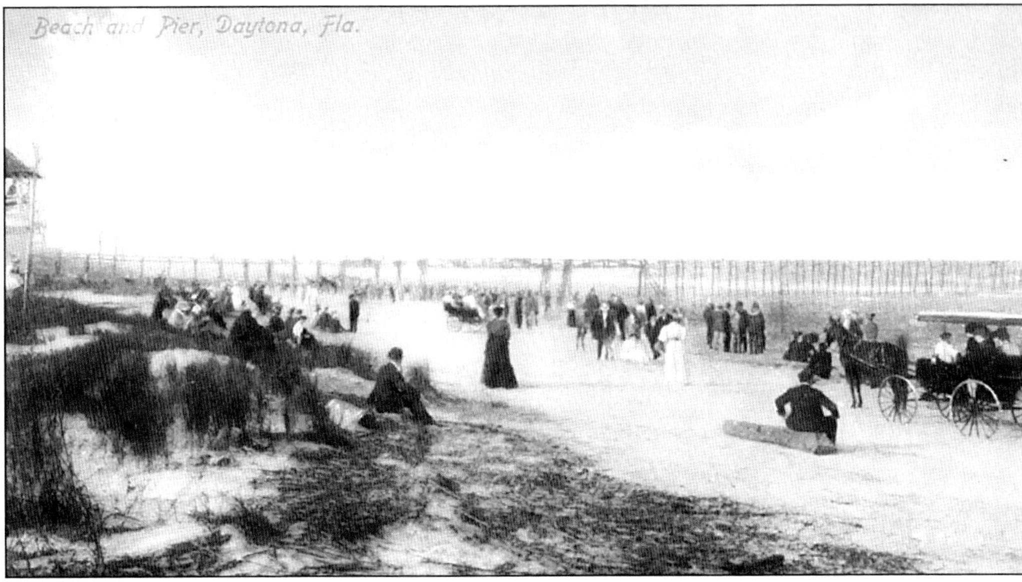

PROMENADE ON THE BEACH, C. 1904, DAYTONA BEACH. Favorite seaside pastimes are depicted here. Sidney Lanier put the beach experience into perspective more than one hundred years ago with this comment that has stood the test of time: "Here one has an instinct that it is one's duty to repose broad-faced upward . . . to lie fallow under suns and airs that shed unspeakable fertilizations upon body and spirit." His 1875 guidebook, *Florida: Its Scenery and Climate*, was written for a railroad company.

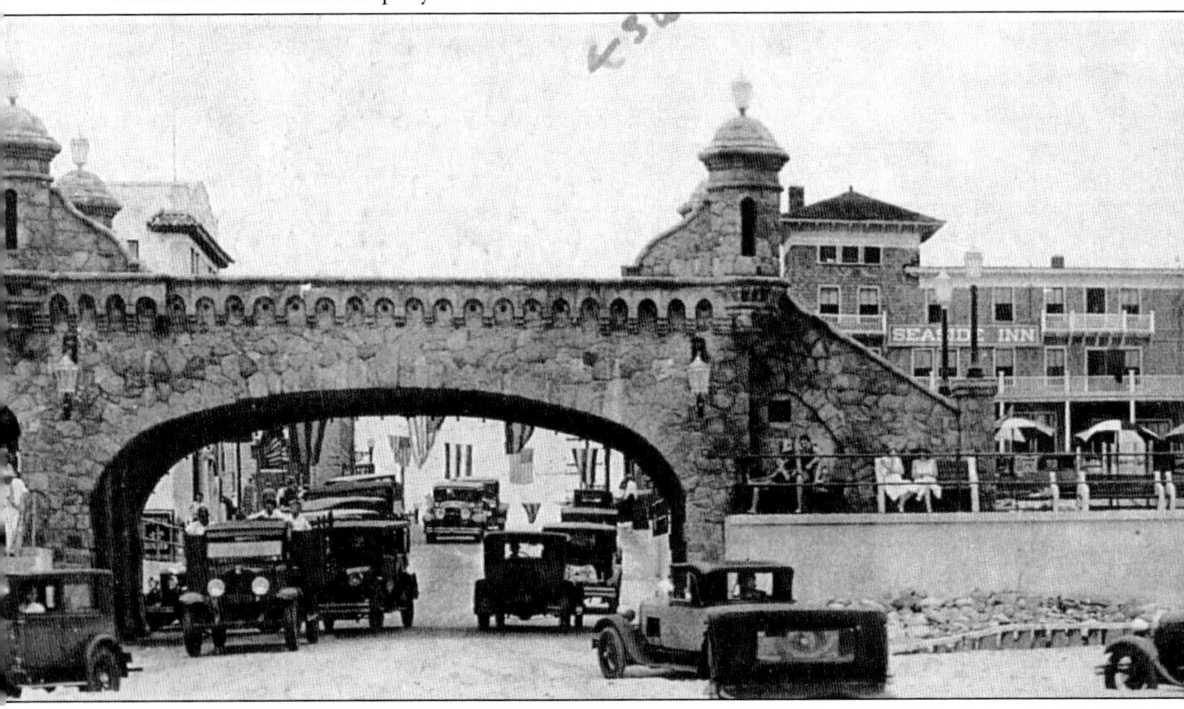

MAIN STREET APPROACH TO THE BEACH. This is a late 1920s picture of the Main Street approach to the beach, showing the Seaside Inn in the background. Entrance to the beach was free back then, unlike today. The arches still stand, and a boardwalk extends north along

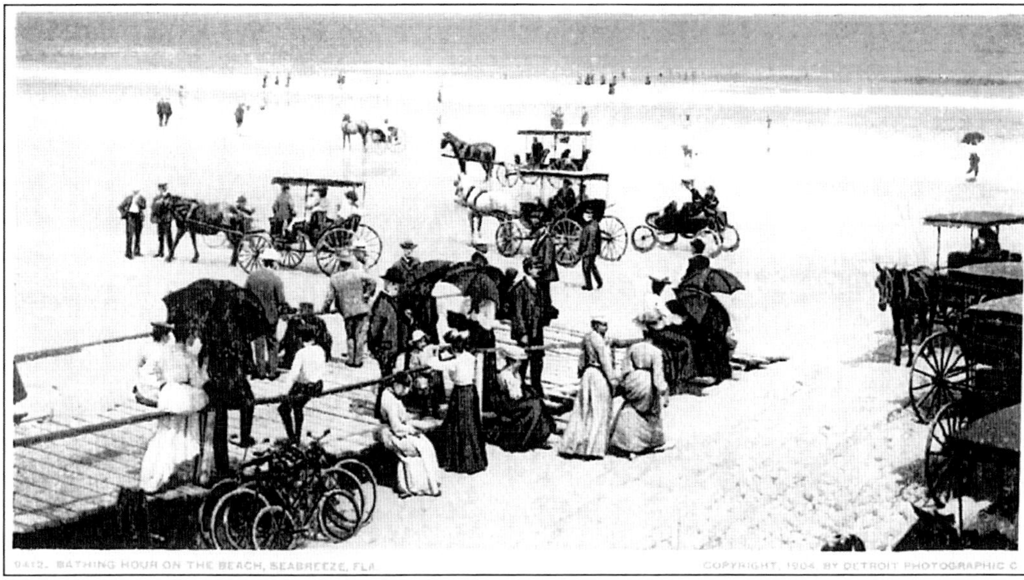

BATHING HOUR ON THE SEABREEZE BEACH, *c.* 1904. On an 1894 trip to Daytona, New England visitor and writer Bradford Torrey overheard a resident make this observation about winter surf bathing, which also is appropriate commentary for the activity depicted on this postcard: "We who live here don't think the water is warm enough yet; but for these Northern folks it is a great thing to go into the surf in February, and you can't keep them out." Torrey wrote *Florida: A Sketchbook.* (Postcard courtesy Richard Dragoni.)

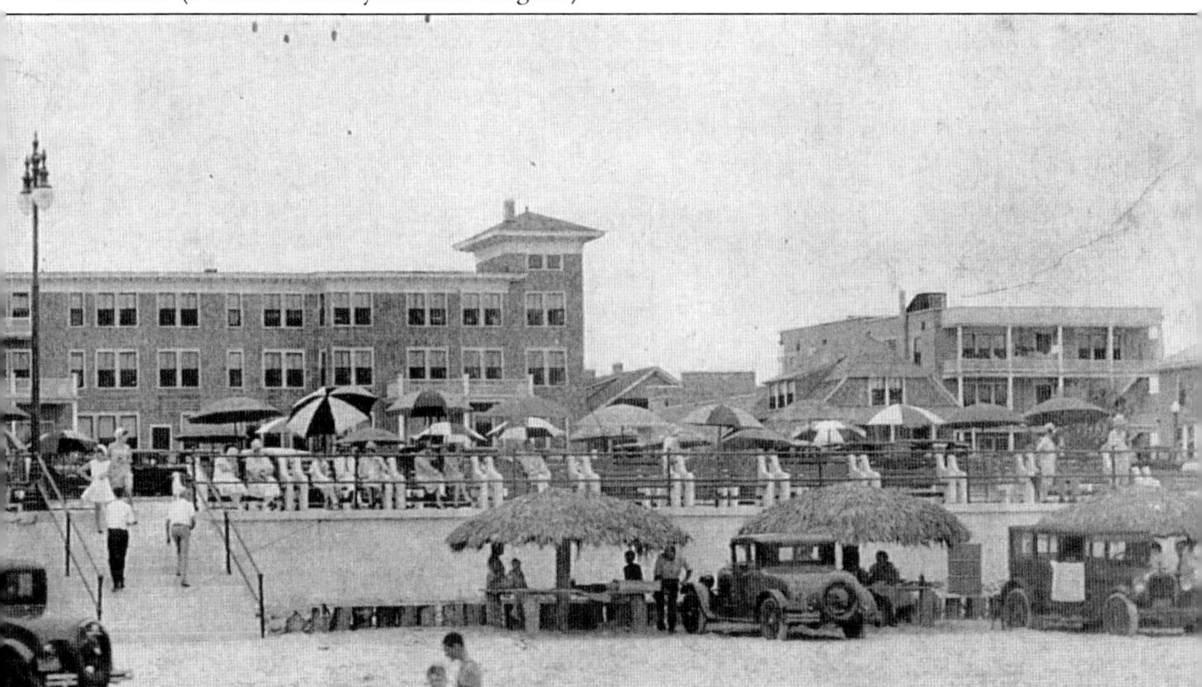

the beach where the seawall is shown. The Ocean Pier is at the end of Main Street. (Postcard courtesy David Findlay.)

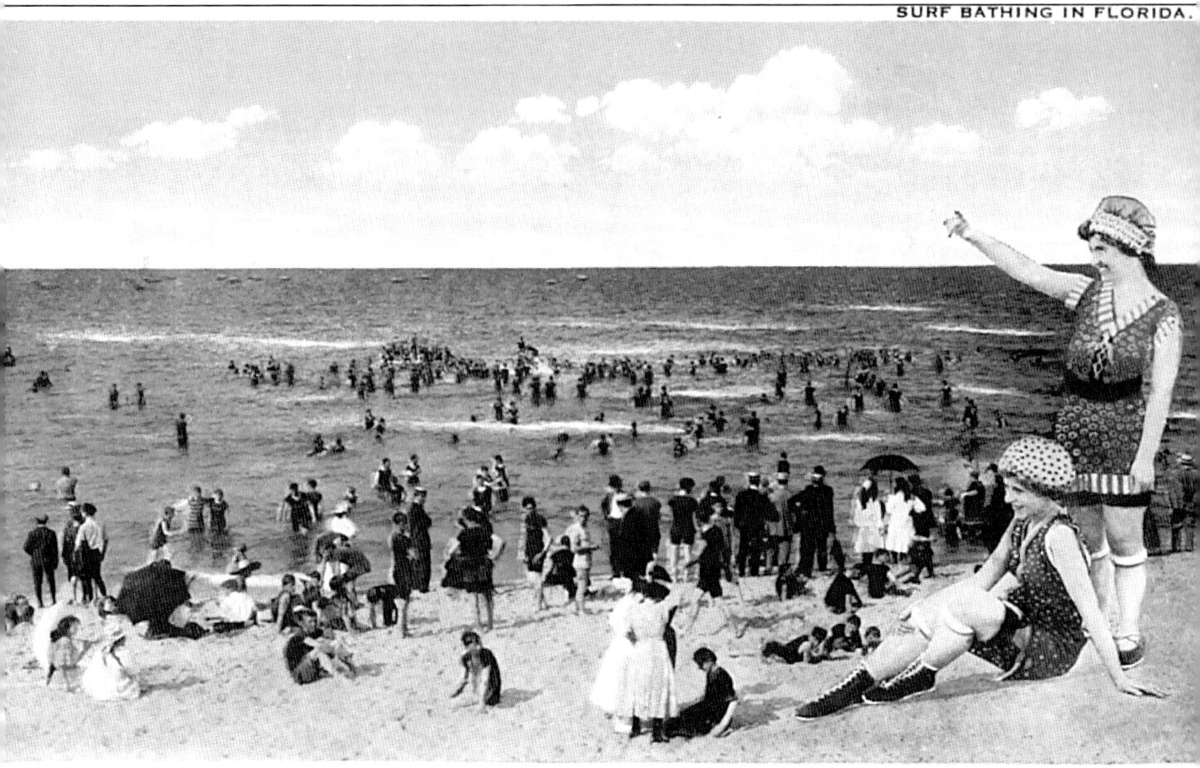

BATHING IN FLORIDA. Early 20th-century beach attire is depicted here. Avril Landsdell, author of *Seaside Fashions 1860–1929*, observed this about swimming outfits such as those worn by the women in the foreground: "For women with less than perfect figures, the two-piece costume was much more decorative and kinder to the average figure." Mob caps, stockings, and beach shoes were *de rigueur*.

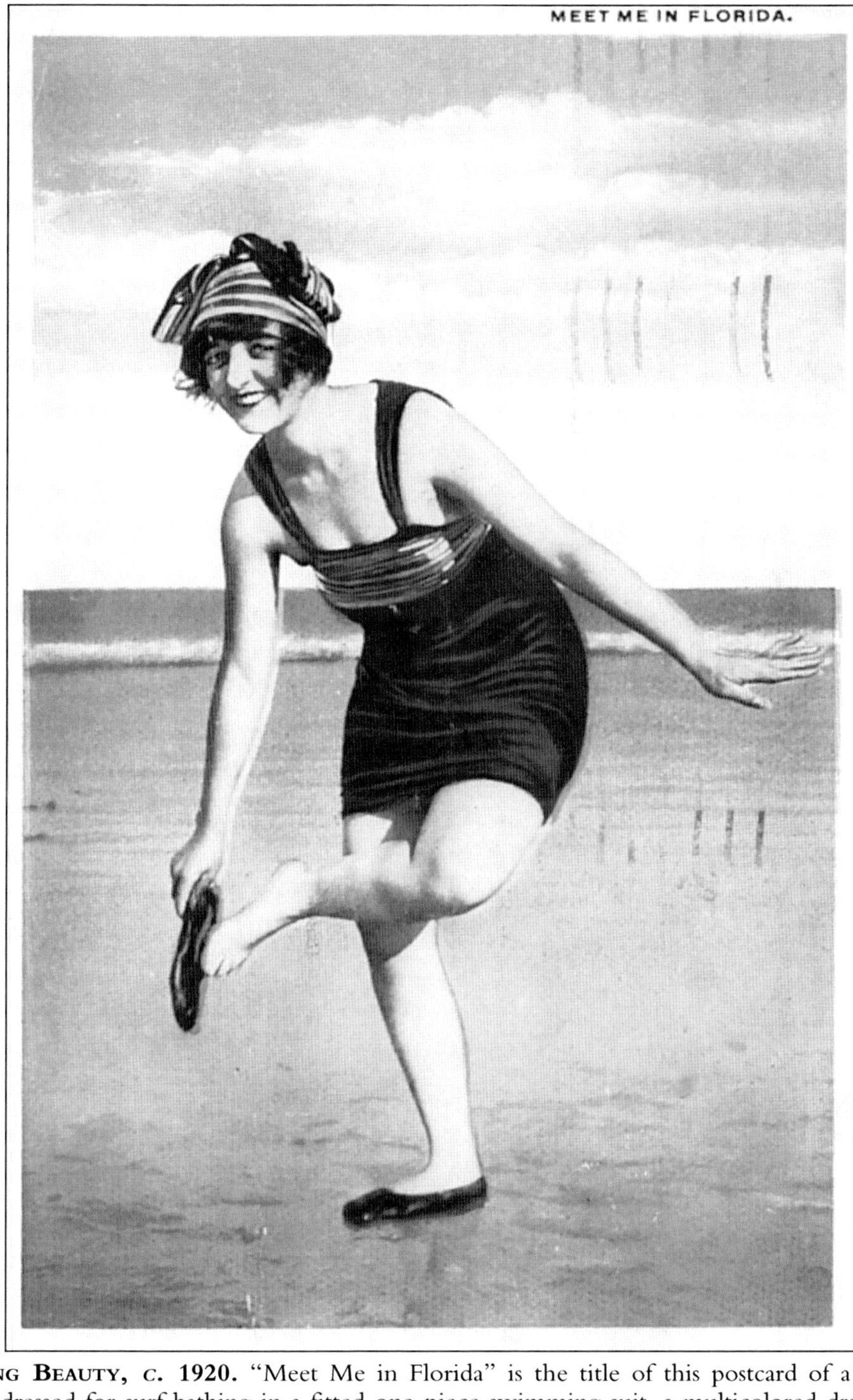

BATHING BEAUTY, C. 1920. "Meet Me in Florida" is the title of this postcard of a bathing beauty dressed for surf bathing in a fitted one-piece swimming suit, a multicolored draped silk turban, and rubber beach slippers. The message on the back from John to a chum reads: "I certainly wish you were here. This life would suit you, I know. Next year you are coming with me. It doesn't cost much to live here." Seems John chose an appropriate card to entice his friend.

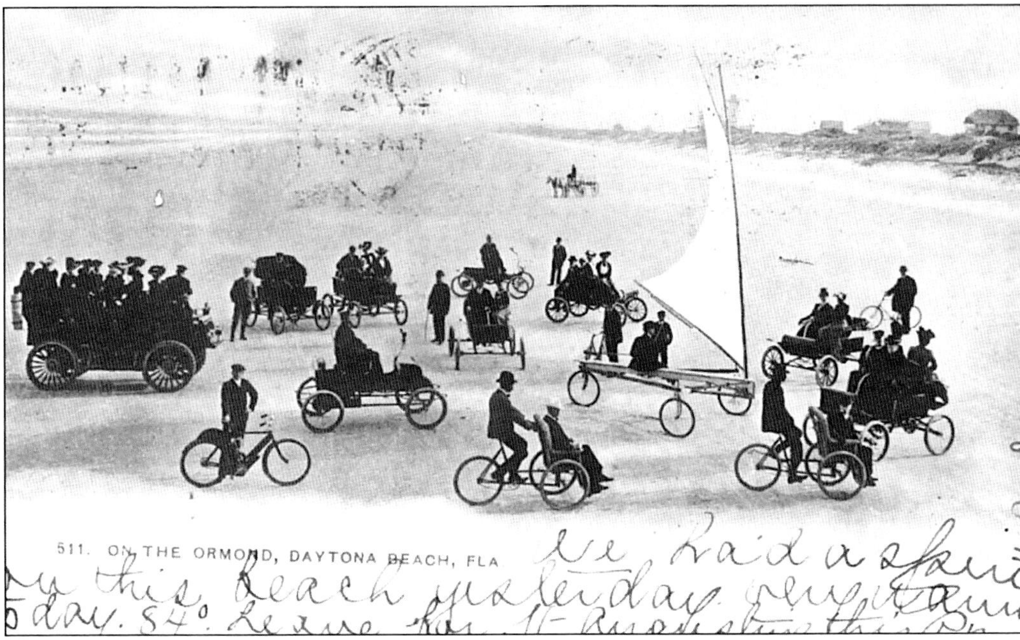

Beach-going Vehicles. Whether powered by motor, muscle, or merely the wind, the wheeled conveyances in this picture rolled with more ease and speed on the sand than on most roads of the day. The curious looking three-wheeled launch with the sail was called a sand sailer. This very popular card bears a 1908 postmark; however, postmark dates on identical cards indicate the photograph was taken a few years earlier.

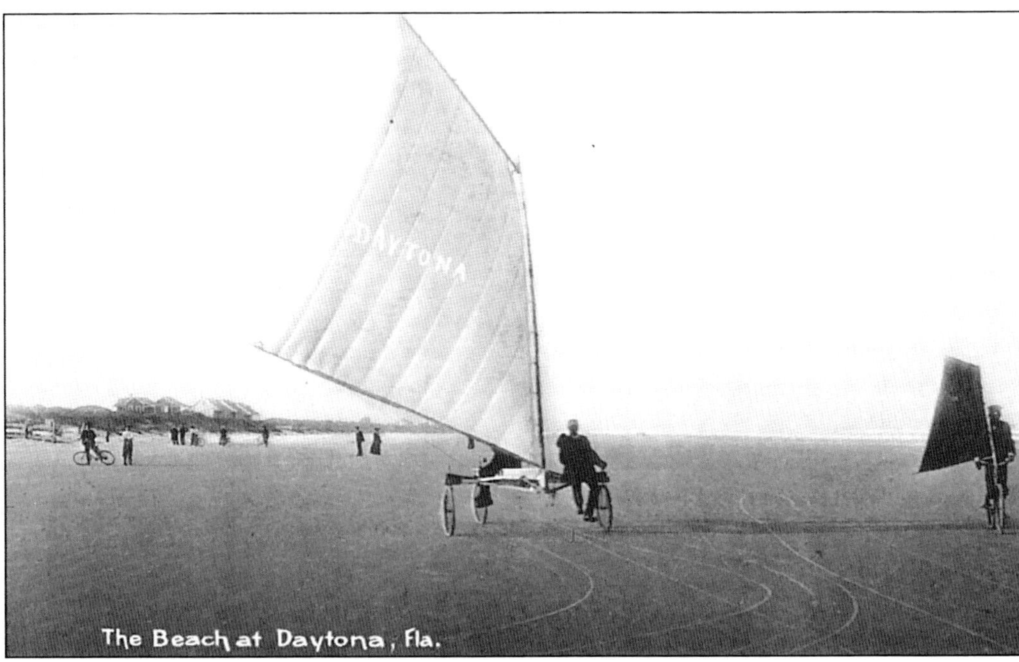

Sand Sailers. The sand sailer is shown here with a driver and passenger alongside a two-wheeled version of a wind-powered cycle.

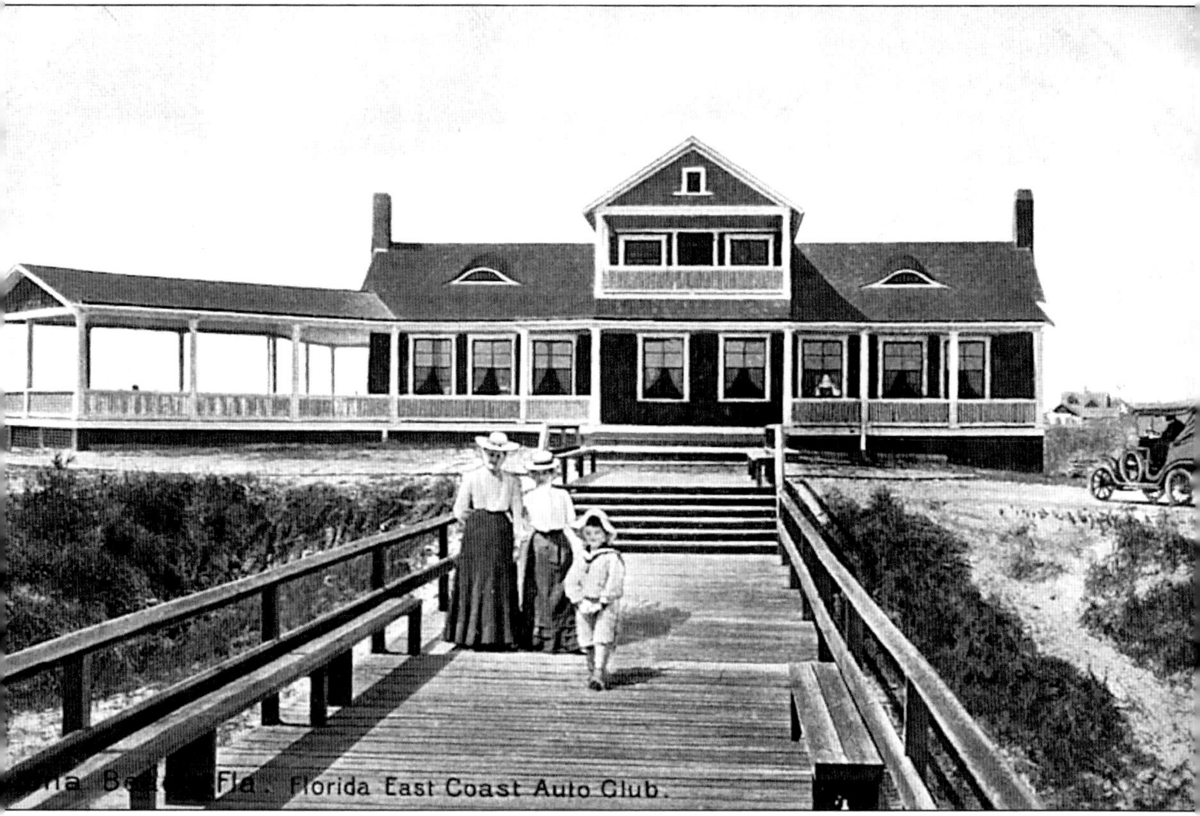

Florida East Coast Automobile Association Clubhouse, *c.* 1903. The club was formed after the first race season in 1903 to promote the new sport of automobile racing on sand. Some of the country's wealthiest men, including John Jacob Astor, as well as racing luminaries and local supporters were members. Daytona's Commodore Burgoyne served as president of the organization at one time.

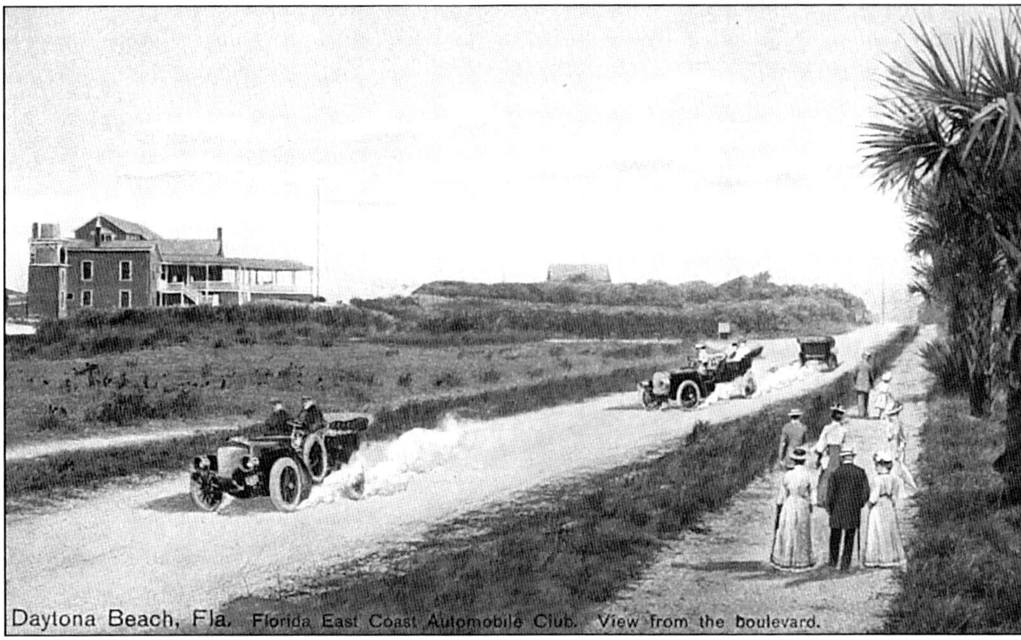

View of Clubhouse at Silver Beach Avenue. Ormond was the true "Birthplace of Speed," and the Ormond Hotel was racing headquarters until the clubhouse was erected near the south end of the speedway.

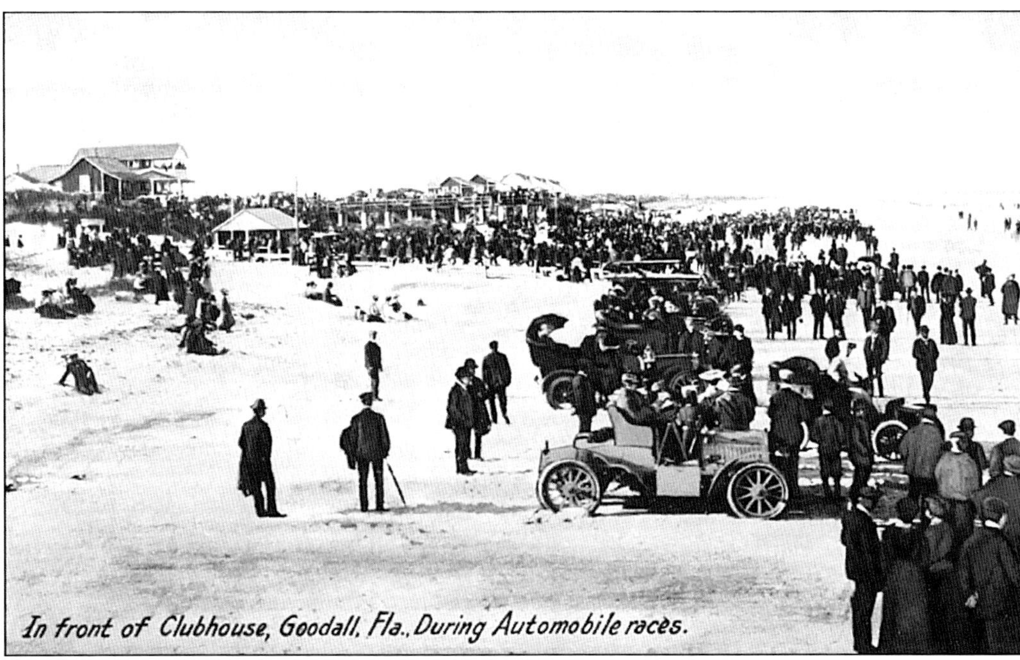

Race Day in front of the Clubhouse. In the early years of beach racing, the starting line was alternated between Ormond and Daytona Beach during the meets. Note that the card gives the location as Goodall, which later became Daytona Beach.

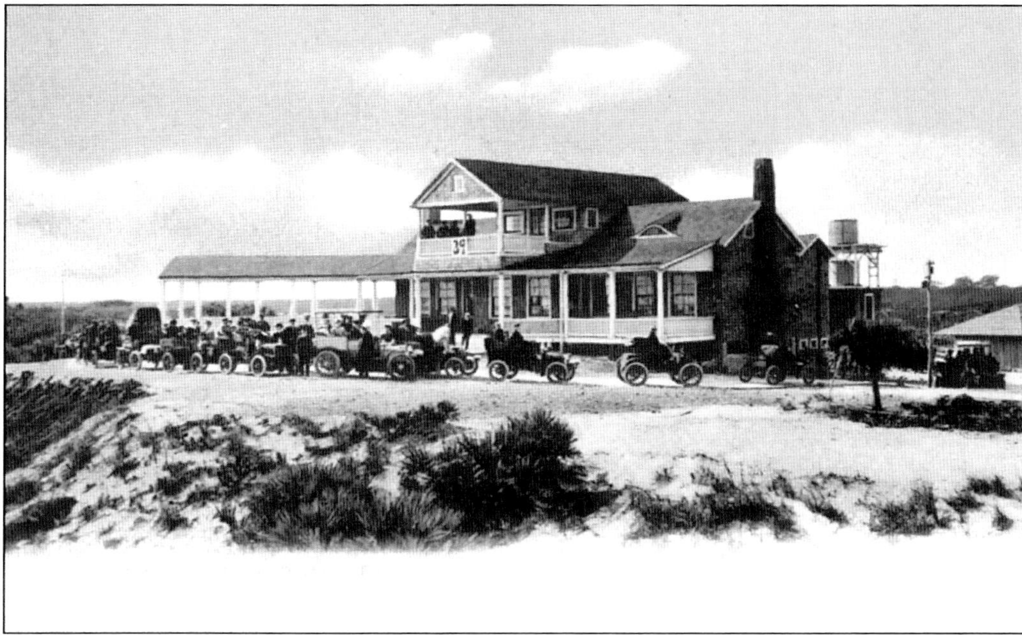

Front View of Automobile Clubhouse. The number 39 on the balcony of the clubhouse was not the building's address; it represented the number of seconds it took William K. Vanderbilt Jr. to race 1 mile in his Mercedes. Vanderbilt's 1904 glory was short-lived, but number 39 remained on display even after the record was broken.

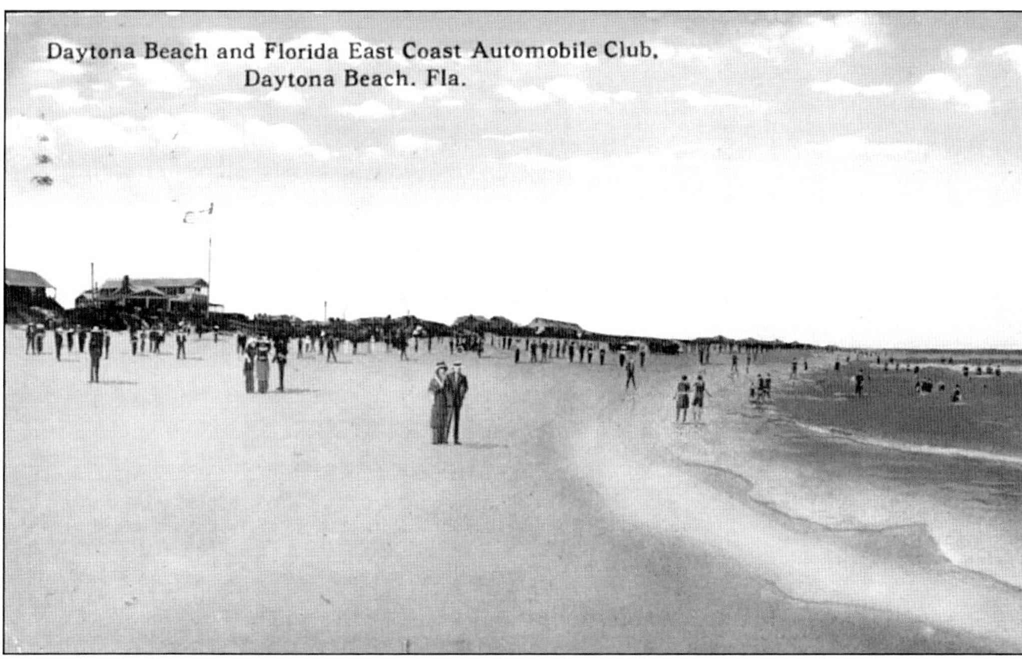

Looking North Along Beach in front of Automobile Clubhouse, *c.* 1914. This card carried an interesting message: "Am spending a few days over here at the beach. Mother and I are going home tomorrow in the car. Don't know whether we'll get there or not." By the way, home to the writer was Augusta, Maine.

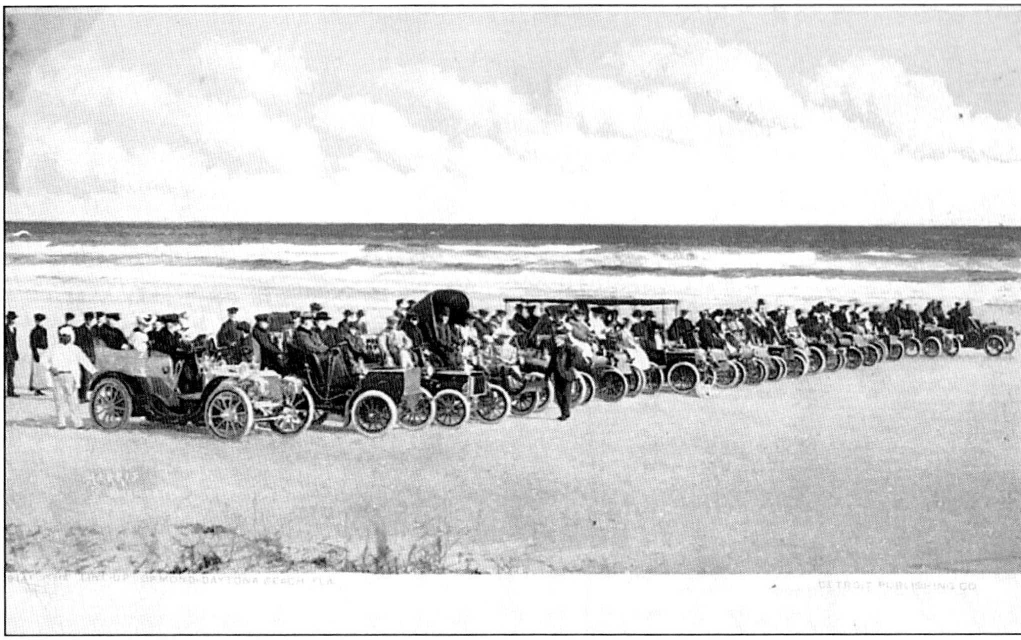

Lineup of Automobiles on the Ormond-Daytona Beach. Nearly 20 vehicles were lined up for this picture taken about 1904–1906, probably at low tide when the beach was at its widest and the sand at its hardest. It is unlikely that this lineup had anything to do with an official race, but exactly what was about to take place is left to one's imagination.

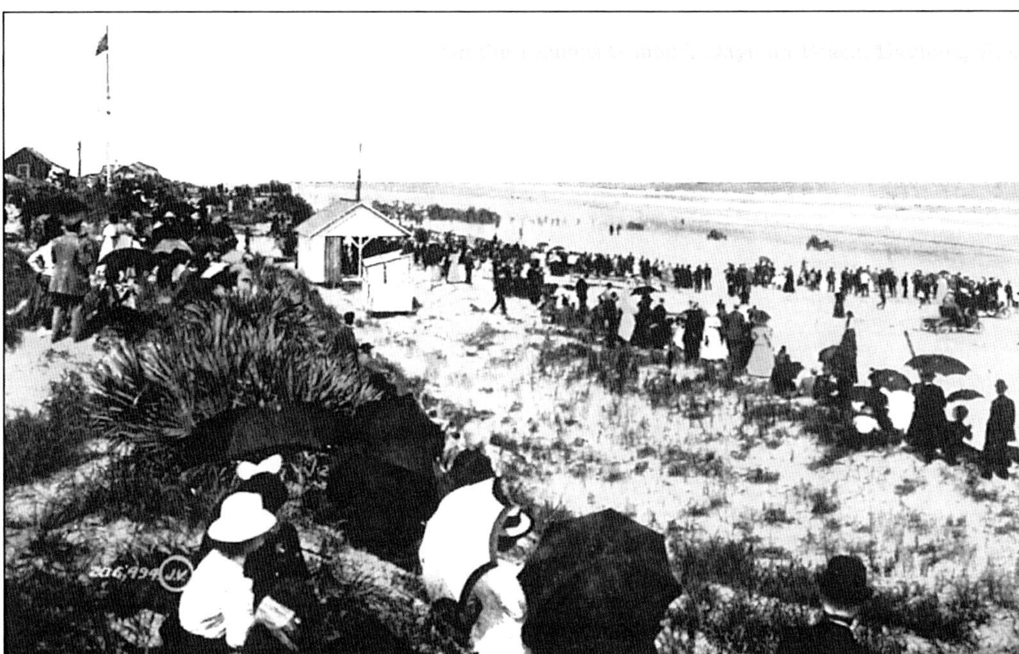

Crowds Watching a Race Near the Clubhouse, *c.* 1904–1905. The dunes served as grandstand seating on race day. As the cars approached, all eyes were fixed on the horizon. (Postcard courtesy Richard Dragoni.)

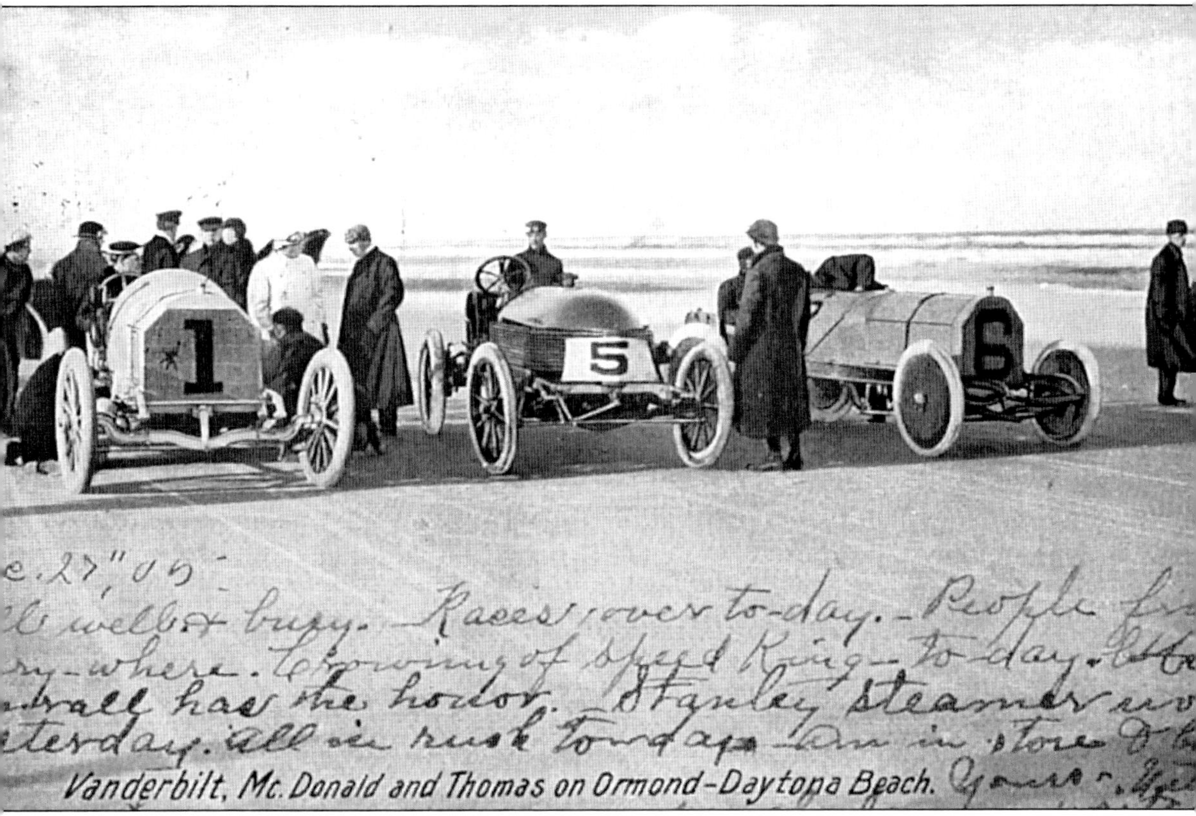

VANDERBILT, MCDONALD, AND THOMAS ON ORMOND-DAYTONA BEACH, C. 1904–1905. This card shows three important figures in racing history. Millionaire William K. Vanderbilt Jr. raced his Mercedes (#1) against Englishman Arthur McDonald's Napier (#5) and another Mercedes (#6) driven by E.R. Thomas. The card's message, written December 27, 1905, provides a spectator's account of racing activity that season: "Races over today. People from everywhere. Crowning of Speed King today. Miss Simrall has the honor. Stanley Steamer won yesterday." (Postcard courtesy David Findlay.)

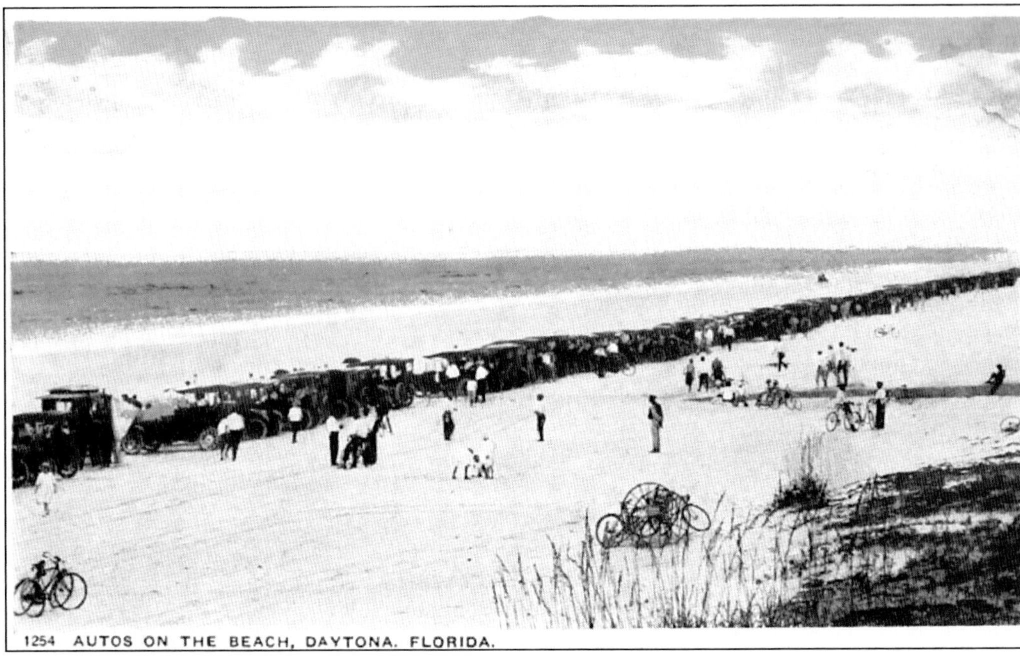

AUTOMOBILES ON THE BEACH. "Lineups" were popular photographic subjects because the public was fascinated with the notion of driving vehicles on the hard sand. The subject was worthy of recording on film because it represented a phenomenon unique to the area.

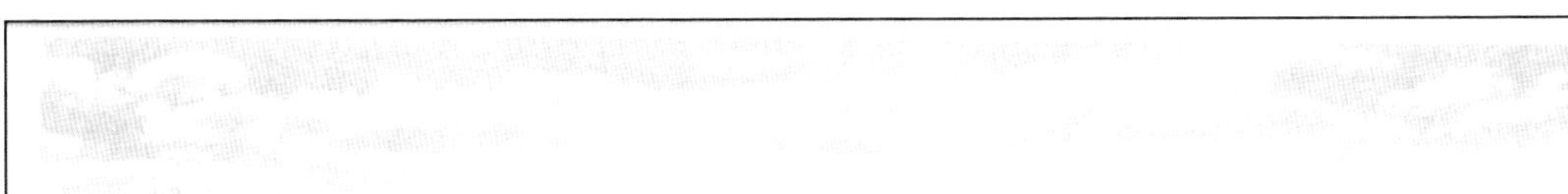

BATHERS AND AUTOMOBILES ON THE BEACH. The activity suggested by this *c.* 1920 card can be compared to modern times. The rules are much the same as they were then: Park facing east; drive north and south, and look both ways before going from the surf to the dunes! (From Curt Teich and Company souvenir booklet.)

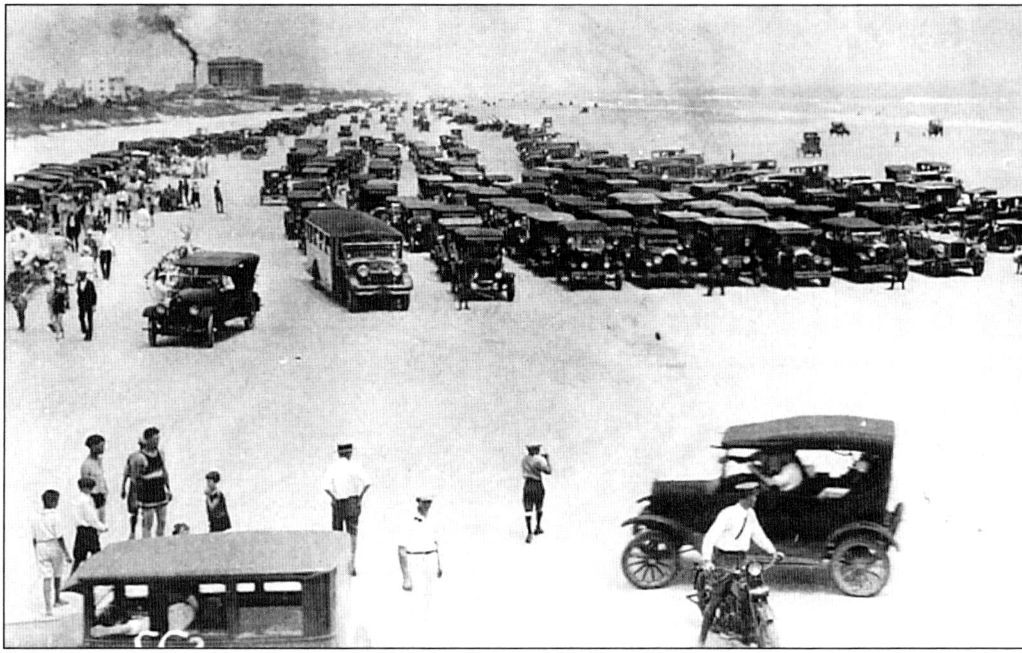

The Beach Near Main Street. This photograph of an eventful day at the beach in the mid-1920s may have been taken from the pier. (Postcard courtesy David Findlay.)

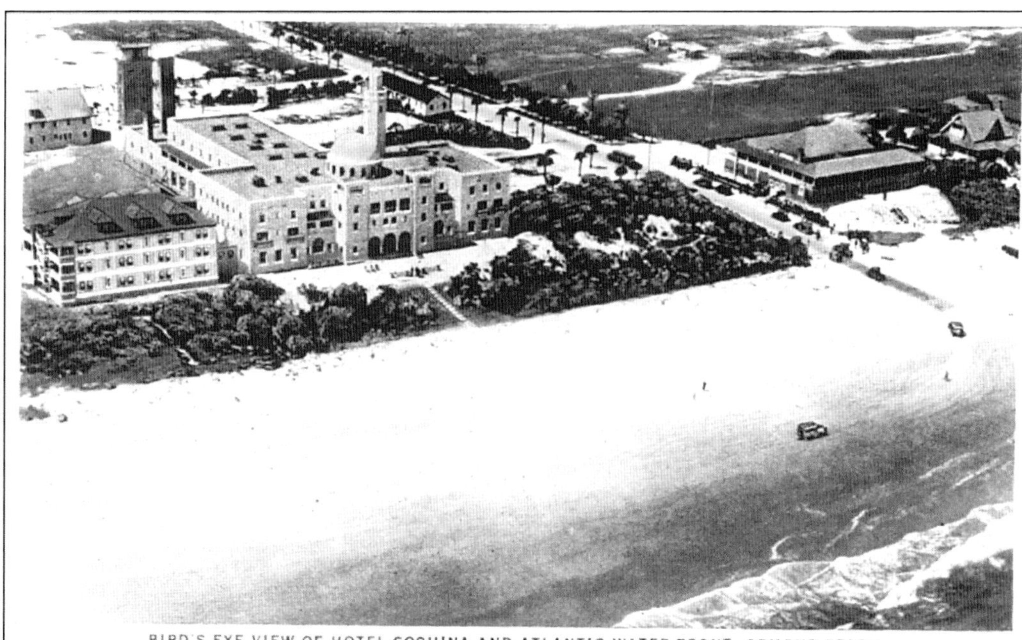

Aerial View of Beach at Ormond, c. Mid-1920s. Automobiles approached the Ormond beach using Granada Avenue. The Coquina Hotel was south of the approach and the Ormond Hotel's golf course and clubhouse were on the north side. The Ormond Hotel was farther west on the north side of Granada Avenue at the river. This area of beach was the northern end of the race course for many years. (From Curt Teich and Company souvenir booklet.)

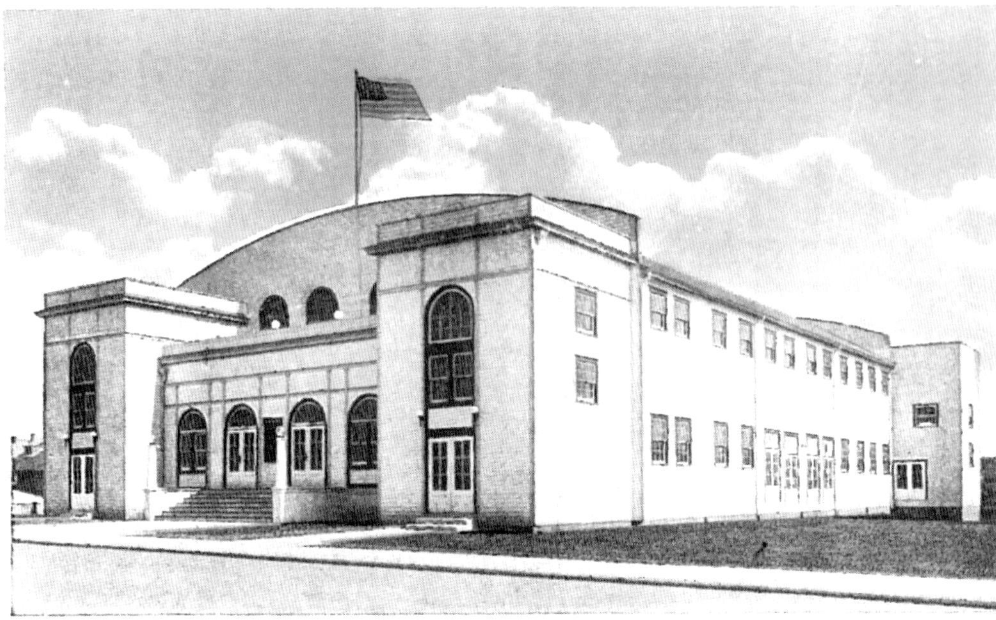

New Auditorium, Daytona Beach.

PEABODY AUDITORIUM, DAYTONA BEACH. The auditorium was built 1919–1920 to house the Florida Open Forum meetings, a popular form of entertainment and enlightenment during the early 1900s. Modeled after the Chautauqua movement, cultural forums featured performing artists and renowned speakers for three months during winter. They were organized and funded by winter residents including Simon J. Peabody. The auditorium burned in 1946, but was immediately replaced.

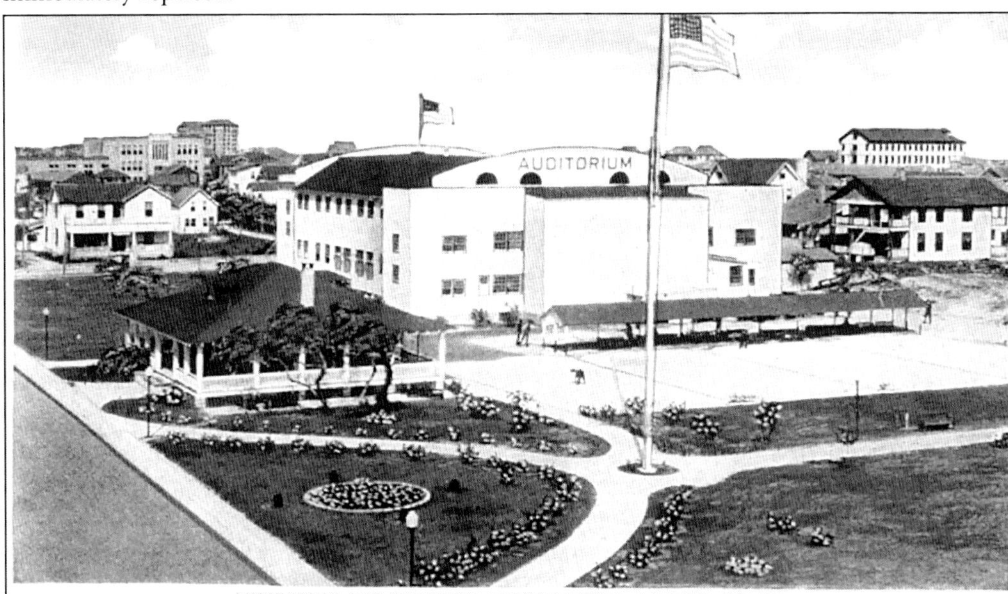

AUDITORIUM AND TOURISTS' HEADQUARTERS DAYTONA BEACH

PEABODY AUDITORIUM, *c.* 1923. The auditorium was just north of Main Street, the apparent vantage point for this view looking north along Wild Olive Street. The Clarendon Hotel, the tallest building in Seabreeze, could be seen from the auditorium.

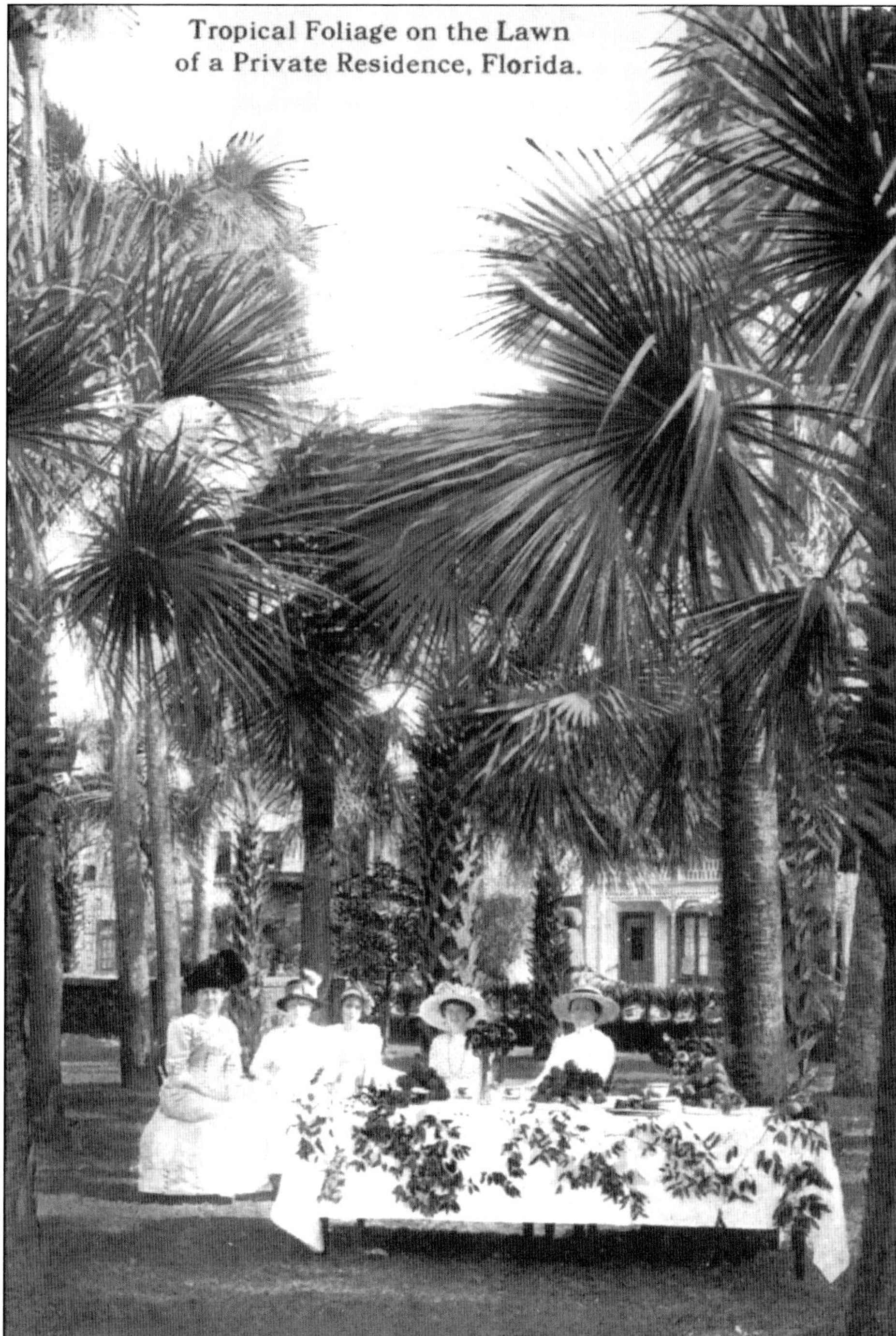

LADIES ON THE LAWN OF A PRIVATE RESIDENCE, C. 1917. One can only imagine what this group of leisurely ladies had gathered to discuss over tea. Perhaps they were members of the garden club, a church group, or even a civic organization like Daytona's Palmetto Club. Daytona's gentlemen congregated at the Benevolent and Protective Order of Elks lodge on Volusia Avenue or the Masonic Hall on Orange Avenue.

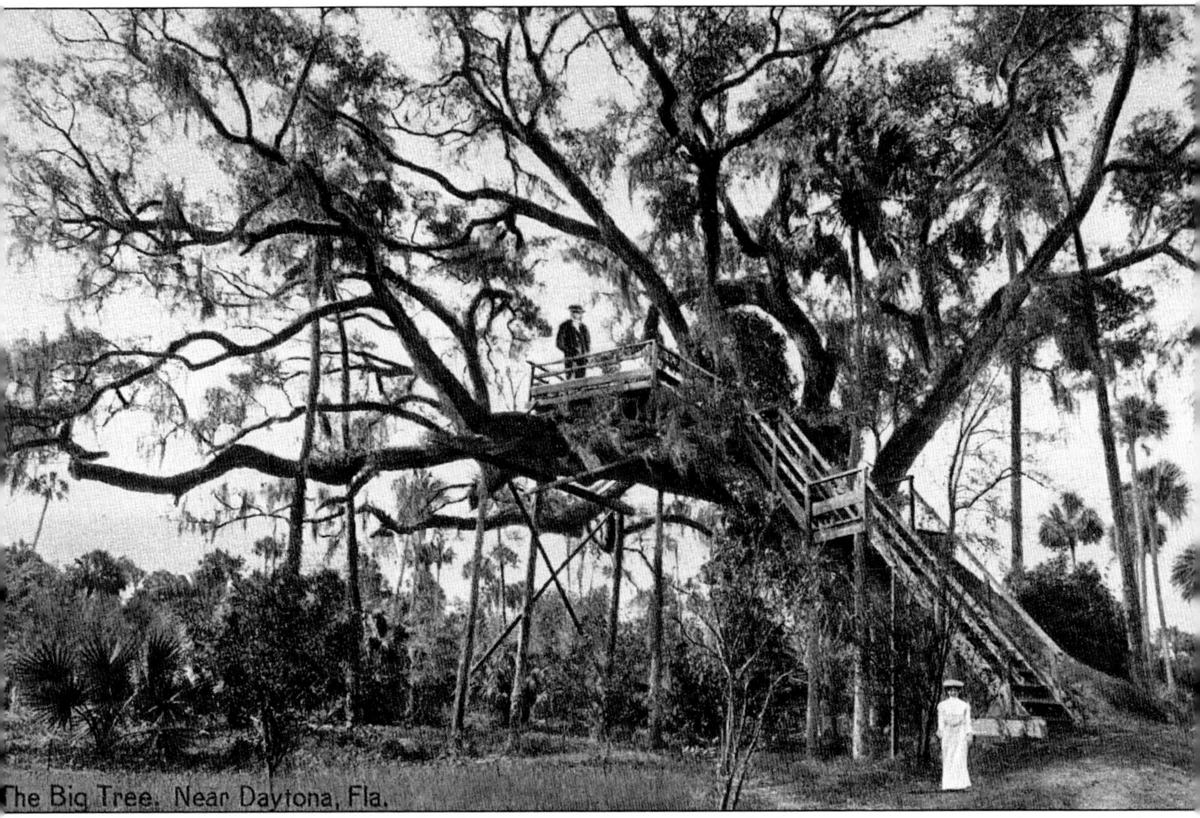

The Big Tree. Visiting a natural attraction such as this enormous live oak tree 2 miles south of Daytona was a recommended excursion in the early 1900s. Although no longer there, the tree was honored by having a street named for it—Big Tree Road.

Bibliography

American Motorist, The. January 1910; February 1912.

Brinton, Daniel G. *A Guide-book of Florida and the South.* Philadelphia: George Maclean, 1869.

Celebration of Old Daytona. Daytona Beach: Old Daytona Civic Association, 1995.

Charles Grover Burgoyne, The Man Who Brought Tourism to Daytona. Daytona Beach: Halifax Historical Society.

City Directories, City of Daytona; 1909, 1914–15, 1920–21, 1926.

Davis, T. Frederick. *History of Jacksonville, Florida and Vicinity, 1513–1924.* Reprint Jacksonville: San Marco Bookstore, 1990.

Fitzgerald, T.E. *Volusia County Past and Present.* Daytona Beach: The Observer Press, 1937.

Gold, Pleasant Daniel. *History of Volusia County, Florida.* DeLand, Florida: The E.O. Painter Printing Co., 1927.

Hallock, Charles (compiler). *Camp Life in Florida: A Handbook for Sportsmen and Settlers.* New York: Smith and McDougal, 1875.

Halifax Historical Society vertical files, documents and photographs.

Hebel, Ianthe Bond (editor). *Centennial History of Volusia County, Florida.* Daytona Beach: College Publishing Company, 1955.

Historic Daytona Beach. Daytona Beach: Halifax Historical Society, 1992.

Historical and Descriptive of Volusia County and its Settlements. Jacksonville: DaCosta Printing and Publishing House, 1888; facsimile reproduction, DeLand, Fla: Saint Johns-Oklawaha Rivers Trading Company.

Into Tropical Florida. New York. Leve and Alden's Publication Department; reprint, DeLand, Fla.: Saint Johns-Oklawaha Rivers Trading Company.

Kennedy, Stetson. *Palmetto Country.* New York: Duell, Sloan and Pearce, 1942.

Lanier, Sidney. *Florida: Its Scenery, Climate and History*. Philadelphia: J.B. Lippincott and Co., 1875.

Martin, Sidney Walter. *Florida's Flagler*. Athens: The University of Georgia Press, 1949.

Miller, George and Dorothy. *Picture Postcards in the United States, 1893–1918*. New York: Clarkson N. Potter, Inc. 1975.

Patrick, Rembert W. and Morris, Allen. *Florida Under Five Flags*. Gainesville: University of Florida Press, 1967.

St. Augustine Historical Society. *The Oldest City: St. Augustine, Saga of Survival*. 1983.

Stockbridge, Frank Parker and Perry, John Holliday. *Florida in the Making*. New York: The de Bower Publishing Company, 1926.

The Story of a Pioneer. Centennial edition, Florida East Coast Railway.

Strickland, Alice. *Ormond-on-the-Halifax*. Ormond Beach, 1980; reprint 1995.

Strickland, Alice. *The Valiant Pioneers*. Miami: Center Printing Co., 1963.

Swanson, Henry F. *Countdown for Agriculture*. Orlando: Designers Press of Orlando, Inc., 1975
Torrey, Bradford. *A Florida Sketch-book*. Boston and New York: Houghton, Mifflin and Company, 1894.

Tuthill, William R. *Speed on Sand*. Daytona Beach: Museum of Speed, 1969.

Watson, Henry B. *Bicentennial Pictorial History of Volusia County*. Daytona Beach: The News-Journal Corporation, 1976.